THE GREAT TRADITION

F(rank) R(aymond) LEAVIS was born in England in 1895 and educated at Perse School, and Emmanuel College, Cambridge. He has been a Fellow of Downing College, Cambridge, and University Lecturer in English since 1936. Dr. Leavis was the founder and editor of *Scrutiny*, which was for fourteen years a leading quarterly journal of literary criticism. His published works include *Mass Civilization and Minority Culture* (1930), *D. H. Lawrence* (1930), *New Bearings in English Poetry* (1932), *For Continuity* (1933), *Culture and Environment* (with Denys Thompson—1933), *Revaluation: Tradition and Development in English Poetry* (1936), *Education and the University* (1943), and *The Common Pursuit* (1952).

THE GREAT TRADITION was first published in 1948.

THE GREAT TRADITION

by F. R. Leavis

FELLOW OF DOWNING COLLEGE
CAMBRIDGE

Doubleday Anchor Books

DOUBLEDAY & COMPANY, INC., GARDEN CITY, N.Y., 1954

Reprinted with the permission of
George W. Stewart, Publisher, Inc.
Design: Joseph P. Ascherl

Printed in the United States

CONTENTS

ACKNOWLEDGEMENTS   The greater part of this book appeared first in *Scrutiny,* and for permission to use this matter I am indebted to the Editors. The second part of the critique of Henry James appeared in the issue for March, 1937. That of Conrad appeared in June and October, 1941, and that of George Eliot in 1945 and 1946. I have also to thank Messrs. John Farquharson, acting on behalf of the Henry James' estate, for kind permission to reprint *Daniel Deronda: A Conversation,* as an Appendix to this volume.

My sense of my immeasurable indebtedness, in every page of this book, to my wife cannot be adequately expressed, and I cannot express it at all without an accompanying consciousness of shortcomings—no one but myself has any part in them —that makes me insist at the same time on my claim to all the responsibility.

F. R. L.

'I know how hard it is. One needs something to make one's mood deep and sincere. There are so many little frets that prevent our coming at the real naked essence of our vision. It sounds boshy, doesn't it? I often think one ought to be able to pray, before one works—and then leave it to the Lord. Isn't it hard, hard work to come to real grips with one's imagination— throw everything overboard. I always feel as if I stood naked for the fire of Almighty God to go through me—and it's rather an awful feeling. One has to be so terribly religious, to be an artist. I often think of my dear Saint Lawrence on his gridiron, when he said, "Turn me over, brothers, I am done enough on this side".'

To Ernest Collings. *Feb. 24, 1913*
THE LETTERS OF D. H. LAWRENCE

I. THE GREAT TRADITION

'. . . not dogmatically but deliberately . . .'
JOHNSON: Preface to Shakespeare

THE great English novelists are Jane Austen, George Eliot, Henry James and Joseph Conrad—to stop for the moment at that comparatively safe point in history. Since Jane Austen, for special reasons, needs to be studied at considerable length, I confine myself in this book to the last three. Critics have found me narrow, and I have no doubt that my opening proposition, whatever I may say to explain and justify it, will be adduced in reinforcement of their strictures. It passes as fact (in spite of the printed evidence) that I pronounce Milton negligible, dismiss 'the Romantics,' and hold that, since Donne, there is no poet we need bother about except Hopkins and Eliot. The view, I suppose, will be as confidently attributed to me that, except Jane Austen, George Eliot, James and Conrad, there are no novelists in English worth reading.

The only way to escape misrepresentation is never to commit oneself to any critical judgment that makes an impact—that is, never to *say* anything. I still, however, think that the best way to promote profitable discussion is to be as clear as possible with oneself about what one sees and judges, to try and establish the essential discriminations in the given field of interest, and to state them as clearly as one can (for disagreement, if necessary). And it seems to me that in the field of fiction some challenging discriminations are very much called for; the field is so large and offers such insidious temptations to complacent confusions of judgment and to critical indolence. It is of the field of fiction belonging to Literature that I am thinking, and I am thinking in particular of the present vogue of the Victorian age. Trollope, Charlotte Yonge, Mrs. Gaskell, Wilkie Collins, Charles Reade, Charles and Henry Kingsley,

Marryat, Shorthouse[1]—one after another the minor novelists of that period are being commended to our attention,
written up, and publicized by broadcast, and there is a
marked tendency to suggest that they not only have various
kinds of interest to offer but that they are living classics.
(Are not they all in the literary histories?) There are Jane
Austen, Mrs. Gaskell, Scott, 'the Brontës,'[2] Dickens,
Thackeray, George Eliot, Trollope and so on, all, one gathers, classical novelists.

It is necessary to insist, then, that there are important
distinctions to be made, and that far from all of the names
in the literary histories really belong to the realm of significant creative achievement. And as a recall to a due
sense of differences it is well to start by distinguishing the
few really great—the major novelists who count in the
same way as the major poets, in the sense that they not
only change the possibilities of the art for practitioners
and readers, but that they are significant in terms of the
human awareness they promote; awareness of the possibilities of life.[3]

---

[1] The novelist who has not been revived is Disraeli. Yet,
though he is not one of the great novelists, he is so alive and
intelligent as to deserve permanent currency, at any rate in
the trilogy *Coningsby, Sybil* and *Tancred*: his own interests
as expressed in these books—the interests of a supremely intelligent politician who has a sociologist's understanding of
civilization and its movement in his time—are so mature.

[2] See note 'The Brontës,' page 41 below.

[3] Characteristic of the confusion I am contending against is
the fashion (for which the responsibility seems to go back to
Virginia Woolf and Mr. E. M. Forster) of talking of *Moll
Flanders* as a 'great novel.' Defoe was a remarkable writer,
but all that need be said about him as a novelist was said
by Leslie Stephen in *Hours in a Library* (First Series). He
made no pretension to practising the novelist's art, and matters
little as an influence. In fact, the only influence that need be
noted is that represented by the use made of him in the nineteen-twenties by the practitioners of the fantastic *conte* (or
pseudo-moral fable) with its empty pretence of significance.

To insist on the pre-eminent few in this way is not to be indifferent to tradition; on the contrary, it is the way towards understanding what tradition is. 'Tradition,' of course, is a term with many forces—and often very little at all. There is a habit nowadays of suggesting that there is a tradition of 'the English Novel,' and that all that can be said of the tradition (that being its peculiarity) is that 'the English Novel' can be anything you like. To distinguish the major novelists in the spirit proposed is to form a more useful idea of tradition (and to recognize that the conventionally established view of the past of English fiction needs to be drastically revised). It is in terms of the major novelists, those significant in the way suggested, that tradition, in any serious sense, has its significance.

To be important historically is not, of course, to be necessarily one of the significant few. Fielding deserves the place of importance given him in the literary histories, but he hasn't the kind of classical distinction we are also

---

Associated with this use of Defoe is the use that was made in much the same *milieu* of Sterne, in whose irresponsible (and nasty) trifling, regarded as in some way extraordinarily significant and mature, was found a sanction for attributing value to other trifling.

The use of Bunyan by T. F. Powys is quite another matter. It is a mark of the genuine nature of Mr. Powys's creative gift (his work seems to me not to have had due recognition) that he has been able to achieve a kind of traditional relation to Bunyan—especially, of course, in *Mr. Weston's Good Wine.* Otherwise there is little that can be said with confidence about Bunyan as an influence. And yet we know him to have been for two centuries one of the most frequented of all classics, and in such a way that he counts immeasurably in the English-speaking consciousness. It is, perhaps, worth saying that his influence would tend strongly to reinforce the un-Flaubertian quality of the line of English classical fiction (Bunyan, Lord David Cecil might point out—see p. 18 below—was a Puritan), as well as to co-operate with the Jonsonian tradition of morally significant typicality in characters.

invited to credit him with. He is important not because he leads to Mr. J. B. Priestley but because he leads to Jane Austen, to appreciate whose distinction is to feel that life isn't long enough to permit of one's giving much time to Fielding or any to Mr. Priestley.

Fielding made Jane Austen possible by opening the central tradition of English fiction. In fact, to say that the English novel began with him is as reasonable as such propositions ever are. He completed the work begun by *The Tatler* and *The Spectator,* in the pages of which we see the drama turning into the novel—that this development should occur by way of journalism being in the natural course of things. To the art of presenting character and *mœurs* learnt in that school (he himself, before he became a novelist, was both playwright and periodical essayist) he joined a narrative habit the nature of which is sufficiently indicated by his own phrase, 'comic epic in prose.' That the eighteenth century, which hadn't much lively reading to choose from, but had much leisure, should have found *Tom Jones* exhilarating is not surprising; nor is it that Scott, and Coleridge, should have been able to give that work superlative praise. Standards are formed in comparison, and what opportunities had they for that? But the conventional talk about the 'perfect construction' of *Tom Jones* (the late Hugh Walpole brought it out triumphantly and you may hear it in almost any course of lectures on 'the English Novel') is absurd. There can't be subtlety of organization without richer matter to organize, and subtler interests, than Fielding has to offer. He is credited with range and variety and it is true that some episodes take place in the country and some in Town, some in the churchyard and some in the inn, some on the high-road and some in the bed-chamber, and so on. But we haven't to read a very large proportion of *Tom Jones* in order to discover the limits of the essential interests it has to offer us. Fielding's attitudes, and his concern with human nature, are simple, and not such as to produce an effect of anything but monotony (on a mind,

that is, demanding more than external action) when exhibited at the length of an 'epic in prose.' What he *can*
do appears to best advantage in *Joseph Andrews*. *Jonathan
Wild*, with its famous irony, seem to me mere hobbledehoydom (much as one applauds the determination to
explode the gangster-hero), and by *Amelia* Fielding has
gone soft.

We all know that if we want a more inward interest it is
to Richardson we must go. And there is more to be said
for Johnson's preference, and his emphatic way of expressing it at Fielding's expense, than is generally recognized. Richardson's strength in the analysis of emotional
and moral states is in any case a matter of common
acceptance; and *Clarissa* is a really impressive work. But
it's no use pretending that Richardson can ever be made
a current classic again. The substance of interest that he
too has to offer is in its own way extremely limited in
range and variety, and the demand he makes on the reader's time is in proportion—and absolutely—so immense as
to be found, in general, prohibitive (though I don't know
that I wouldn't sooner read through again *Clarissa* than
A la recherche du temps perdu). But we can understand
well enough why his reputation and influence should
have been so great throughout Europe; and his immediately relevant historical importance is plain: he too is a
major fact in the background of Jane Austen.

The social gap between them was too wide, however,
for his work to be usable by her directly: the more he tries
to deal with ladies and gentlemen, the more immitigably
vulgar he is. It was Fanny Burney who, by transposing
him into educated life, made it possible for Jane Austen
to absorb what he had to teach her. Here we have one of
the important lines of English literary history—Richardson
-Fanny Burney-Jane Austen. It is important because Jane
Austen is one of the truly great writers, and herself a major fact in the background of other great writers. Not that
Fanny Burney is the only other novelist who counts in her
formation; she read all there was to read, and took all that

was useful to her—which wasn't only lessons.[4] In fact, Jane Austen, in her indebtedness to others, provides an exceptionally illuminating study of the nature of originality, and she exemplifies beautifully the relations of 'the individual talent' to tradition. If the influences bearing on her hadn't comprised something fairly to be called tradition she couldn't have found herself and her true direction; but her relation to tradition is a creative one. She not only makes tradition for those coming after, but her achievement has for us a retroactive effect: as we look back beyond her we see in what goes before, and see because of her, potentialities and significances brought out in such a way that, for us, she creates the tradition we see leading down to her. Her work, like the work of all great creative writers, gives a meaning to the past.

Having, in examination-papers and undergraduate essays, come much too often on the proposition that 'George Eliot is the first modern novelist,' I finally tracked it down to Lord David Cecil's *Early Victorian Novelists*. In so far as it is possible to extract anything clear and coherent from the variety of things that Lord David Cecil says by way of explaining the phrase, it is this: that George Eliot, being concerned, not to offer 'primarily an entertainment,' but to explore a significant theme—a theme significant in its bearing on the 'serious problems and preoccupations of mature life' (p. 291)—breaks with 'those fundamental conventions both of form and matter within which the English novel up till then had been constructed' (p. 288). What account, then, are we to assume of Jane Austen? Clearly, one that appears to be the most commonly held: she creates delightful characters ('Compare Jane Austen's characterization with Scott's'[5]—a recurrent examination-

---

[4] For the relation of Jane Austen to other writers see the essay by Q. D. Leavis, *A Critical Theory of Jane Austen's Writings*, in *Scrutiny*, Vol. X, No. 1.

[5] Scott was primarily a kind of inspired folk-lorist, qualified to have done in fiction something analogous to the ballad-opera: the only live part of *Redgauntlet* now is 'Wandering

question) and lets us forget our cares and moral tensions in the comedy of pre-eminently civilized life. The idea of 'civilization' invoked appears to be closely related to that expounded by Mr. Clive Bell.[6]

Lord David Cecil actually compares George Eliot with Jane Austen. The passage is worth quoting because the inadequate ideas of form ('composition') and moral inter-

---

Willie's Tale,' and 'The Two Drovers' remains in esteem while the heroics of the historical novels can no longer command respect. He was a great and very intelligent man; but, not having the creative writer's interest in literature, he made no serious attempt to work out his own form and break away from the bad tradition of the eighteenth-century romance. Of his books, *The Heart of Midlothian* comes the nearest to being a great novel, but hardly *is* that: too many allowances and deductions have to be made. Out of Scott a bad tradition came. It spoiled Fenimore Cooper, who had new and first-hand interests and the makings of a distinguished novelist. And with Stevenson it took on 'literary' sophistication and fine writing.

[6] ' "As for the revolt against Nature," he continued, "that, too, has its uses. If it conduces to the cult of the stylized, the con-ventionalized, the artificial, just for their own sakes, it also, more broadly, makes for civilization."

' "Civilization?" I asked. "At what point between barbarism and decadence does civilization reign? If a civilized commu-nity be defined as one where you find aesthetic preoccupa-tions, subtle thought, and polished intercourse, is civilization necessarily desirable? Aesthetic preoccupations are not incon-sistent with a wholly inadequate conception of the range and power of art; thought may be subtle and yet trivial; and pol-ished intercourse may be singularly uninteresting." '—L. H. Myers, *The Root and the Flower*, p. 418.

Myers hasn't the great novelist's technical interest in method and presentment; he slips very easily into using the novel as a *vehicle*. That is, we feel that he is not primarily a novelist. Yet he is sufficiently one to have made of *The Root and the Flower* a very remarkable novel. Anyone seriously interested in literature is likely to have found the first reading a memorable experience and to have found also that repeated re-readings have not exhausted the interest.

est it implies—ideas of the relation between 'art' and 'life' as it concerns the novelist—are very representative. (Its consistency with what has been said about George Eliot earlier in the same essay isn't obvious, but that doesn't disturb the reader by the time he has got here.)

'It is also easy to see why her form doesn't satisfy us as Jane Austen's does. Life is chaotic, art is orderly. The novelist's problem is to evoke an orderly composition which is also a convincing picture of life. It is Jane Austen's triumph that she solves this problem perfectly, fully satisfies the rival claims of life and art. Now George Eliot does not. She sacrifices life to art. Her plots are too neat and symmetrical to be true. We do not feel them to have grown naturally from their situation like a flower, but to have been put together deliberately and calculatedly like a building.' (p. 322.)

Jane Austen's plots, and her novels in general, were put together very 'deliberately and calculatedly' (if not 'like a building').[7] But her interest in 'composition' is not something to be put over against her interest in life; nor does she offer an 'aesthetic' value that is separable from moral significance. The principle of organization, and the principle of development, in her work is an intense moral interest of her own in life that is in the first place a preoccupation with certain problems that life compels on her as personal ones.[8] She is intelligent and serious enough to be able to impersonalize her moral tensions as she strives, in her art, to become more fully conscious of them, and to learn what, in the interests of life, she ought to do with them. Without her intense moral preoccupation she wouldn't have been a great novelist.

This account of her would, if I had cared to use the

---

[7] See 'Lady Susan' into 'Mansfield Park' by Q. D. Leavis in *Scrutiny*, Vol. X, No. 2.
[8] D. W. Harding deals illuminatingly with this matter in *Regulated Hatred: An Aspect of the Work of Jane Austen* (see *Scrutiny*, Vol. VIII, No. 4).

formula, have been my case for calling Jane Austen, and not anyone later, 'the first modern novelist.' In applying it to George Eliot, Lord David Cecil says: 'In fact, the laws conditioning the form of George Eliot's novels are the same laws that condition those of Henry James and Wells and Conrad and Arnold Bennett.' I don't know what Wells is doing in that sentence; there is an elementary distinction to be made between the *discussion* of problems and ideas, and what we find in the great novelists. And, for all the generous sense of common humanity to be found in his best work, Bennett seems to me never to have been disturbed enough by life to come anywhere near greatness. But it would certainly be reasonable to say that 'the laws conditioning the form of Jane Austen's novels are the same laws that condition those of George Eliot and Henry James and Conrad.' Jane Austen, in fact, is the inaugurator of the great tradition of the English novel—and by 'great tradition' I mean the tradition to which what is great in English fiction belongs.

The great novelists in that tradition are all very much concerned with 'form'; they are all very original technically, having turned their genius to the working out of their own appropriate methods and procedures. But the peculiar quality of their preoccupation with 'form' may be brought out by a contrasting reference to Flaubert. Reviewing Thomas Mann's *Der Tod in Venedig*, D. H. Lawrence[9] adduces Flaubert as figuring to the world the 'will of the writer to be greater than and undisputed lord over the stuff he writes.' This attitude in art, as Lawrence points out, is indicative of an attitude in life—or towards life. Flaubert, he comments, 'stood away from life as from a leprosy.' For the later Aesthetic writers, who, in general, represent in a weak kind of way the attitude that Flaubert maintained with a perverse heroism, 'form' and 'style' are ends to be sought for themselves, and the chief preoccupation is with elaborating a beautiful style to apply to the chosen subject. There is George Moore, who in the best circles, I gather (from a distance), is still held to be among the very greatest masters of prose, though—I give my own limited experience for what it is worth—it is very hard to find an admirer who, being pressed, will lay his hand on his heart and swear he has read one of the 'beautiful' novels through. 'The novelist's problem is to evolve an orderly composition which is also a convincing picture of life'—this is the way an admirer of George Moore sees it. Lord David Cecil, attributing this way to Jane Austen, and crediting her with a superiority over George Eliot in 'satisfying the rival claims of life and art,' explains this superiority, we gather, by a freedom from moral preoccupations that he supposes her to enjoy. (George Eliot, he tells us, was a Puritan, and earnestly bent on instruction.[10])

As a matter of fact, when we examine the formal perfection of *Emma,* we find that it can be appreciated only in terms of the moral preoccupations that characterize the novelist's peculiar interest in life. Those who suppose it to be an 'aesthetic matter,' a beauty of 'composition' that is combined, miraculously, with 'truth to life,' can give no adequate reason for the view that *Emma* is a great novel, and no intelligent account of its perfection of form. It is in the same way true of the other great English novelists that their interest in their art gives them the opposite of an affinity with Pater and George Moore; it is, brought to an intense focus, an unusually developed interest in life. For, far from having anything of Flaubert's disgust or disdain or boredom, they are all distinguished by a vital capacity for experience, a kind of reverent openness before life, and a marked moral intensity.

It might be commented that what I have said of Jane Austen and her successors is only what can be said of any novelist of unqualified greatness. That is true. But there

---

[10] She is a moralist and a highbrow, the two handicaps going together. 'Her humour is less affected by her intellectual approach. Jokes, thank heaven, need not be instructive.'—*Early Victorian Novelists,* p. 299.

is—and this is the point—an English tradition, and these great classics of English fiction belong to it; a tradition that, in the talk about 'creating characters' and 'creating worlds,' and the appreciation of Trollope and Mrs. Gaskell and Thackeray and Meredith and Hardy and Virginia Woolf, appears to go unrecognized. It is not merely that we have no Flaubert (and I hope I haven't seemed to suggest that a Flaubert is no more worth having than a George Moore). Positively, there is a continuity from Jane Austen. It is not for nothing that George Eliot admired her work profoundly, and wrote one of the earliest appreciations of it to be published. The writer whose intellectual weight and moral earnestness strike some critics as her handicap certainly saw in Jane Austen something more than an ideal contemporary of Lytton Strachey.[11] What one great original artist learns from another, whose genius and problems are necessarily very different, is the hardest kind of 'influence' to define, even when we see it to have been of the profoundest importance. The obvious manifestation of influence is to be seen in this kind of passage:

> 'A little daily embroidery had been a constant element in Mrs. Transome's life; that soothing occupation of taking stitches to produce what neither she nor any one else wanted, was then the resource of many a well-born and unhappy woman.'

> 'In short, he felt himself to be in love in the right place, and was ready to endure a great deal of predominance, which, after all, a man could always put down when he liked. Sir James had no idea that he should

---

[11] It is perhaps worth insisting that Peacock is more than that too. He is not at all in the same class as the Norman Douglas of *South Wind* and *They Went*. In his ironical treatment of contemporary society and civilization he is seriously applying serious standards, so that his books, which are obviously not novels in the same sense as Jane Austen's, have a permanent life as light reading—indefinitely re-readable—for minds with mature interests.

ever like to put down the predominance of this hand-some girl, in whose cleverness he delighted. Why not? A man's mind—what there is of it—has always the ad-vantage of being masculine,—as the smallest birch-tree is of a higher kind than the most soaring palm—and even his ignorance is of a sounder quality. Sir James might not have originated this estimate; but a kind Providence furnishes the limpest personality with a lit-tle gum or starch in the form of tradition.'

The kind of irony here is plainly akin to Jane Austen's—though it is characteristic enough of George Eliot; what she found was readily assimilated to her own needs. In Jane Austen herself the irony has a serious background, and is no mere display of 'civilization.' George Eliot wouldn't have been interested in it if she hadn't perceived its full significance—its relation to the essential moral in-terest offered by Jane Austen's art. And here we come to the profoundest kind of influence, that which is not man-ifested in likeness. One of the supreme debts one great writer can owe another is the realization of unlikeness (there is, of course, no significant unlikeness without the common concern—and the common seriousness of concern —with essential human issues). One way of putting the difference between George Eliot and the Trollopes whom we are invited to consider along with her is to say that she was capable of understanding Jane Austen's greatness and capable of learning from her. And except for Jane Austen there was no novelist to learn from—none whose work had any bearing on her own essential problems as a novelist.

Henry James also was a great admirer of Jane Austen,[12] and in his case too there is that obvious aspect of influence which can be brought out by quotation. And there is for

---

[12] He can't have failed to note with interest that *Emma* fulfils, by anticipation, a prescription of his own: everything is pre-sented through Emma's dramatized consciousness, and the essential effects depend on that.

him George Eliot as well, coming between. In seeing him in an English tradition I am not slighting the fact of his American origin; an origin that doesn't make him less of an English novelist, of the great tradition, than Conrad later. That he was an American is a fact of the first importance for the critic, as Mr. Yvor Winters brings out admirably in his book, *Maule's Curse*.[13] Mr. Winters discusses him as a product of the New England ethos in its last phase, when a habit of moral strenuousness remained after dogmatic Puritanism had evaporated and the vestigial moral code was evaporating too. This throws a good deal of light on the elusiveness that attends James's peculiar ethical sensibility. We have, characteristically, in reading him, a sense that important choices are in question and that our finest discrimination is being challenged, while at the same time we can't easily produce for discussion any issues that have moral substance to correspond.

It seems relevant also to note that James was actually a New Yorker. In any case, he belonged by birth and upbringing to that refined civilization of the old European America which we have learnt from Mrs. Wharton to associate with New York. His bent was to find a field for his ethical sensibility in the appreciative study of such a civilization—the 'civilization' in question being a matter of personal relations between members of a mature and sophisticated Society. It is doubtful whether at any time in any place he could have found what would have satisfied his implicit demand: the actual fine art of civilized social intercourse that would have justified the flattering inten-

---

[13] New Directions, Norfolk, Conn. (1938). To insist that James is in the English tradition is not to deny that he is in an American tradition too. He is in the tradition that includes Hawthorne and Melville. He is related to Hawthorne even more closely than Mr. Winters suggests. A study of the very early work shows Hawthorne as a major influence—as *the* major influence. The influence is apparent there in James's use of symbolism; and this use develops into something that characterizes his later work as a whole.

sity of expectation he brought to it in the form of his curiously transposed and subtilized ethical sensibility.

History, it is plain, was already leaving him *déraciné* in his own country, so that it is absurd to censure him, as some American critics have done, for pulling up his roots. He could hardly become deeply rooted elsewhere, but the congenial soil and climate were in Europe rather than in the country of his birth. There is still some idealizing charm about his English country-house[14] in *The Portrait of a Lady*, but that book is one of the classics of the language, and we can't simply regret the conditions that produced something so finely imagined. It is what *The Egoist* is supposed to be. Compare the two books, and the greatness of Henry James as intellectual poet-novelist[15] of 'high civilization' comes out in a way that, even for the most innocently deferential reader, should dispose of Meredith's pretensions for ever. James's wit is

---

[14] Though it has in justice to be remembered that the inhabitants of the house in *The Portrait of a Lady*, the Touchetts, are Americans, and that there is critical significance in the difference between the atmosphere of intellectual aliveness they establish and the quite other English atmosphere of the Warburton home. Moreover, Isabel rejects the admirable Lord Warburton for reasons much like those for which the heroine of *An International Episode* rejects the nice English lord, who, by Touchett standards (shall we say?), is not good enough. And in story after story James, with the exasperation of an intellectual writer, expresses his disdainful sense of the utter unintellectuality of the country-house class. He always knew that he hadn't really found the ideal civilization he looked for; so that there is something like a tragic significance in the two juxtaposed notes of this passage from an early letter:

'But don't envy me too much; for the British country-house has at moments, for a cosmopolitanized American, an insuperable flatness. On the other hand, to do it justice, there is no doubt of its being one of the ripest fruits of time . . . of the highest results of civilization.'—To Miss Alice James, 15th Dec. 1877: *The Letters of Henry James*, Vol. I, p. 64.

[15] See p. 157-58 below.

real and always natural, his poetry intelligent as well as truly rich, and there is nothing bogus, cheap or vulgar about his idealizations: certain human potentialities are nobly celebrated.

That he is a novelist who has closely studied his fellow-craftsmen is plain—and got from them more than lessons in the craft. It is plain, for instance, in *The Portrait of a Lady* that he sees England through literature. We know that he turned an attentive professional eye on the French masters. He has (in his early mature work) an easy and well-bred technical sophistication, a freedom from any marks of provinciality, and a quiet air of knowing his way about the world that distinguish him from among his contemporaries in the language. If from the English point of view he is unmistakably an American, he is also very much a European.

But there could be no question of his becoming a French master in English, and the help he could get from the Continent towards solving his peculiar problem was obviously limited.[16] It was James who put his finger on the weakness in *Madame Bovary*: the discrepancy between the technical ('aesthetic') intensity, with the im-

---

[16] 'Your remarks on my French tricks in my letters are doubtless most just, and shall be heeded. But it's an odd thing that such tricks should grow at a time when my last layers of resistance to a long-encroaching weariness and satiety with the French mind and its utterance has fallen from me like a garment. I have done with 'em, forever, and am turning English all over. I desire only to feed on English life and the contact of English minds—I wish greatly I knew some. Easy and smooth-flowing as life is in Paris, I would throw it over to-morrow for an even very small chance to plant myself for a while in England. I have got nothing important out of Paris nor am likely to. . . . I know the Théâtre Français by heart! 'Daniel Deronda (Dan'l himself) is indeed a dead, though amiable, failure. But the book is a large affair; I shall write an article of some sort about it. All desire is dead within me to produce something on George Sand.'—To William James, 29th July 1876: *The Letters*, Vol. I, p. 51.

plied attribution of interest to the subject, and the actual
moral and human paucity of this subject on any mature
valuation. His own problem was to justify in terms of an
intense interest in sophisticated 'civilization' his New England ethical sensibility. The author who offered a congenial study would have to be very different from Flaubert.
It was, as a matter of fact, a very English novelist, the
living representative of the great tradition—a writer as unlike Flaubert as George Eliot.

George Eliot's reputation being what it is, this suggestion won't recommend itself to everyone immediately.
'Like most writers, George Eliot could only create from
the world of her personal experience—in her case middle-
and lower-class rural England of the nineteenth-century
Midlands.' [17] Moreover, she was confined by a Puritanism
such as James (apart from the fact that he wasn't lower-
middle-class) had left a generation or two behind him:
'the enlightened person of to-day must forget his dislike
of Puritanism when he reads George Eliot.' Weighty, provincial, and pledged to the 'school-teacher's virtues,' she
was not qualified by nature or breeding to appreciate high
civilization, even if she had been privileged to make its
acquaintance. These seem to be accepted commonplaces—
which shows how little even those who write about her
have read her work.

Actually, though 'Puritan' is a word used with many
intentions, it is misleading to call her a Puritan at all,[18]

---

[17] All the quotations in this paragraph are from Lord David
Cecil.
[18] Unless you specify that, of the definitions Lord David
Cecil gives us to choose from, the one you have in mind is
that given here: 'But the moral code founded on that Puritan theology had soaked itself too deeply into the fibre of
her thought and feeling for her to give it up as well. She
might not believe in heaven and hell and miracles, but she
believed in right and wrong, and man's paramount obliga-
tion to follow right, as strictly as if she were Bunyan himself.
And her standards of right and wrong were the Puritan standards. She admired truthfulness and chastity and industry

and utterly false to say that her 'imagination had to scrape what nourishment it could from the bare bones of Puritan ethics.' There was nothing restrictive or timid about her ethical habit; what she brought from her Evangelical background was a radically reverent attitude towards life, a profound seriousness of the kind that is a first condition of any real intelligence, and an interest in human nature that made her a great psychologist. Such a psychologist, with such a relation to Puritanism, was, of all the novelists open to his study, the one peculiarly relevant to James's interests and problems. That, at any rate, becomes an irresistible proposition when it is added that, in her most mature work, she deals and (in spite of the accepted commonplaces about her) deals consummately, with just that 'civilization' which was James's chosen field. To say this is to have the confident wisdom of hindsight, for it can be shown, with a conclusiveness rarely possible in these matters, that James did actually go to school to George Eliot.[19]

---

and self-restraint, she disapproved of loose living and recklessness and deceit and self-indulgence.' I had better confess that I differ (apparently) from Lord David Cecil in sharing these beliefs, admirations and disapprovals, so that the reader knows my bias at once. And they seem to me favourable to the production of great literature. I will add (exposing myself completely) that the enlightenment or aestheticism or sophistication that feels an amused superiority to them leads, in my view, to triviality and boredom, and that out of triviality comes evil (as L. H. Myers notes in the preface to *The Root and the Flower*, and illustrates in the novel itself, especially in the sections dealing with the 'Camp').

[19] So the footnote on p. 23 above takes on a marked significance—a significance confirmed very strikingly by Percy Lubbock's summary of letters written at about the same time: 'In Paris he settled therefore, in the autumn of 1875, taking rooms at 29 Rue du Luxembourg. He began to write *The American*, to contribute Parisian Letters to the *New York Tribune*, and to frequent the society of a few of his compatriots. He made the valued acquaintance of Ivan Turgenev, and through him of the group which surrounded Gustave

That is a fair way of putting the significance of the
relation between *The Portrait of a Lady* and *Daniel Deronda* that I discuss in my examination of the latter book.
That relation demonstrated, nothing more is needed in
order to establish the general relation I posit between the
two novelists. James's distinctive bent proclaims itself un-
compromisingly in what he does with *Daniel Deronda*
(on the good part of which—I call it *Gwendolen Harleth*
—*The Portrait of a Lady* is a variation; for the plain fact
I point out amounts to that). The moral substance of
George Eliot's theme is subtilized into something going
with the value James sets on 'high civilization'; her study
of conscience has disappeared. A charming and intelligent
girl, determined to live 'finely,' confidently exercises her
'free ethical sensibility' (Mr. Winters' phrase) and discovers that she is capable of disastrous misvaluation
(which is not surprising, seeing not only how inexperi-
enced she is, but how much an affair of inexplicitnesses,
overtones and fine shades is the world of discourse she
moves in). It is a tragedy in which, for her, neither remorse
is involved, nor, in the ordinary sense, the painful growth
of conscience, though no doubt her 'ethical sensibility'
matures.

Along the line revealed by the contrast between the
two novels James develops an art so unlike George Eliot's
that, but for the fact (which seems to have escaped notice)
of the relation of *The Portrait of a Lady* to *Daniel Der-*

Flaubert—Edmond de Goncourt, Alphonse Daudet, Guy de
Maupassant, Zola and others. But the letters which follow
will show the kind of doubts that began to arise after a winter
in Paris—doubts of the possibility of Paris as a place where
an American imagination could really take root and flourish.
He found the circle of literature tightly closed to outside influences; it seemed to exclude all culture but its own after a
fashion that aroused his opposition; he speaks sarcastically on
one occasion of having watched Turgenev and Flaubert seriously discussing Daudet's *Jack*, while he reflected that none
of the three had read, or knew English enough to read,
Daniel Deronda.'—*The Letters of Henry James*, Vol. I, p. 41.

onda, it would, argument being necessary, have been difficult to argue at all convincingly that there was the significant relation between the novelists. And I had better insist that I am not concerned to establish *indebtedness.* What I have in mind is the fact of the great tradition and the apartness of the two great novelists above the ruck of Gaskells and Trollopes and Merediths. Of the earlier novelists it was George Eliot alone (if we except the minor relevance of Jane Austen) whose work had a direct and significant bearing on his own problem. It had this bearing because she *was* a great novelist, and because in her maturest work she handled with unprecedented subtlety and refinement the personal relations of sophisticated characters exhibiting the 'civilization' of the 'best society,' and used, in so doing, an original psychological notation corresponding to the fineness of her psychological and moral insight. Her moral seriousness was for James very far from a disqualification; it qualified her for a kind of influence that neither Flaubert nor the admired Turgenev could have.

Circumstances discussed above made James peculiarly dependent on literature; the contact with George Eliot's distinctive kind of greatness was correspondingly important for him. It is significant that *Madame de Mauves* (1874), the early story in which he uses something like the theme of *The Portrait of a Lady,* has a wordy quality premonitory (one can't help feeling) of the cobwebbiness that afflicted him in his late phase. We can't doubt that George Eliot counts for something in the incomparably superior concreteness of *The Portrait of a Lady.* In that book, and in its successor, *The Bostonians,* his art is at its most concrete, and least subject to the weakness attendant on his subtlety. It is not derivativeness that is in question, but the relation between two original geniuses. 'We cannot attempt to trace,' says Mr. Van Wyck Brooks in *The Pilgrimage of Henry James,* 'the astonishing development of a creative faculty which, in the course of a dozen years, transcended the simple plot-maker's art of *The American,* the factitious local-colourism of *Roderick Hudson,* and rendered itself capable of the serene beauty of *The Portrait of a Lady*, the masterly assurance of *The Bostonians*, the mature perfection of *Washington Square*.'—It is more than a guess that, in that development, George Eliot had some part.

The reader is likely to comment, I suppose, on the degree in which my treatment of James is taken up with discussing his limitations and the regrettable aspects of his later development. Since it will also be noted that, of my three novelists, he, in terms of space, gets least attention, it might be concluded that a corresponding relative valuation is implied. I had, then, perhaps better say that there is no such relation intended between valuation and length of treatment. I will not, however, deny that, of the three, James seems to me to give decidedly most cause for dissatisfaction and qualification. He is, all the same, one of the great. His registration of sophisticated human consciousness is one of the classical creative achievements: it *added* something as only genius can. And when he is at his best that something is seen to be of great human significance. He creates an ideal civilized sensibility; a humanity capable of communicating by the finest shades of inflection and implication: a nuance may engage a whole complex moral economy and the perceptive response be the index of a major valuation or choice. Even *The Awkward Age*, in which the extremely developed subtlety of treatment is not as remote as one would wish from the hypertrophy that finally overcame him, seems to me a classic; in no other work can we find anything like that astonishing—in so astonishing a measure successful—use of sophisticated 'society' dialogue.

In considering James's due status, in fact, it is not easy to say just where the interest of the classical artist turns into the interest of the classical 'case.' But it seems to me obvious that the 'case' becomes in some places boring to the point of unreadableness. Yet there is a tacit conspiracy to admire some of the works that fall, partly, at any rate (wholly, one must conclude, for the admirers who risk explanatory comment on them), under this description.

And here is sufficient reason why an attempt to promote a due appreciation of James's genius should give a good deal of discriminatory attention to the tendencies that, as they develop, turn vital subtlety into something else.

When we come to Conrad we can't, by way of insisting that he is indeed significantly 'in' the tradition—in and of it, neatly and conclusively relate him to any one English novelist. Rather, we have to stress his foreignness—that he was a Pole, whose first other language was French.[20] I remember remarking to André Chevrillon how surprising a choice it was on Conrad's part to write in English, especially seeing he was so clearly a student of the French masters. And I remember the reply, to the effect that it wasn't at all surprising, since Conrad's work couldn't have been written in French. M. Chevrillon, with the authority of a perfect bilingual, went on to explain in terms of the characteristics of the two languages why it had to be English. Conrad's themes and interests demanded the concreteness and action—the dramatic energy—of English. We might go further and say that Conrad chose to write his novels in English for the reasons that led him to become a British Master Mariner.

---

[20] 'The politeness of Conrad to James and of James to Conrad was of the most impressive kind. Even if they had been addressing each other from the tribunal of the Académie Française their phrases could not have been more elaborate or delivered more *ore rotundo*. James always addressed Conrad as "Mon cher confrère," Conrad almost bleated with the peculiar tone that the Marseillais get into their compliments "Mon cher maître" . . . Every thirty seconds. When James spoke of me to Conrad he always said: "Votre ami, le jeune homme modeste." They always spoke French together, James using an admirably pronounced, correct and rather stilted idiom such as prevailed in Paris in the 'seventies. Conrad spoke with extraordinary speed, fluency and incomprehensibility, a meridional French with as strong a Southern accent as that of garlic in *aioli*. . . . Speaking English he had so strong a French accent that few who did not know him well could understand him at first.' —Ford Madox Ford, *Return to Yesterday*, pp. 23-4.

I am not, in making this point, concurring in the emphasis generally laid on the Prose Laureate of the Merchant Service. What needs to be stressed is the great novelist. Conrad's great novels, if they deal with the sea at all, deal with it only incidentally. But the Merchant Service is for him both a spiritual fact and a spiritual symbol, and the interests that made it so for him control and animate his art everywhere. Here, then, we have a master of the English language, who chose it for its distinctive qualities and because of the moral tradition associated with it, and whose concern with art—he being like Jane Austen and George Eliot and Henry James an innovator in 'form' and method—is the servant of a profoundly serious interest in life. To justify our speaking of such a novelist as in the tradition, that represented by those three, we are not called on to establish particular relations with any one of them. Like James, he brought a great deal from outside, but it was of the utmost importance to him that he found a serious art of fiction there in English, and that there *were*, in English, great novelists to study. He drew from English literature what he needed, and learnt in that peculiar way of genius which is so different from imitation. And for us, who have *him* as well as the others, there he is, unquestionably a constitutive part of the tradition, belonging in the full sense.

As being technically sophisticated he may be supposed to have found fortifying stimulus in James, whom he is quite unlike (though James, in his old age, was able to take a connoisseur's interest in *Chance* and appreciate with a professional eye the sophistication of the 'doing').[21] But

---

[21] Here is the testimony of Conrad's collaborator, Ford Madox Ford: 'Conrad had the most unbounded, the most generous and the most understanding admiration for the Master's work but he did not much like James personally. I imagine that was because at bottom James was a New Englander *pur sang*, though he was actually born in New York. James on the other hand liked neither Conrad nor his work very much. . . . James on the other hand never made fun of Conrad in

actually, the one influence at all obvious is that of a writer
at the other end of the scale from sophistication, Dickens.
As I point out in my discussion of him, Conrad is in certain respects so like Dickens that it is difficult to say for
just how much influence Dickens counts. He is undoubtedly there in the London of *The Secret Agent*, though—
except for the unfortunate *macabre* of the cab-journey,
and one or two local mannerisms—he has been transmuted
into Conrad. This co-presence of obvious influence with
assimilation suggests that Dickens may have counted for
more in Conrad's mature art (we don't find much to suggest Dickens in the early adjectival phase) than seems at
first probable: it suggests that Dickens may have encour-
aged the development in Conrad's art of that extraordinary
energy of vision and registration in which they are akin.
('When people say that Dickens exaggerates,' says Mr.
Santayana, 'it seems to me that they can have no eyes and
no ears. They probably have only *notions* of what things
and people are; they accept them conventionally, at their
diplomatic value.') We may reasonably, too, in the same
way see some Dickensian influence, closely related and of
the same order, in Conrad's use of melodrama, or what
would have been melodrama in Dickens; for in Conrad
the end is a total significance of a profoundly serious kind.

The reason for not including Dickens in the line of
great novelists is implicit in this last phrase. The kind of
greatness in question has been sufficiently defined. That
Dickens was a great genius and is permanently among the
classics is certain. But the genius was that of a great entertainer, and he had for the most part no profounder respon-

---

private. Conrad was never for him "poor dear old" as were
Flaubert, Mrs. Humphry Ward, Meredith, Hardy or Sir Edmund Gosse. He once expressed to me as regards Conrad
something like an immense respect for his character and
achievements. I cannot remember his exact words, but they
were something to the effect that Conrad's works impressed
him very disagreeably, but he could find no technical fault
or awkwardness about them.'—*Return to Yesterday*, p. 24.

sibility as a creative artist than this description suggests. Praising him magnificently in a very fine critique,[22] Mr. Santayana, in concluding, says: 'In every English-speaking home, in the four quarters of the globe, parents and children would do well to read Dickens aloud of a winter's evening.' This note is right and significant. The adult mind doesn't as a rule find in Dickens a challenge to an unusual and sustained seriousness. I can think of only one of his books in which his distinctive creative genius is controlled throughout to a unifying and organizing significance, and that is *Hard Times*, which seems, because of its unusualness and comparatively small scale, to have escaped recognition for the great thing it is. Conrad's views on it, supposing it to have caught his attention, would have been interesting; he was qualified to have written an apt appreciation.

It has a kind of perfection as a work of art that we don't associate with Dickens—a perfection that is one with the sustained and complete seriousness for which among his productions it is unique. Though in length it makes a good-sized modern novel, it is on a small scale for Dickens: it leaves no room for the usual repetitive overdoing and loose inclusiveness. It is plain that he felt no temptation to these, he was too urgently possessed by his themes; the themes were too rich, too tightly knit in their variety and too commanding. Certain key characteristics of Victorian civilization had clearly come home to him with overwhelming force, embodied in concrete manifestations that suggested to him connexions and significances he had never realized so fully before. The fable is perfect; the symbolic and representative values are inevitable, and, sufficiently plain at once, yield fresh subtleties as the action develops naturally in its convincing historical way.

In Gradgrind and Bounderby we have, in significant relation, two aspects of Victorian Utilitarianism. In Gradgrind it is a serious creed, devoutly held, and so, if repellent (as the name conveys), not wholly unrespectable; but

---

[22] See *Soliloquies in England*.

we are shown Gradgrind as on the most intimate and uncritical terms with Josiah Bounderby, in whom we have the grossest and crassest, the most utterly unspiritual egotism, and the most blatant thrusting and bullying, to which a period of 'rugged individualism' gave scope. Gradgrind, in fact, marries his daughter to Bounderby. Yet he is represented as a kind of James Mill; an intellectual who gives his children, on theory, an education that reminds us in a very significant way of the *Autobiography* of the younger Mill. And it is hardly possible to question the justice of this vision of the tendency of James Mill's kind of Utilitarianism, so blind in its onesidedness, so unaware of its bent and its blindness. The generous uncalculating spontaneity, the warm flow of life, towards which Gradgrindery, practical and intellectual, must be hostile, is symbolized by Sleary's Horse-riding.

The richness in symbolic significance of *Hard Times* is far from adequately suggested by this account. The prose is that of one of the greatest masters of English, and the dialogue—very much a test in such an undertaking—is consummate; beautifully natural in its stylization. But there is only one *Hard Times* in the Dickensian *œuvre*.

Though the greatness of *Hard Times* passed unnoticed, Dickens couldn't fail to have a wide influence. We have remarked his presence in *The Secret Agent*. It is there again, in a minor way, in George Eliot, in some of her less felicitous characterization; and it is there in Henry James, most patently, perhaps, in *The Princess Casamassima*, but most importantly in *Roderick Hudson*.[23] It is there once more, and even more interestingly, in D. H. Lawrence, in *The Lost Girl*. The ironic humour, and the presentation in general, in the first part of that book bear a clear relation to the Dickensian, but are incomparably more mature, and belong to a total serious significance.

I take the opportunity, at this point, to remark parenthetically, that, whereas Dickens's greatness has been confirmed by time, it is quite otherwise with his rival. 'It is

---

23 See pp. 160-72 below.

usual,' says Mr. Santayana, 'to compare Dickens with Thackeray, which is like comparing the grape with the gooseberry; there are obvious points of resemblance, and the gooseberry has some superior qualities of its own; but you can't make red wine of it.' It seems to me that Thackeray's place is fairly enough indicated, even if his peculiar quality isn't precisely defined, by inverting a phrase I found the other day on an examination-paper: 'Trollope is a lesser Thackeray.' Thackeray is a greater Trollope; that is, he has (apart from some social history) nothing to offer the reader whose demand goes beyond the 'creation of characters' and so on. His attitudes, and the essential substance of interest, are so limited that (though, of course, he provides incident and plot) for the reader it is merely a matter of going on and on; nothing has been done by the close to justify the space taken—except, of course, that time has been killed (which seems to be all that even some academic critics demand of a novel). It will be fair enough to Thackeray if *Vanity Fair* is kept current as, in a minor way, a classic: the conventional estimate that puts him among the great won't stand the touch of criticism. The kind of thing that Thackeray is credited with is done at a mature level by James's friend, Howard Sturgis, in *Belchamber*, a novel about Edwardian society (it is, with an appropriateness not always observed in that series, included in *The World's Classics*).

To come back to Conrad and his major quality: he is one of those creative geniuses whose distinction is manifested in their being peculiarly alive in their time—peculiarly alive *to* it; not 'in the vanguard' in the manner of Shaw and Wells and Aldous Huxley, but sensitive to the stresses of the changing spiritual climate as they begin to be registered by the most conscious. His interest in the tradition of the Merchant Service as a constructive triumph of the human spirit is correlative with his intense consciousness of the dependence, not only of the distinctive humanities at all levels, but of sanity itself and our sense of a normal outer world, on an analogous creative collaboration. His Robinson Crusoe cannot bear a few days alone on his island, and blows out his brains. We are a long way from Jane Austen, for whom the problem was not to rescue the highly conscious individual from his isolation, but much the contrary. Conrad, of course, was a *déraciné*, which no doubt counts for a good deal in the intensity with which he renders his favourite theme of isolation. But then a state of something like deracination is common to-day among those to whom the question of who the great novelists are is likely to matter. Conrad is representative in the way genius is, which is not the way of those writers in whom journalist-critics acclaim the Zeitgeist. (It is relevant to note here that in the early hey-day of Wells and Shaw Conrad wrote *Nostromo*—a great creative masterpiece which, among other things, is essentially an implicit comment on their preoccupations, made from a very much profounder level of preoccupation than theirs. And it is also relevant to venture that in Mr. Arthur Koestler's very distinguished novel, *Darkness at Noon,* we have the work of a writer—also, we note, not born to the language—who knows and admires Conrad, especially the Conrad of *Nostromo* and *Under Western Eyes.*

Conrad is incomparably closer to us to-day than Hardy and Meredith are. So, for that matter, is George Eliot. I specify Hardy and Meredith because they are both offered to us among the great novelists, and they are both supposed to be philosophically profound about life. It will have been gathered that I think neither can support his reputation. On Hardy (who owes enormously to George Eliot) the appropriately sympathetic note is struck by Henry James: 'The good little Thomas Hardy has scored a great success with *Tess of the d'Urbervilles,* which is chock-full of faults and falsity, and yet has a singular charm.' This concedes by implication all that properly can be conceded—unless we claim more for *Jude the Obscure,* which, of all Hardy's works of a major philosophic-tragic ambition, comes nearer to sustaining it, and, in its clumsy way—which hasn't the rightness with which the great novelists show their profound sureness of their essential

purpose—is impressive.[24] It is all the same a little comic
that Hardy should have been taken in the early nineteen-
twenties—the Chekhov period—as pre-eminently the representative of the 'modern consciousness' or the modern
'sense of the human situation.' As for Meredith, I needn't
add anything to what is said about him by Mr. E. M.
Forster,[25] who, having belonged to the original *milieu*
in which Meredith was erected into a great master, enjoys
peculiar advantages for the necessary demolition-work.

Is there no name later than Conrad's to be included in
the great tradition? There is, I am convinced, one: D. H.
Lawrence. Lawrence, in the English language, was the
great genius of our time (I mean the age, or climatic phase,

---

[24] Arthur Mizener's essay, '*Jude the Obscure* as a Tragedy,'
in the Thomas Hardy Centennial Issue of *The Southern Review* (Summer 1940), puts interestingly the case for a serious
estimate of the book.

[25] See *Aspects of the Novel*. And here is James on *Lord
Ormont and his Aminta*: 'Moreover, I have vowed not to open
Lourdes till I shall have closed with a furious final bang the
unspeakable *Lord Ormont*, which I have been reading at the
maximum rate of ten pages—ten insufferable and unprofitable
pages—a day. It fills me with a critical rage, an artistic fury,
utterly blighting in me the indispensable principle of *respect*.
I have finished, at this rate, but the first volume—whereof I
am moved to declare that I doubt if any equal quantity of
extravagant verbiage, of airs and graces, of phrases and attitudes, of obscurities and alembications, ever *started* less their
subject, ever contributed less of a statement—told the reader
less of what the reader needs to know. All the elaborate pred-
icates of exposition without the ghost of a nominative to hook
themselves to; and not a difficulty met, not a figure presented,
not a scene constituted—not a dim shadow condensing once
either into audible or into visible reality—making you hear for
an instant the tap of its feet on the earth. Of course there are
pretty things, but for what they are they come so much too
dear, and so many of the profundities and tortuosities prove
when threshed out to be only pretentious statements of the
very simplest propositions.'—To Edmund Gosse: *The Letters
of Henry James*, Vol. I, p. 224.

following Conrad's). It would be difficult to separate the
novelist off for consideration, but it was in the novel that
he committed himself to the hardest and most sustained
creative labour, and he was, as a novelist, the representative of vital and significant development. He might, he
has shown conclusively, have gone on writing novels
with the kind of 'character creation' and psychology that
the conventional cultivated reader immediately appre-
ciates—novels that demanded no unfamiliar effort of approach. He might—if his genius had let him. In nothing
is the genius more manifest than in the way in which,
after the great success—and *succès d'estime*—of *Sons and
Lovers* he gives up that mode and devotes himself to the
exhausting toil of working out the new things, the devel-
opments, that as the highly conscious and intelligent servant of life he saw to be necessary. Writing to Edward
Garnett of the work that was to become *Women in Love*
he says: 'It is *very* different from *Sons and Lovers*: written
in another language almost. I shall be sorry if you don't
like it, but am prepared. I shan't write in the same manner
as *Sons and Lovers* again, I think—in that hard, violent
style full of sensation and presentation.' [26]

Describing at length what he is trying to do he says:

'You mustn't look in my novel for the old stable *ego*
of the character. There is another *ego*, according to
whose action the individual is unrecognizable, and
passes through, as it were, allotropic states which it
needs a deeper sense than any we've been used to exercise, to discover are states of the same single radically
unchanged element. (Like as diamond and coal are the
same pure simple element of carbon. The ordinary novel
would trace the history of the diamond—but I say, "Diamond, what! This is carbon." And my diamond might
be coal or soot, and my theme is carbon.) You must not
say my novel is shaky—it is not perfect, because I am
not expert in what I want to do. But it is the real thing,

[26] *The Letters of D. H. Lawrence*, p. 172.

say what you like. And I shall get my reception, if not now, then before long. Again I say, don't look for the development of the novel to follow the lines of certain characters: the characters fall into the form of some other rhythmic form, as when one draws a fiddle-bow across a fine tray delicately sanded, the sand takes lines unknown.' [27]

He is a most daring and radical innovator in 'form,' method, technique. And his innovations and experiments are dictated by the most serious and urgent kind of interest in life. This is the spirit of it:

'Do you know Cassandra in Aeschylus and Homer? She is one of the world's great figures, and what the Greeks and Agamemnon did to her is symbolic of what mankind has done to her since—raped and despoiled her, to their own ruin. It is not your brain that you must trust to, nor your will—but to that fundamental pathetic faculty for receiving the hidden waves that come from the depths of life, and for transferring them to the unreceptive world. It is something which happens below the consciousness, and below the range of the will—it is something which is unrecognizable and frustrated and destroyed.' [28]

It is a spirit that, for all the unlikeness, relates Lawrence closely to George Eliot.[29] He writes, again, to Edward Garnett[30]:

'You see—you tell me I am half a Frenchman and one-eighth a Cockney. But that isn't it. I have very often the vulgarity and disagreeableness of the common people, as you say Cockney, and I may be a Frenchman. But primarily I am a passionately religious man, and my novels must be written from the depth of my religious

---

[27] *Letters*, p. 198.
[28] *Letters*, p. 232.
[29] Lawrence too has been called a Puritan.
[30] *Letters*, p. 190.

experience. That I must keep to, because I can only work like that. And my Cockneyism and commonness are only when the deep feeling doesn't find its way out, and a sort of jeer comes instead, and sentimentality and purplism. But you should see the religious, earnest, suffering man in me first, and then the flippant or common things after. Mrs. Garnett says I have no true nobility—with all my cleverness and charm. But that is not true. It is there, in spite of all the littlenesses and commonnesses.'

It is this spirit, by virtue of which he can truly say that what he writes must be written from the depth of his religious experience, that makes him, in my opinion, so much more significant in relation to the past and future, so much more truly creative as a technical inventor, an innovator, a master of language, than James Joyce. I know that Mr. T. S. Eliot has found in Joyce's work something that recommends Joyce to him as positively religious in tendency (see *After Strange Gods*). But it seems plain to me that there is no organic principle determining, informing, and controlling into a vital whole, the elaborate analogical structure, the extraordinary variety of technical devices, the attempts at an exhaustive rendering of consciousness, for which *Ulysses* is remarkable, and which got it accepted by a cosmopolitan literary world as a new start. It is rather, I think, a dead end, or at least a pointer to disintegration—a view strengthened by Joyce's own development (for I think it significant and appropriate that *Work in Progress—Finnegans Wake*, as it became—should have engaged the interest of the inventor of Basic English).

It is true that we can point to the influence of Joyce in a line of writers to which there is no parallel issuing from Lawrence. But I find here further confirmation of my view. For I think that in these writers, in whom a regrettable (if minor) strain of Mr. Eliot's influence seems to me to join with that of Joyce, we have, in so far as we have anything significant, the wrong kind of reaction against liberal idealism.[31] I have in mind writers in whom Mr. Eliot has expressed an interest in strongly favourable terms: Djuna Barnes of *Nightwood,* Henry Miller, Lawrence Durrell of *The Black Book.* In these writers —at any rate in the last two (and the first seems to me insignificant)—the spirit of what we are offered affects me as being essentially a desire, in Laurentian phrase, to 'do dirt' on life. It seems to me important that one should, in all modesty, bear one's witness in these matters. 'One must speak for life and growth, amid all this mass of destruction and disintegration.' [32] This is Lawrence, and it is the spirit of all his work. It is the spirit of the originality that gives his novels their disconcerting quality, and gives them the significance of works of genius.

I am not contending that he isn't, as a novelist, open to a great deal of criticism, or that his achievement is as a whole satisfactory (the potentiality being what it was). He wrote his later books far too hurriedly. But I know from experience that it is far too easy to conclude that his very aim and intention condemned him to artistic unsatisfactoriness. I am thinking in particular of two books at which he worked very hard, and in which he developed his disconcertingly original interests and approaches—*The Rainbow* and *Women in Love.* Re-read, they seem to me astonishing works of genius, and very much more largely successful than they did when I read them (say) fifteen years ago. I still think that *The Rainbow* doesn't build up sufficiently into a whole. But I shouldn't be quick to offer my criticism of *Women in Love,* being pretty sure that I should in any case have once more to convict myself of stupidity and habit-blindness on later re-reading. And after these novels there comes, written, perhaps, with an ease earned by this hard work done, a large body of short stories and *nouvelles* that are as indubitably successful works of genius as any the world has to show.

---

[31] See D. H. Lawrence's *Fantasia of the Unconscious,* especially Chapter XI.
[32] *The Letters of D. H. Lawrence,* p. 256.

I have, then, given my hostages. What I think and judge I have stated as responsibly and clearly as I can. Jane Austen, George Eliot, Henry James, Conrad, and D. H. Lawrence: the great tradition of the English novel is *there*.

NOTE: 'THE BRONTËS'

It is tempting to retort that there is only one Brontë. Actually, Charlotte, though claiming no part in the great line of English fiction (it is significant that she couldn't see why any value should be attached to Jane Austen), has a permanent interest of a minor kind. She had a remarkable talent that enabled her to do something firsthand and new in the rendering of personal experience, above all in *Villette*.

The genius, of course, was Emily. I have said nothing about *Wuthering Heights* because that astonishing work seems to me a kind of sport. It may, all the same, very well have had some influence of an essentially undetectable kind: she broke completely, and in the most challenging way, both with the Scott tradition that imposed on the novelist a romantic resolution of his themes, and with the tradition coming down from the eighteenth century that demanded a plane-mirror reflection of the surface of 'real' life. Out of her a minor tradition comes, to which belongs, most notably, *The House with the Green Shutters*.

II. GEORGE ELIOT

(i) The Early Phase

THERE is general agreement that an appraisal of George
Eliot must be a good deal preoccupied with major discriminations—that the body of her work exhibits within
itself striking differences not merely of kind, but between
the more and the less satisfactory, and exhibits them in
such a way that the history of her art has to be seen as
something less happy in its main lines than just an unfolding of her genius, a prosperous development of her
distinctive powers, with growing maturity. It is generally
assumed that this aspect of her performance is significantly
related to the fact of her having displayed impressive intellectual gifts outside her art, so that she was a distinguished
figure in the world of Herbert Spencer and the *Westminster Review* before she became a novelist. And there is
something like a unanimity to the effect that it is distinctive of her, among great novelists, to be peculiarly addicted
to moral preoccupations.

The force of this last—what it amounts to or intends,
and the significance it has for criticism—is elusive; and it
seems well to start with a preliminary glance at what, from
his hours with the critics, the reader is likely to recall as a
large established blur across the field of vision. Henry
James seems to me to have shown finer intelligence than
anyone else in writing about George Eliot, and he, in his
review of the Cross *Life* of her, tells us that, for her, the
novel 'was not primarily a picture of life, capable of deriving a high value from its form, but a moralized fable,
the last word of a philosophy endeavouring to teach by
example.' [1] The blur is seen here in that misleading antithesis, which, illusory as it is, James's commentary insists

---

[1] *Partial Portraits*, p. 50.

on. What, we ask, is the 'form' from which a 'picture of life' derives its value? As we should expect, the term 'aesthetic,' with its trail of confusion, turns up in the neighbourhood (it is a term the literary critic would do well to abjure). James notes, as characterizing 'that side of George Eliot's nature which was weakest,' the 'absence of free aesthetic life,' and he says that her 'figures and situations' are 'not *seen* in the irresponsible plastic way.' But, we ask, in what great, in what interesting, novel *are* the figures and situations seen in an 'irresponsible plastic way' (a useful determination of one of the intentions of 'aesthetic')? Is there any great novelist whose preoccupation with 'form' is not a matter of his responsibility towards a rich human interest, or complexity of interests, profoundly realized?—a responsibility involving, of its very nature, imaginative sympathy, moral discrimination and judgment of relative human value?

The art distinguished by the corresponding irresponsibility might be supposed to be represented by the dreary brilliance of *Salammbô* and *La Tentation*. But we know that this is so far from James's intention that he finds even *Madame Bovary*, much as he admires it, an instance of a preoccupation with 'form' that is insufficiently a preoccupation with human value and moral interest.[2] In fact, his verdict on *Madame Bovary* may fairly be taken to be of no very different order from that implied when George Eliot finds *Le Père Goriot* 'a hateful book'—the phrase that, curiously enough, provides the occasion for James's remarks about her lack of 'free aesthetic life.'[3]

---

[2] See his essay on Flaubert in *Notes on Novelists*.

[3] I had better say that my judgment of *Le Père Goriot* clearly differs from Henry James's. The impressiveness of the famous passions Balzac presents seems to me to be too much of the order of Shelley's

> BEATRICE (wildly)   O
> My God! Can it be possible . . . *etc.*

Balzac's art here seems to me an essentially rhetorical art in a

That the antithesis I quote from Henry James is unsatis-factory and doesn't promote clear thinking is no doubt obvious enough. And the reader may note that James's essay dates sixty years back. Yet his handling of the matter seems to me representative: I don't know of anything writ-ten about George Eliot that, touching on this matter of her distinctive moral preoccupation, does anything essen-tially more helpful towards defining the distinctive quality of her art. James, then, is a critic one reads with close attention, and, coming on so challenging a formula-tion in so intelligent a context, one is provoked to com-ment that, while, among the great novelists, George Eliot must certainly have her difference, it can hardly be of the kind such an antithetical way of putting things suggests. Though such formulations may have their colourable grounds, there must, one reflects, be something more im-portant to say about the moral seriousness of George El-iot's novels; otherwise she would hardly be the great novel-ist one knows her to be. There are certain conditions of art from which she cannot be exempt while remaining an artist.

A tentative comparison or two may help to define the direction in which the appraising critic should turn his inquiries. Consider her against, not Flaubert, but two nov-elists concerning whose greatness one has no uneasy sense of a need to hedge. In her own language she ranks with Jane Austen and Conrad, both of whom, in their different ways, present sharp contrasts with her. To take Conrad first: there is no novelist of whom it can more fitly be said that his figures and situations are *seen,* and James would have testified to his intense and triumphant preoccupation with 'form.' [4] He went to school to the French masters, and

---

pejorative sense of the adjective: romantic rhetoric is the life and spirit of the sublimities and degradations he exhibits. They depend for their effect, that is, not on any profound realiza-tion of human emotions, but on excited emphasis, top-level assertion and explicit insistence.

[4] Actually James salutes *Chance* in *The New Novel,* an article written in 1914 (see *Notes on Novelists*).

is in the tradition of Flaubert. But he is a greater novelist than Flaubert because of the greater range and depth of his interest in humanity and the greater intensity of his moral preoccupation: he is not open to the kind of criticism that James brings against *Madame Bovary*. *Nostromo* is a masterpiece of 'form' in senses of the term congenial to the discussion of Flaubert's art, but to appreciate Conrad's 'form' is to take stock of a process of relative valuation conducted by him in the face of life: what do men live by? what *can* men live by?—these are the questions that animate his theme. His organization is devoted to exhibiting in the concrete a representative set of radical attitudes, so ordered as to bring out the significance of each in relation to a total sense of human life. The dramatic imagination at work is an intensely moral imagination, the vividness of which is inalienably a judging and a valuing. With such economy has each 'figure' and 'situation' its significance in a taut inclusive scheme that *Nostromo* might more reasonably than any of George Eliot's fictions except *Silas Marner* (which has something of the fairy-tale about it, and is in any case a minor work) be called a 'moralized fable.'

What, then, in this matter of the relation between their moral interests and their art, is the difference between Conrad and George Eliot? (Their sensibilities, of course, differ, but that is not the question.) I had better here give the whole of the sentence of James's, of which above I quoted a part:

'Still, what even a jotting may *not* have said after a first perusal of *Le Père Goriot* is eloquent; it illuminates the author's general attitude with regard to the novel, which, for her, was not primarily a picture of life, capable of deriving a high value from its form, but a moralized fable, the last word of a philosophy endeavouring to teach by example.'

—To find the difference in didactism doesn't take us very far; not much to the point is said about a work of art in calling it didactic—unless one is meaning to judge it adversely. In that case one is judging that the intention to communicate an attitude hasn't become sufficiently more than an intention; hasn't, that is, justified itself as art in the realized concreteness that speaks for itself and *enacts* its moral significance. But whatever criticism the weaker parts of George Eliot may lie open to no one is going to characterize her by an inclusive judgment of that kind. And it is her greatness we are concerned with.

James speaks of a 'philosophy endeavouring to teach by example': perhaps, it may be suggested, the clue we want is to be found in the 'philosophy?' And the context shows that James does, in attempting to define her peculiar quality, intend to stress George Eliot's robust powers of intellectual labour and her stamina in the realm of abstract thought—he speaks elsewhere of her 'exemption from cerebral lassitude.' But actually it is not easy to see how, in so far as her intellectual distinction appears in the strength of her art, it constitutes an essential difference between her and Conrad. She has no more of a philosophy than he has, and he, on the other hand, is, in his work, clearly a man of great intelligence and confirmed intellectual habit, whose 'picture of life' embodies much reflective analysis and sustained thought about fundamentals.

What can, nevertheless, be said, with obvious truth, is that Conrad is more completely an artist. It is not that he had no intellectual career outside his art—that he did nothing comparable to translating Strauss, Spinoza and Feuerbach, and editing *The Westminster Review*. It is that he transmutes more completely into the created work the interests he brings in. No doubt the two facts are related: the fact that he was novelist and seaman and not novelist and high-level intellectual middleman has a bearing on the fact that he achieved a wholeness in art (it will be observed that the change of phrase involves a certain change of force, but the shift is legitimate, I think) not characteristic of George Eliot. But it must not be concluded that the point about her is that her novels contain unabsorbed intellectual elements—patches, say, of tough or drily abstract thinking undigested by her art. The relevant characteristic, rather, is apt to strike the reader as something quite other than toughness or dryness; we note it as an emotional quality, something that strikes us as the direct (and sometimes embarrassing) presence of the author's own personal need. Conrad, we know, had been in his time hard-pressed; the evidence is everywhere in his work, but, in any one of the great novels, it comes to us out of the complex impersonalized whole. There can, of course, be no question of saying simply that the opposite is true of George Eliot: she is a great novelist, and has achieved her triumphs of creative art. Nor is it quite simply a matter of distinguishing between what is strong in her work and what is weak. At her best she has the impersonality of genius, but there is characteristic work of hers that is rightly admired where the quality of the sensibility can often be felt to have intimate relations with her weakness.

That is, the critic appraising her is faced with a task of discrimination. I began by reporting general agreement to this effect. The point of my comparison is to suggest that the discriminating actually needing to be done will be on different lines from those generally assumed.

And that is equally the conclusion prompted by a comparative glance at Jane Austen. Though the fashionable cult tends to suggest otherwise, she doesn't differ from George Eliot by not being earnestly moral. The vitality of her art is a matter of a preoccupation with moral problems that is subtle and intense because of the pressure of personal need. As for the essential difference (leaving aside the differences in the nature of the need and in range of interests), is it something that can be related to the fact that Jane Austen, while unmistakably very intelligent, can lay no claim to a massive intellect like George Eliot's, capable of maintaining a specialized intellectual life? Perhaps; but what again strikes us in the intellectual writer is an emotional quality, one to which there is no equivalent in Jane Austen. And it is not merely a matter of a difference of theme and interest—of George Eliot's dealing with (say) the agonized conscience and with re-

ligious need as Jane Austen doesn't. There could be this
difference without what is as a matter of fact associated
with it in George Eliot's work: a tendency towards that
kind of direct presence of the author which has to be stig-
matized as weakness.

But this is to anticipate.

The large discrimination generally made in respect of
George Eliot is a simple one. Henry James's account is
subtler than any other I know, but isn't worked out to
consistency. He says[5] (though the generalization is implicitly criticized by the context, being inadequate to his
perception):

> 'We feel in her, always, that she proceeds from the
> abstract to the concrete; that her figures and situations
> are evolved, as the phrase is, from her moral conscious-
> ness, and are only indirectly the products of observation.'

What this gives us is, according to the accepted view,
one half of her—the unsatisfactory half. The great George
Eliot, according to this view, is the novelist of reminiscence; the George Eliot who writes out of her memories
of childhood and youth, renders the poignancy and charm
of personal experience, and gives us, in a mellow light,
the England of her young days, and of the days then still
alive in family tradition. Her classics are *Scenes of Clerical
Life, Adam Bede, The Mill on the Floss,* and *Silas Marner.* With these books she exhausted her material, and in
order to continue a novelist had to bring the other half
of herself into play—to hand over, in fact, to the intellectual. *Romola* is the product of an exhausting and misguided labour of excogitation and historical reconstruction
(a judgment no one is likely to dispute). *Felix Holt* and
Daniel Deronda also represent the distinguished intellectual rather than the great novelist; in them she 'proceeds
from the abstract to the concrete,' 'her figures and situa-

---

[5] *Partial Portraits,* p. 51.

tions are evolved from her moral consciousness,' they 'are
deeply studied and massively supported, but . . .'—Henry
James's phrases fairly convey the accepted view.

It should be said at once that he is not to be identified
with it (he discriminates firmly, for instance, in respect
of *Daniel Deronda*). Still, he expresses for us admirably
what has for long been the current idea of her development, and he does in such passages as this endorse the
view that, in the later novels, the intellectual gets the
upper hand:

> 'The truth is, perception and reflection at the outset
> divided George Eliot's great talent between them; but
> as time went on circumstances led the latter to develop
> itself at the expense of the former—one of these cir-
> cumstances being apparently the influence of George
> Henry Lewes.'

And we don't feel that he is inclined to dissociate himself
to any significant extent when, in the *Conversation*[6] about
Daniel Deronda, he makes Constantius say:

> 'She strikes me as a person who certainly has naturally
> a taste for general considerations, but who has fallen
> upon an age and a circle which have compelled her to
> give them an exaggerated attention. She does not strike
> me as naturally a critic, less still as naturally a sceptic;
> her spontaneous part is to observe life and to feel it—to
> feel it with admirable depth. Contemplation, sympathy
> and faith—something like that, I should say, would have
> been her natural scale.'

At any rate, that gives what appears to be still the established notion of George Eliot.

It will have been noted above that I left out *Middlemarch*. And it will have been commented that *Middlemarch*, which, with *Felix Holt* between, comes in order
of production after *Romola* and doesn't at all represent a
reversion to the phase of 'spontaneity,' has for at least two

---

[6] See Appendix, p. 300 below.

decades been pretty generally acclaimed as one of the great masterpieces of English fiction. That is true. Virginia Woolf, a good index of cultivated acceptance in that period, writes (in *The Common Reader,* first series):

> 'It is not that her power diminishes, for, to our thinking, it is at its highest in the mature *Middlemarch,* the magnificent book which, with all its imperfections, is one of the few English novels written for grown-up people.'

This judgment, in a characteristic and not very satisfactory essay on George Eliot, must be set to Mrs. Woolf's credit as a critic; there is no doubt that it has had a good deal to do with the established recognition of *Middlemarch.*

But Mrs. Woolf makes no serious attempt at the work of general revision such a judgment implies, and the appreciation of George Eliot's *œuvre* has not been put on a critical basis and reduced to consistency. For if you think so highly of *Middlemarch,* then, to be consistent, you must be more qualified in your praise of the early things than persisting convention recognizes. Isn't there, in fact, a certain devaluing to be done? The key word in that sentence quoted from Mrs. Woolf is 'mature.' Her distinguished father (whose book on George Eliot in *The English Men of Letters* has his characteristic virtues) supplies, where their popularity is concerned, the key word for the earlier works when he speaks of a 'loss of charm' involved in her development after *The Mill on the Floss.* At the risk of appearing priggish one may suggest that there is a tendency to overrate charm. Certainly charm is overrated when it is preferred to maturity.

Going back in one's mind over the earlier works, what can one note as their attractions and their claims? There is *Scenes of Clerical Life,* which is to-day, perhaps, not much read. And indeed only with an effort can one appreciate why these stories should have made such an impact when they came out. One of them, *Mr. Gilfil's Love-Story,* is charming in a rather slight way. Without the charm the pathos would hardly be very memorable, and the charm is characteristic of the earlier George Eliot: it is the atmospheric richness of the past seen through home tradition and the associations of childhood. Of the other two, *The Sad Fortunes of the Rev. Amos Barton* and *Janet's Repentance,* one feels that they might have appeared in any Victorian family magazine. This is unfair, no doubt; the imaginative and morally earnest sympathy that finds a moving theme in the ordinariness of undistinguished lives —there we have the essential George Eliot; the magazine writer would not have had that touch in pathos and humour, and there is some justice in Leslie Stephen's finding an 'indication of a profoundly reflective intellect' in 'the constant, though not obtrusive, suggestion of the depths below the surface of trivial life.' But *Scenes of Clerical Life* would not have been remembered if nothing had followed.

George Eliot did no more prentice-work (the greater part of the *Scenes* may fairly be called that): *Adam Bede* is unmistakably qualified to be a popular classic—which, in so far as there are such to-day, it still is. There is no need here to offer an appreciation of its attractions; they are as plain as they are genuine, and they have had full critical justice done them. Criticism, it seems to me, is faced with the ungrateful office of asking whether, much as *Adam Bede* deserves its currency as a classic (and of the classical English novels it has been among the most widely read), the implicit valuation it enjoys in general acceptance doesn't represent something more than justice. The point can perhaps be made by suggesting that the book is too much the sum of its specifiable attractions to be among the great novels—that it is too resolvable into the separate interests that we can see the author to have started with. Of these, a main one, clearly, is given in Mrs. Poyser and that mellow presentation of rustic life (as George Eliot recalled it from her childhood) for which Mrs. Poyser's kitchen is the centre. This deserves all the admiration it has received. And this is the moment to say that juxtaposition with George Eliot is a test that disposes finally of the

'Shakespearean' Hardy: if the adjective is to be used at all, it applies much more fitly to the rich creativeness of the art that seems truly to draw its sap from life and is free from all suspicion of Shakespeareanizing. George Eliot's rustic life is convincingly real even when most charming (and she doesn't always mellow her presentation of it with charm).

We have another of the main interests with which George Eliot started in Dinah, that idealized recollection of the Methodist aunt. Dinah, a delicate undertaking, is sufficiently successful, but one has, in appraising her in relation to the total significance of the book, to observe, with a stress on the limiting implications of the word, that the success is conditioned by the 'charm' that invests her as it does the world she moves in and belongs to. She is idealized as Adam is idealized; they are in keeping. Adam, we know, is a tribute to her father; but he is also the Ideal Craftsman, embodying the Dignity of Labour. He too is *réussi*, but compare him with George Eliot's other tribute to her father, Caleb Garth of *Middlemarch*, who is in keeping with *his* context, and the suggestion that the idealizing element in the book named after Adam involves limiting judgments for the critic gets, I think, an obvious force.

Mrs. Poyser, Dinah and Adam—these three represent interests that George Eliot wanted to use in a novel. To make a novel out of them she had to provide something else. The Dinah theme entails the scene in prison, and so there had to be a love-story and a seduction. George Eliot works them into her given material with convincing skill; the entanglement of Arthur Donnithorne with Hetty Sorrel—the first casual self-indulgence, the progressive yielding to temptation, the inexorable Nemesis—involves a favourite moral-psychological theme of hers, and she handles it in a personal way. And yet—does one want ever to read that large part of the book again? does it gain by re-reading? doesn't this only confirm one's feeling that, while as Victorian fiction—a means of passing the time—the love-story must be granted its distinction, yet, judged

by the expectations with which one approaches a great
novelist, it offers nothing proportionate to the time it takes
(even if we cut the large amount of general reflection)?
Satisfactory at its own level as the unity is that the author
has induced in her materials, there is not at work in the
whole any pressure from her profounder experience to
compel an inevitable development; so that we don't feel
moved to discuss with any warmth whether or not she was
right to take Lewes's suggestion, and whether or not Dinah
would really have become Mrs. Adam Bede. We are not
engaged in such a way as to give any force to the question
whether the marriage is convincing or otherwise; there is
no sense of inevitability to outrage. These comments of
Henry James's seem to me just:

> 'In *Silas Marner*, in *Adam Bede*, the quality seems
> gilded by a sort of autumn haze, an afternoon light, of
> meditation, which mitigates the sharpness of the portrai-
> ture. I doubt very much whether the author herself had
> a clear vision, for instance, of the marriage of Dinah
> Morris to Adam, or of the rescue of Hetty from the
> scaffold at the eleventh hour. The reason of this may
> be, indeed, that her perception was a perception of na-
> ture much more than of art, and that these particular
> incidents do not belong to nature (to my sense at least);
> by which I do not mean that they belong to a very happy
> art. I cite them, on the contrary, as an evidence of artistic
> weakness; they are a very good example of the view in
> which a story must have marriages and rescues in the
> nick of time, as a matter of course.'

James indicates here the relation between the charm and
what he calls the 'art.' They are not identical, of course;
but what I have called 'charm' and described as an idealizing element means an abeyance of the profounder responsibility, so that, without being shocked, we can have
together in the same book the 'art' to which James refers—
the vaguely realized that draws its confidence from convention—and such genuinely moving things as the story
of Hetty Sorrel's wanderings. And here I will anticipate

and make the point that it is because the notorious scandal of Stephen Guest in *The Mill on the Floss* has nothing to do with 'art,' but is a different kind of thing altogether, that it is interesting and significant.

It is a related point that if 'charm' prevails in *Adam Bede* (and, as Henry James indicates, in *Silas Marner*), there should be another word for what we find in *The Mill on the Floss*. The fresh directness of a child's vision that we have there, in the autobiographical part, is something very different from the 'afternoon light' of reminiscence. This recaptured early vision, in its combination of clarity with rich 'significance,' is for us, no doubt, enchanting; but it doesn't idealize, or soften with a haze of sentiment (and it can't consort with 'art'). Instead of Mrs. Poyser and her setting we have the uncles and aunts. The bearing of the change is plain if we ask whether there could have been a Dinah in this company. Could there have been an Adam? They both belong to a different world.

In fact, the Gleggs and the Pullets and the Dodson clan associate, not with the frequenters of Mrs. Poyser's kitchen, but with the tribe that forgathers at Stone Court waiting for Peter Featherstone to die. The intensity of Maggie's naïve vision is rendered with the convincing truth of genius; but the rendering brings in the intelligence that goes with the genius and is *of* it, and the force of the whole effect is the product of understanding. This is an obvious enough point. I make it because I want to observe that, although the supremely mature mind of *Middlemarch* is not yet manifested in *The Mill on the Floss*, the creative powers at work here owe their successes as much to a very fine intelligence as to powers of feeling and remembering—a fact that, even if it is an obvious one, the customary stress nevertheless leaves unattended to, though it is one that must get its full value if George Eliot's development is to be understood. I will underline it by saying that the presentment of the Dodson clan is of marked sociological interest—not accidentally, but because of the intellectual qualifications of the novelist.

But of course the most striking quality of *The Mill on the Floss* is that which goes with the strong autobiographical element. It strikes us as an emotional tone. We feel an urgency, a resonance, a personal vibration, adverting us of the poignantly immediate presence of the author. Since the vividness, the penetration and the irresistible truth of the best of the book are clearly bound up with this quality, to suggest that it also entails limitations that the critic cannot ignore, since they in turn are inseparable from disastrous weaknesses in George Eliot's handling of her themes, is perhaps a delicate business. But the case is so: the emotional quality represents something, a need or hunger in George Eliot, that shows itself to be insidious company for her intelligence—apt to supplant it and take command. The acknowledged weaknesses and faults of *The Mill on the Floss*, in fact, are of a more interesting kind than the accepted view recognizes.

That Maggie Tulliver is essentially identical with the young Mary Ann Evans we all know. She has the intellectual potentiality for which the environment into which she is born doesn't provide much encouragement; she has the desperate need for affection and intimate personal relations; and above all she has the need for an emotional exaltation, a religious enthusiasm, that shall transfigure the ordinariness of daily life and sweep her up in an inspired devotion of self to some ideal purpose. There is, however, a difference between Maggie Tulliver and Mary Ann Evans: Maggie is beautiful. She is triumphantly beautiful, after having been the ugly duckling. The experience of a sensitive child in this latter rôle among insensitive adults is evoked with great poignancy: George Eliot had only to remember. The glow that comes with imagining the duckling turned swan hardly needs analysing; it can be felt in every relevant page, and it is innocent enough. But it is intimately related to things in the book that common consent finds deplorable, and it is necessary to realize this in order to realize their nature and significance and see what the weaknesses of *The Mill on the Floss* really are.

There is Stephen Guest, who is universally recognized

to be a sad lapse on George Eliot's part. He is a more significant lapse, I think, than criticism commonly allows. Here is Leslie Stephen (*George Eliot*, p. 104):

> 'George Eliot did not herself understand what a mere hairdresser's block she was describing in Mr. Stephen Guest. He is another instance of her incapacity for portraying the opposite sex. No man could have introduced such a character without perceiving what an impression must be made upon his readers. We cannot help regretting Maggie's fate; she is touching and attractive to the last; but I, at least, cannot help wishing that the third volume could have been suppressed. I am inclined to sympathize with the readers of *Clarissa Harlowe* when they entreated Richardson to save Lovelace's soul. Do, I mentally exclaim, save this charming Maggie from damning herself by this irrelevant and discordant degradation.'

That the presentment of Stephen Guest is unmistakably feminine no one will be disposed to deny, but not only is the assumption of a general incapacity refuted by a whole gallery of triumphs, Stephen himself is sufficiently 'there' to give the drama a convincing force. Animus against him for his success with Maggie and exasperation with George Eliot for allowing it shouldn't lead us to dispute that plain fact—they don't really amount to a judgment of his unreality. To call him a 'mere hairdresser's block' is to express a valuation—a valuation extremely different from George Eliot's. And if we ourselves differ from her in the same way (who doesn't?), we must be careful about the implication of the adjective when we agree that her valuation is surprising. For Leslie Stephen Maggie's entanglement with Stephen Guest is an 'irrelevant and discordant degradation.'—Irrelevant to what and discordant with what?—

> 'The whole theme of the book is surely the contrast between the "beautiful soul" and the commonplace sur-

roundings. It is the awakening of the spiritual and imaginative nature and the need of finding some room for
the play of the higher faculties, whether in the direction
of religious mysticism or of human affection.'

—It is bad enough that the girl who is distinguished not
only by beauty but by intelligence should be made to fall
for a provincial dandy; the scandal or incredibility (runs
the argument) becomes even worse when we add that she
is addicted to Thomas à Kempis and has an exalted spiritual nature. Renunciation is a main theme in her history
and in her daily meditations; but—when temptation takes
the form of Mr. Stephen Guest! It is incredible, or insufferable in so far as we have to accept it, for temptation at
this level can have nothing to do with the theme of renunciation as we have become familiar with it in Maggie's
spiritual life—it is 'irrelevant and discordant.' This is the
position.

Actually, the soulful side of Maggie, her hunger for
ideal exaltations, as it is given us in the earlier part of the
book, is just what should make us say, on reflection, that
her weakness for Stephen Guest is not so surprising after
all. It is commonly accepted, this soulful side of Maggie,
with what seems to me a remarkable absence of criticism.
It is offered by George Eliot herself—and this of course is
the main point—with a remarkable absence of criticism.
There *is*, somewhere, a discordance, a discrepancy, a
failure to reduce things to a due relevance: it is a characteristic and significant failure in George Eliot. It is a
discordance, not between her ability to present Maggie's
yearnings and her ability to present Stephen Guest as an
irresistible temptation, but between her presentment of
those yearnings on the one hand and her own distinction
of intelligence on the other.

That part of Maggie's make-up is done convincingly
enough; it is done from the inside. One's criticism is that it
is done too purely from the inside. Maggie's emotional
and spiritual stresses, her exaltations and renunciations,

exhibit, naturally, all the marks of immaturity; they involve confusions and immature valuations; they belong to a stage of development at which the capacity to make some essential distinctions has not yet been arrived at—at which the poised impersonality that is one of the conditions of being able to make them can't be achieved. There is nothing against George Eliot's presenting this immaturity with tender sympathy; but we ask, and ought to ask, of a great novelist something more. 'Sympathy and understanding' is the common formula of praise, but understanding, in any strict sense, is just what she doesn't show. To understand immaturity would be to 'place' it, with however subtle an implication, by relating it to mature experience. But when George Eliot touches on these given intensities of Maggie's inner life the vibration comes directly and simply from the novelist, precluding the presence of a maturer intelligence than Maggie's own. It is in these places that we are most likely to make with conscious critical intent the comment that in George Eliot's presentment of Maggie there is an element of self-idealization. The criticism sharpens itself when we say that with the self-idealization there goes an element of self-pity. George Eliot's attitude to her own immaturity as represented by Maggie is the reverse of a mature one.

Maggie Tulliver, in fact, represents an immaturity that George Eliot never leaves safely behind her. We have it wherever we have this note, and where it prevails her intelligence and mature judgment are out of action:

'Maggie in her brown frock, with her eyes reddened and her heavy hair pushed back, looking from the bed where her father lay, to the dull walls of this sad chamber which was the centre of her world, was a creature full of eager, passionate longings for all that was beautiful and glad; thirsty for all knowledge; with an ear straining after dreamy music that died away and would not come nearer to her; with a blind, unconscious yearning for something that would link together the wonderful impressions of this mysterious life, and give her soul a sense of home in it.' [7]

This 'blind, unconscious yearning' never, for all the intellectual contacts it makes as Maggie grows up and from which it acquires a sense of consciousness, learns to understand itself: Maggie remains quite naïve about its nature. She is quite incapable of analysing it into the varied potentialities it associates. In the earlier part of the book, from which the passage just quoted comes, the religious and idealistic aspect of the yearning is not complicated by any disconcerting insurgence from out of the depths beneath its vagueness. But with that passage compare this:

'In poor Maggie's highly-strung, hungry nature—just come away from a third-rate schoolroom, with all its jarring sounds and petty round of tasks—these apparently trivial causes had the effect of rousing and exalting her imagination in a way that was mysterious to herself. It was not that she thought distinctly of Mr. Stephen Guest, or dwelt on the indications that he looked at her with admiration; it was rather that she felt the half-remote presence of a world of love and beauty and delight, made up of vague, mingled images from all the poetry she had ever read, or had ever woven in her dreamy reveries.' [8]

The juxtaposition of the two passages makes us revert to a sentence quoted above from Leslie Stephen, and see in it a hint that he, pretty plainly, missed:

'It is the awakening of the spiritual and imaginative nature and the need of finding some room for the play of the higher faculties, whether in the direction of religious mysticism or of human affection.'

—For the second alternative we need to couple with 're-

---

[7] *The Mill on the Floss*, Book III, Chapter V, the end.
[8] Book VI, Chapter III, third paragraph.

ligious mysticism' a phrase more suggestive of emotional
intensity than Leslie Stephen's. And we then can't help
asking whether the 'play of the higher faculties' that is as
intimately associated with a passion for Stephen Guest as
the two last-quoted paragraphs together bring out can be
as purely concerned with the 'higher' as Maggie and
George Eliot believe (unchallenged, it seems, by Leslie
Stephen).

Obviously there is a large lack of self-knowledge in
Maggie—a very natural one, but shared, more remarkably,
by George Eliot. Maggie, it is true, has the most painful
throes of conscience and they ultimately prevail. But she
has no sense that Stephen Guest (apart, of course, from
the insufficient strength of moral fibre betrayed under the
strain of temptation—and it is to Maggie he succumbs)
is not worthy of her spiritual and idealistic nature. There
is no hint that, if Fate had allowed them to come together
innocently, she wouldn't have found him a pretty satisfactory soul-mate; there, for George Eliot, lies the tragedy—
it is conscience opposes. Yet the ordinary nature of the
fascination is made quite plain:

'And then, to have the footstool placed carefully by
a too self-confident personage—not any self-confident
personage, but one in particular, who suddenly looks
humble and anxious, and lingers, bending still, to ask if
there is not some draught in that position between the
window and the fireplace, and if he may not be allowed
to move the work-table for her—these things will summon a little of the too-ready, traitorous tenderness into
a woman's eyes, compelled as she is in her girlish time
to learn her life-lessons in very trivial language.' (Book
VI, Chapter VII.)

And it is quite plan that George Eliot shares to the full
the sense of Stephen's irresistibleness—the vibration establishes it beyond a doubt:

'For hours Maggie felt as if her struggle had been in
vain. For hours every other thought that she strove to

summon was thrust aside by the image of Stephen waiting for the single word that would bring him to her.
She did not *read* the letter: she heard him uttering it,
and the voice shook her with its old strange power.
. . . And yet that promise of joy in the place of sadness
did not make the dire force of the temptation to Maggie.
It was Stephen's tone of misery, it was the doubt in the
justice of her own resolve, that made the balance trem-
ble, and made her once start from her seat to reach the
pen and paper, and write "Come." '

There is no suggestion of any antipathy between this
fascination and Maggie's 'higher faculties,' apart from the
moral veto that imposes renunciation. The positive counterpart of renunciation in the 'higher' realm to which this
last is supposed to belong is the exaltation, transcending
all conflicts and quotidian stalenesses, that goes with an
irresistibly ideal self-devotion. It is significant that the
passages describing such an exaltation, whether as longed
for or as attained—and there are many in George Eliot's
works—have a close affinity in tone and feeling with this
(from the chapter significantly headed, *Borne along by
the tide*):

'And they went. Maggie felt that she was being led
down the garden among the roses, being helped with
firm tender care into the boat, having the cushion and
cloak arranged for her feet, and her parasol opened for
her (which she had forgotten)—all this by the stronger
presence that seemed to bear her along without any act
of her own will, like the added self which comes with
the sudden exalting influence of a strong tonic—and
she felt nothing else.' (Book VI, Chapter XIII.)

—The satisfaction got by George Eliot from imaginative
participation in exalted enthusiasms and self-devotions
would, if she could suddenly have gained the power of
analysis that in these regions she lacked, have surprised her
by the association of elements it represented.

The passage just quoted gives the start of the expedition

with Stephen in which chance, the stream and the tide are allowed, temporarily, to decide Maggie's inner conflict. It has been remarked that George Eliot has a fondness for using boats, water and chance in this way. But there are distinctions to be made. The way in which Maggie, exhausted by the struggle, surrenders to the chance that leaves her to embark alone with Stephen, and then, with inert will, lets the boat carry her down-stream until it is too late, so that the choice seems taken from her and the decision compelled—all this is admirable. *This* is insight and understanding, and comes from the psychologist who is to analyse for us Gwendolen Harleth's acceptance of Grandcourt. But the end of *The Mill on the Floss* belongs to another kind of art. Some might place it under the 'art' referred to by Henry James. And it is certainly a 'dramatic' close of a kind congenial to the Victorian novel-reader. But it has for the critic more significance than this suggests: George Eliot is, emotionally, fully engaged in it. The qualifying 'emotionally' is necessary because of the criticism that has to be urged: something so like a kind of daydream indulgence we are all familiar with could not have imposed itself on the novelist as the right ending if her mature intelligence had been fully engaged, giving her full self-knowledge. The flooded river has no symbolic or metaphorical value. It is only the dreamed-of perfect accident that gives us the opportunity for the dreamed-of heroic act—the act that shall vindicate us against a harshly misjudging world, bring emotional fulfilment and (in others) changes of heart, and provide a gloriously tragic curtain. Not that the sentimental in it is embarrassingly gross, but the finality is not that of great art, and the significance is what I have suggested—a revealed immaturity.

The success of *Silas Marner*, that charming minor masterpiece, is conditioned by the absence of personal immediacy; it is a success of reminiscent and enchanted re-creation: *Silas Marner* has in it, in its solid way, something of the fairy tale. That 'solid' presents itself because of the way in which the moral fable is realized in terms of a substantial real world. But this, though re-seen through adult experience, is the world of childhood and youth—the world as directly known then, and what is hardly distinguishable from that, the world as known through family reminiscence, conveyed in anecdote and fireside history. The mood of enchanted adult reminiscence blends with the re-captured traditional aura to give the world of *Silas Marner* its atmosphere. And it is this atmosphere that conditions the success of the moral intention. We take this intention quite seriously, or, rather, we are duly affected by a realized moral significance; the whole history has been conceived in a profoundly and essentially moral imagination. But the atmosphere precludes too direct a reference to our working standards of probability—that is, to our everyday sense of how things happen; so that there is an answer to Leslie Stephen when he comments on *Silas Marner* in its quality of moral fable:

> 'The supposed event—the moral recovery of a nature reduced by injustice and isolation to the borders of sanity—strikes one perhaps as more pretty than probable. At least, if one had to dispose of a deserted child, the experiment of dropping it by the cottage of a solitary in the hope that he would bring it up to its advantage and to his own regeneration would hardly be tried by a judicious philanthropist.'

Leslie Stephen, of course, is really concerned to make a limiting judgment, that which is made in effect when he says:

> 'But in truth the whole story is conceived in a way which makes a pleasant conclusion natural and harmonious.'

There is nothing that strikes us as false about the story; its charm depends upon our being convinced of its moral truth. But in our description of the satisfaction got from it, 'charm' remains the significant word.

The force of the limiting implication may be brought out by a comparative reference to another masterpiece of fiction that it is natural to bring under the head of 'moral fable': Dickens's *Hard Times*. The heightened reality of that great book (which combines a perfection of 'art' in the Flaubertian sense with an un-Flaubertian moral strength and human richness) has in it nothing of the fairy tale, and is such as to preclude pleasantness altogether; the satisfaction given depends on a moral significance that can have no relations with charm. But the comparison is, of course, unfair: *Hard Times* has a large and complex theme, involving its author's profoundest response to contemporary civilization, while *Silas Marner* is modestly conscious of its minor quality.

The unfairness may be compensated by taking up Leslie Stephen's suggestion that '*Silas Marner* is . . . scarcely equalled in English literature, unless by Mr. Hardy's rustics, in *Far from the Madding Crowd* and other early works.' Actually, the comparison is to George Eliot's advantage (enormously so), and to Hardy's detriment, in ways already suggested. The praises that have been given to George Eliot for the talk at the Rainbow are deserved. It is indeed remarkable that a woman should have been able to present so convincingly an exclusively masculine *milieu*. It is the more remarkable when we recall the deplorable Bob Jakin of *The Mill on the Floss*, who is so obviously and embarrassingly a feminine product.

Silas Marner closes the first phase of George Eliot's creative life. She finds that, if she is to go on being a novelist, it must be one of a very different kind. And *Romola*, her first attempt to achieve the necessary inventiveness, might well have justified the conviction that her creative life was over.

(ii) '*Romola*' to '*Middlemarch*'

If we hesitated to judge that in *Romola* George Eliot 'proceeds from the abstract to the concrete' it would be because 'proceed' might seem to imply 'attain.' Of this monument of excogitation and reconstruction Henry James himself says: 'More than any of her novels it was evolved from her moral consciousness—a moral consciousness encircled by a prodigious amount of literary research.' The 'figures and situations' are indeed 'deeply studied and massively supported,' and they represent characteristic preoccupations of the novelist, but they fail to emerge from the state of generalized interest: they are not brought to any sharp edge of realization. Tito Melema, developing a mere mild insufficiency of positive unselfishness into a positive and lethal viciousness, illustrates a favourite theme, moral and psychological, but he remains an illustration, thought of, thought out, and painstakingly specified; never becoming anything like a prior reality that embodies the theme and presents it as life. The analogous and worse failure in respect of Savonarola is fairly suggested by such passages of laborious analytic prose as Leslie Stephen quotes (*George Eliot*, p. 134), with the comment:

> 'this almost Germanic concatenation of clauses not only puts such obvious truths languidly, but keeps Savonarola himself at a distance. We are not listening to a Hamlet, but to a judicious critic analysing the state of mind which prompts "to be or not to be."'

—There is no presence, that is; the analysis serves instead. Romola herself Leslie Stephen judges more favourably —indeed, very favourably. And it is true that she represents something other than the failure of a powerful mind to warm analysis into creation; she is a palpably emotional presence: Romola, in fact, is another idealized George Eliot—less real than Maggie Tulliver and more idealized. While patrician and commandingly beautiful, she has also George Eliot's combination of intellectual power, emancipation, inherent piety, and hunger for exaltations.

'The pressing problem for Romola just then was . . . to keep alive that flame of unselfish emotion by which a life of sadness might still be a life of active love.'

—With 'Maggie' substituted for 'Romola,' that might have come as a patently autobiographical note from *The Mill on the Floss*. And it is the immediate presence of the yearning translator of Strauss that we feel in such situations as this:

'Romola, kneeling with buried face on the altar step, was enduring one of those sickening moments when the enthusiasm which had come to her as the only energy strong enough to make life worthy, seemed to be inevitably bound up with vain dreams and wilful eyeshutting.'

And when we read that 'tender fellow-feeling for the nearest has its danger too, and is apt to be timid and sceptical towards the larger aims without which life cannot rise into religion' we know that we are in direct contact with the 'pressing problem' of the nineteenth-century intellectual, contemporary of Mill, Matthew Arnold and Comte. So that we can hardly help being pryingly personal in our conjectures when, going on, we read:

'No one who has ever known what it is thus to lose faith in a fellow man whom he has profoundly loved and reverenced, will lightly say that the shock can leave the faith in the Invisible Goodness unshaken. With the sinking of high human trust, the dignity of life sinks too: we cease to believe in our own better self, since that also is part of the common nature which is degraded in our thought; and all the finer impulses of the soul are dulled.'

—Dr. John Chapman? we ask.

The answer, of course, doesn't matter. The point we have to make is that this closeness of relation between heroine and author is no more here than elsewhere in George Eliot a strength. Romola, in fact, has none of the reality associated with Maggie Tulliver, but she brings in the weakness, associated with Maggie, that embarrasses us in *The Mill on the Floss*.

The passage just quoted opens the episode in which Romola, lying down in an open boat, abandons herself to the winds and tides—'To be freed from the burden of choice when all motive was bruised, to commit herself, sleeping, to destiny which would either bring death or else new necessities that might rouse a new life in her.' 'Had she,' she asks, as she lies in the gliding boat, 'found anything like the dream of her girlhood? No.' But she is to find now, in alleged actuality, something embarrassingly like a girlhood dream. She drifts ashore at the plague-stricken village, and, a ministering Madonna—'the Mother with the glory about her tending the sick'—is a miracle for the villagers. It is a miracle for her too, rescuing her from her 'pressing problem' with a 'flame of unselfish emotion,' provided by a heaven-sent chance out of the void.

Few will want to read *Romola* a second time, and few can ever have got through it once without some groans. It is indubitably the work of a very gifted mind, but of a mind misusing itself; and it is the one novel answering to the kind of account of George Eliot that became current during the swing of the pendulum against her after her death.

Yet *Romola* has habitually been included in the lists of cheap reprints, and probably a good many more readers have tackled it than have ever taken up *Felix Holt*. In writing *Felix Holt*, which brings us back to England, George Eliot did look up *The Times* for 1830 or thereabouts; but there was no tremendous and exhausting labour of historical reconstruction. What called for the most uncongenial hard work on her part was the elaboration of the plot—work (it strikes us to-day) about as perversely, if not as desiccatingly, misdirected as that which went to evoking life at Florence in the time of Savonarola. The complications of the thorough-paced Victorian plot depend, with painful correctness (professional advice having been taken of the Positivist friend, Frederic Harrison), on some esoteric subtleties of the law of entail, and they demand of the reader a strenuousness of attention that, if he is an admirer of George Eliot, he is unwilling to devote.

It is in the theme represented by the title of the book that the 'reflective' preponderance of the 'moral consciousness,' working from the 'abstract' without being able to turn it into convincing perception, notably manifests itself. Felix Holt is the ideal working man. Though educated, he is wholly loyal to his class (to the extent of remaining shaggy in appearance and manners), and dedicates his life to its betterment; but, while proposing to take an active part in politics, he refuses to countenance any of the compromises of organized political action. He denounces the Radical agent for fighting the constituency in the usual way. Rational appeal to unalloyed principle —that alone can be permitted; the time-honoured methods of party warfare, defended as practical necessities for party success, debase and betray the people's cause, and there must be no truck with them. Felix is as noble and courageous in act as in ideal, and is wholly endorsed by his creator. That in presenting these unrealities George Eliot gives proof of a keen interest in political, social and economic history, and in the total complex movement of civilization, and exhibits an impressive command of the facts, would seem to confirm the deprecatory view commonly taken of the relation between intellectual and novelist. Here is the way Felix Holt, Radical, talks:

'"Oh, yes, your ringed and scented men of the people! —I won't be one of them. Let a man throttle himself with a satin stock, and he'll get new wants and new motives. Metamorphosis will have begun at his neck-joint, and it will go on till it has changed his likings first and then his reasoning, which will follow his likings as the feet of a hungry dog follow his nose. I'll have none of your clerkly gentility. I might end by collecting greasy pence from poor men to buy myself a fine coat and a glutton's dinner, on pretence of serving the poor men. I'd sooner be Paley's fat pigeon than a demagogue all tongue and stomach, though"—here Felix changed his voice a little—"I should like well enough to be another sort of demagogue, if I could."

'"Then you have a strong interest in the great political movements of these times?" said Mr. Lyon, with a perceptible flashing of the eyes.

'"I should think so. I despise every man who has not —or, having it, doesn't try to rouse it in other men."'

Here he is addressing a young lady at their first meeting:

'"Oh, your niceties—I know what they are," said Felix, in his usual *fortissimo*. "They all go on your system of make-believe. 'Rottenness' may suggest what is unpleasant, so you'd better say 'sugar-plums,' or something else such a long way off the fact that nobody is obliged to think of it. Those are your roundabout euphuisms that dress up swindling till it looks as well as honesty, and shoot with boiled pease instead of bullets. I hate your gentlemanly speakers."'[9]

The consequences of general intention combined with inexperience are disastrously plain. The idealizing bent seen to be so marked in Adam Bede when we compare him with Caleb Garth of *Middlemarch* is not really a strength; but George Eliot knew the country artisan at first hand and intimately. In offering to present the Dignity of Labour in the ideal town working-man she is relying on her 'moral consciousness' unqualified by first-hand knowledge.

Felix Holt's very unideal mother, though not the same kind of disaster (she's only a minor figure, of course), is not much more convincing; she seems to be done out of Dickens rather than from life. The Reverend Rufus Lyon, the Congregationalist minister, heroically quaint reminder

---

[9] Compare this later address of his to Esther: '"I wonder," he went on, still looking at her, "whether the subtle measuring of forces will ever come to measuring the force there would be in one beautiful woman whose mind was as noble as her face was beautiful—who made a man's passion for her rush in one current with all the great aims of his life."'

of the heroic age of Puritanism (and inspired, one guesses, by Scott), is incredible and a bore—to say which is a severe criticism, since his talk occupies a large proportion of the book. Esther, the beautiful and elegant young lady passing as his daughter, is interesting only in relation to other feminine studies of the author's, and to her treatment in general of feminine charm.

But there is an element in the novel as yet untouched on. It is represented by this, where the dialogue is so different in quality from that in which Felix Holt figures, and the analysis of so different an order (and in so different a prose) from that characteristic of *Romola*:

'"Harold is remarkably acute and clever," he began at last, since Mrs. Transome did not speak. "If he gets into Parliament, I have no doubt he will distinguish himself. He has a quick eye for business of all kinds."

'"That is no comfort to me," said Mrs. Transome. To-day she was more conscious than usual of that bitterness which was always in her mind in Jermyn's presence, but which was carefully suppressed because she could not endure the degradation she inwardly felt should ever become visible or audible in acts or words of her own—should ever be reflected in any word or look of his. For years there had been a deep silence about the past between them: on her side, because she remembered; on his, because he more and more forgot.

'"I trust he is not unkind to you in any way. I know his opinions pain you; but I trust you find him in everything else disposed to be a good son."

'"Oh, to be sure—good as men are disposed to be to women, giving them cushions and carriages, and recommending them to enjoy themselves, and then expecting them to be contented under contempt and neglect. I have no power over him—remember that—none."

'Jermyn turned to look in Mrs. Transome's face: it was long since he had heard her speak to him as if she were losing her self-command.

'"Has he shown any unpleasant feeling about your management of the affairs?"

'"*My* management of the affairs!" Mrs. Transome said, with concentrated rage, flashing a fierce look at Jermyn. She checked herself: she felt as if she were lighting a torch to flare on her own past folly and misery. It was a resolve which had become a habit, that she would never quarrel with this man—never tell him what she saw him to be. She had kept her woman's pride and sensibility intact: through all her life there had vibrated the maiden need to have her hand kissed and be the object of chivalry. And so she sank into silence again, trembling.

'Jermyn felt annoyed—nothing more. There was nothing in his mind corresponding to the intricate meshes of sensitiveness in Mrs. Transome's. He was anything but stupid; yet he always blundered when he wanted to be delicate or magnanimous; he constantly sought to soothe others by praising himself. Moral vulgarity cleaved to him like an hereditary odour. He blundered now.

'"My dear Mrs. Transome," he said, in a tone of bland kindness, "you are agitated—you appear angry with me. Yet I think, if you consider, you will see that you have nothing to complain of in me, unless you will complain of the inevitable course of man's life. I have always met your wishes both in happy circumstances and in unhappy ones. I should be ready to do so now, if it were possible."

'Every sentence was as pleasant to her as if it had been cut in her bared arm. Some men's kindness and love-making are more exasperating, more humiliating than others' derision, but the pitiable woman who has once made herself secretly dependent on a man who is beneath her in feeling must bear that humiliation for fear of worse. Coarse kindness is at least better than coarse anger; and in all private quarrels the duller nature is triumphant by reason of its dulness. Mrs. Transome knew in her inmost soul that those relations which had sealed her lips on Jermyn's conduct in business matters, had been with him a ground for presuming that he should have impunity in any lax dealing into which circumstances had led him. She knew that she herself had endured all the more privation because of his dishonest selfishness. And now, Harold's long-deferred heirship, and his return with startlingly unexpected penetration, activity, and assertion of mastery, had placed them both in the full presence of a difficulty which had been prepared by the years of vague uncertainty as to issues.'

It should be plain from the quality of this that the theme it handles is profoundly felt and sharply realized. This theme concerns Mrs. Transome, her son Harold, and the family lawyer, Matthew Jermyn. It is utterly different in kind from anything else in *Felix Holt* and from anything earlier of George Eliot's, and when we come to it we see finally that Henry James's antithesis, 'perceptive' and 'reflective,' will not do. For if we ask how this art is so astonishingly finer and maturer than anything George Eliot had done before, the answer is in terms of a perception that is so much more clear and profound because the perceiving focuses the profound experience of years—experience worked over by reflective thought, and so made capable of focusing. What we perceive depends on what we bring to the perceiving; and George Eliot brought a magnificent intelligence, functioning here as mature understanding. Intelligence in her was not always worsted by emotional needs; the relation between the artist and the intellectual in her (with the formidable 'exemption from cerebral lassitude') was not always a matter of her intellect being enlisted in the service of her immaturity.

The beneficent relation between artist and intellectual is to be seen in the new impersonality of the Transome theme. The theme is realized with an intensity certainly not inferior to that of the most poignant autobiographical places in George Eliot, but the directly personal vibration —the directly personal engagement of the novelist—that we feel in Maggie Tulliver's intensities even at their most valid is absent here. 'The more perfect the artist, the more completely separate in him will be the man who suffers and the mind which creates': it is in the part of *Felix Holt* dealing with Mrs. Transome that George Eliot becomes one of the great creative artists. She has not here, it will be noted, a heroine with whom she can be tempted to identify herself. Mrs. Transome is County, and how unlike she is to the novelist appears sufficiently in this account of her:

'She had that high-born imperious air which would have marked her as an object of hatred and reviling by a revolutionary mob. Her person was too typical of social distinctions to be passed by with indifference by anyone: it would have fitted an empress in her own right, who had had to rule in spite of faction, to dare the violation of treaties and dread retributive invasions, to grasp after new territories, to be defiant in desperate circumstances, and to feel a woman's hunger of the heart for ever unsatisfied. . . . When she was young she had been thought wonderfully clever and accomplished, and had been rather ambitious of intellectual superiority—had secretly picked out for private reading the lighter parts of dangerous French authors—and in company had been able to talk of Mr. Burke's style, or of Chateaubriand's eloquence—had laughed at the Lyrical Ballads and admired Mr. Southey's Thalaba. She always thought that the dangerous French authors were wicked and that her reading of them was a sin; but many sinful things were highly agreeable to her, and many things which she did not doubt to be good and true were dull and meaningless. She found ridicule of Biblical characters very amusing, and she was interested in stories of illicit passion; but she believed all the while that truth and safety lay in due attendance on prayers and sermons, in the admirable doctrines and ritual of the Church of England, equally remote from Puritanism and Popery; in fact, in such a view of this

world and the next as would preserve the existing arrangements of English society quite unshaken, keeping
down the obtrusiveness of the vulgar and the discontent
of the poor.'

The treatment of Mrs. Transome is not, as this description may suggest, ironical. The irony, a tragic irony, resides in her situation, which is presented with complete
objectivity—though with poignant sympathy, unlike as her
strains and distresses are to the novelist's own. In this sympathy there is not a trace of self-pity or self-indulgence.
Mrs. Transome is a study in Nemesis. And, although her
case is conceived in an imagination that is profoundly
moral, the presentment of it is a matter of psychological
observation—psychological observation so utterly convincing in its significance that the price paid by Mrs. Transome for her sin in inevitable consequences doesn't need
a moralist's insistence, and there is none; to speak of
George Eliot here as a moralist would, one feels, be to
misplace a stress. She is simply a great artist—a great novelist, with a great novelist's psychological insight and fineness of human valuation. Here is one aspect of Mrs. Transome's tragedy:

'The mother's love is at first an absorbing delight,
blunting all other sensibilities; it is an expansion of the
animal existence; it enlarges the imagined range for
self to move in: but in after years it can only continue
to be joy on the same terms as other long-lived love—
that is, by much suppression of self, and power of living in the experience of another. Mrs. Transome had
darkly felt the pressure of that unchangeable fact. Yet
she had clung to the belief that somehow the possession
of this son was the best thing she lived for; to believe
otherwise would have made her memory too ghastly a
companion.'

Mrs. Transome, of course, is not capable of recognizing
the 'unchangeable fact' of which she 'darkly feels the pressure.' She cannot alter herself, and for her the worth and

meaning of life lie in command, and the imposition of her will. This is shown to us, not with any incitement to censure, but as making her, in its inevitable consequences, tragically pitiable. For her feeble-minded husband she can feel little but contempt. That the unsatisfactory elder son who took after him is dead is matter for rejoicing: Harold, the second and quite other son, now becomes the heir, and, returning home from the Levant where he has made a fortune, will be able to put the encumbered family estate on a new footing, so that, belatedly, the lady of Transome Court will assume real dominion, and take her due place in the County. That dream, for many starved years the reason for living, dies as soon as they meet, and the despairing bitterness that engulfs her as she realizes that he is indeed her son,[10] and that for him too command and the exercise of will are the meaning of life, is evoked (notably in the exchanges with Denner, her maid) with an astringently moving power unsurpassed in literature.

To the tormenting frustration and hopelessness is soon added fear. It is not only that Harold, with his poised kindness that is so utterly unaware of her, frustrates her social hopes by proclaiming himself a Radical, and, at home, supersedes her authority, her *raison d'être*; he terrifies her by proposing to follow up his suspicions concerning Matthew Jermyn's custodianship of the family interests. The mine waiting to be detonated will blast them all three. For Harold is also Jermyn's son.

It is remarkable—and it is characteristic of George Eliot's mature art—that the treatment of Mrs. Transome's early lapse should have in it nothing of the Victorian moralist. In the world of this art the atmosphere of the taboo

---

[10] 'Under the shock of discovering her son's Radicalism Mrs. Transome had no impulse to say one thing rather than another; as in a man who has just been branded on the forehead all wonted motives would be uprooted. Harold, on his side, had no wish opposed to filial kindness, but his busy thoughts were imperiously determined by habits which had no reference to any woman's feelings. . . .'

is unknown; there is none of the excited hush, the skirt-
ing round, the thrill of shocked reprobation, or any of
the forms of sentimentality typical of Victorian fiction
when such themes are handled. There is instead an intently matter-of-fact directness: this is human nature, this
is the fact and these are the inexorable consequences.
Apart from the fear, the worst face, as Mrs. Transome
sees it, of regret for the past is what we have here (it
follows on the first long quotation made above from *Felix
Holt*):

> 'In this position, with a great dread hanging over her,
> which Jermyn knew, and ought to have felt that he
> had caused her, she was inclined to lash him with in-
> dignation, to scorch him with the words that were just
> the fit names for his doings—inclined all the more when
> he spoke with an insolent blandness, ignoring all that
> was truly in her heart. But no sooner did the words "You
> have brought it on me" rise within her than she heard
> within also the retort, "You brought it on yourself." Not
> for all the world beside could she bear to hear that retort
> uttered from without. What did she do? With strange
> sequence to all that rapid tumult, after a few moments'
> silence she said, in a gentle and almost tremulous voice—
> ' "Let me take your arm. . . ."
> 'As she took away her hand, Jermyn let his arm fall,
> put both his hands in his pockets, and shrugging his
> shoulders said, "I shall use him as he uses me."
> 'Jermyn had turned round his savage side, and the
> blandness was out of sight. It was this that had always
> frightened Mrs. Transome: there was a possibility of
> fierce insolence in this man who was to pass with those
> nearest to her as her indebted servant, but whose
> brand she secretly bore. She was as powerless with him
> as she was with her son.
> 'This woman, who loved rule, dared not speak an-
> other word of attempted persuasion.'

Mrs. Transome has, and can have, no impulse towards
what the moralist means by repentance:

'She had no ultimate analysis of things that went beyond blood and family—the Herons of Fenshore or the
Badgers of Hillbury. She had never seen behind the
canvas with which her life was hung. In the dim background there was the burning mount and the tables of
the law; in the foreground there was Lady Debarry privately gossiping about her, and Lady Wyvern finally de-
ciding not to send her invitations to dinner.'

She is herself here in her reaction to Jermyn's suggestion
that he shall be saved by her telling Harold:

'"But now you have asked me, I will never tell him!
Be ruined—no—do something more dastardly to save
yourself. If I sinned, my judgment went beforehand—
that I should sin for a man like you."'

This limitation is of the essence of her tragedy; it goes, as
George Eliot presents her, with her being an impressive
and sympathy-commanding figure. Here we have her
enduring the agonized helplessness of a moment of tension:

'When Harold left the table she went into the long
drawing-room, where she might relieve her restlessness
by walking up and down, and catch the sound of
Jermyn's entrance into Harold's room, which was close
by. Here she moved to and fro amongst the rose-coloured
satin of chairs and curtains—the great story of this
world reduced for her to the little tale of her own existence—dull obscurity everywhere, except where the
keen light fell on the narrow track of her own lot, wide
only for a woman's anguish. At last she heard the expected ring and footstep, and the opening and closing
door. Unable to walk about any longer, she sank into
a large cushioned chair, helpless and prayerless. She
was not thinking of God's anger or mercy but of her
son's. She was thinking of what might be brought, not
by death, but by life.'

There is no touch of the homiletic about this; it is dramatic constatation, poignant and utterly convincing, and the implied moral, which is a matter of the enacted inevitability, is that perceived by a psychological realist. As the strain develops for her, our sympathetic interest is painfully engaged, so that when we come to the critical point (Chapter XLII) at which Jermyn says, 'It is not to be supposed that Harold would go against me . . . if he knew the whole truth,' we feel the full atrocity the proposition has for her. Further, we take the full force and finality of the disaster represented by her now breaking her life-long resolve never to quarrel 'with this man—never tell him what she knew him to be.'

The man is perfectly done. For him Nemesis has a face corresponding to his moral quality; it is something he contemplates 'in anger, in exasperation, that Harold, precisely Harold Transome, should have turned out to be the probable instrument of a visitation that would be bad luck, not justice; for is there any justice when ninety-nine men out of a hundred escape? He found himself beginning to hate Harold. . . .' By delicate touches the resemblance between father and son is conveyed to us, and the discrimination made between their respective egoisms.

If we agree that the two men are 'women's men,' it is not in any sense that detracts from their convincingness; it rather in the sense that the penetrating and 'placing' analysis of their masculinity is something, we feel, that it took a woman to do. Jermyn's case is Tito Melema's; this time not thought out in an effort to work from the abstract to the concrete, but presented in the life, with compelling reality; he is unquestionably 'there' in the full concrete, and unquestionably (as Tito, in so far as he exists, is not) a man—one of 'those who are led on through the years by the gradual demands of a selfishness which has spread its fibres far and wide through the intricate vanities and sordid cares of an everyday existence.'

As for Harold, he has 'the energetic will, the quick perception, and the narrow imagination which make what is called the "practical mind."' He is a 'clever, frank, good-natured egoist.'

'His very good-nature was unsympathetic: it never came from any thorough understanding or deep respect for what was in the mind of the person he obliged or indulged; it was like his kindness to his mother—an arrangement of his for the happiness of others, which, if they were sensible, ought to succeed.'

He cannot, of course, help his parentage; the ironic element of Nemesis in his disaster is given here: [11]

' "Confound the fellow—with his Mrs. Jermyn! Does he think we are on a footing for me to know anything about his wife?" '

It is characteristic of George Eliot that she can make such a man the focus of a profoundly moving tragedy: for Harold unquestionably becomes that for us at the point when, turning violently on Jermyn, who has been driven to come out with, 'I am your father!' he catches sight, in the ensuing scuffle, of the two faces side by side in a mirror, and sees 'the hated fatherhood reasserted.' This may sound melodramatic as recapitulated here; that it should come with so final a rightness in the actual text shows with what triumphant success George Eliot has justified her high tragic conception of her theme. It is characteristic of her to be able to make a tragedy out of 'moral mediocrity.' The phrase is used to convey the redeemed Esther Lyon's sense of life at Transome Court, and Esther has been represented earlier as reflecting: 'Mr. Transome had his beetles, but Mrs. Transome—?' There is nothing sentimental about George Eliot's vision of human mediocrity and 'platitude,' but she sees in them matters for compassion, and her dealings with them are assertions of human dig-

---

[11] ' "Why do you wish to shield such a fellow, mother?" ' . . . Mrs. Transome's rising temper was turned into a horrible sensation, as painful as a sudden concussion from something hard and immovable when we have struck out with our fist, intending to hit something warm, soft and breathing like ourselves. Poor Mrs. Transome's strokes were sent jarring back on her by a hard unendurable past.'

nity. To be able to assert human dignity in this way is greatness: the contrast with Flaubert is worth pondering.

Felix Holt is not one of the novels that cultivated persons are supposed to have read, and, if read at all, it is hardly ever mentioned, so that there is reason for saying that one of the finest things in fiction is virtually unknown. It is exasperating that George Eliot should have embedded some of her maturest work in a mass that is so much other—though *Felix Holt* is not, like *Romola*, 'unreadable,' and the superlative quality of the live part ought to have compelled recognition. It is exasperating and it is, again, characteristic of her. Only one book can, as a whole (though not without qualification), be said to represent her mature genius. That, of course, is *Middlemarch*.

The necessary part of great intellectual powers in such a success as *Middlemarch* is obvious. The sub-title of the book is *A Study of Provincial Life*, and it is no idle pretension. The sheer informedness about society, its mechanism, the ways in which people of different classes live and (if they have to) earn their livelihoods, impresses us with its range, and it is real knowledge; that is, it is knowledge alive with understanding. George Eliot had said in *Felix Holt*, by way of apology for the space she devoted to 'social changes' and 'public matters': 'there is no private life which has not been determined by a wider public life.' The aim implicit in this remark is magnificently achieved in *Middlemarch*, and it is achieved by a novelist whose genius manifests itself in a profound analysis of the individual. We can see that here indeed Beatrice Potter, training herself to become a 'sociological investigator,' might have looked without disappointment for what she failed to find in the textbooks.[12]

The intellectual, again, is apparent in the conception of certain of the most strikingly successful themes. Only a novelist who had known from the inside the exhaustions

---

[12] 'For any detailed description of the complexity of human nature . . . I had to turn to novelists and poets . . .': B. Webb, *My Apprenticeship*, p. 138.

and discouragements of long-range intellectual enterprises
could have conveyed the pathos of Dr. Casaubon's predicament. Not that Casaubon is supposed to have a remarkable intellect; he is an intellectual *manqué*:

> 'Nay, are there many situations more sublimely tragic
> than the struggle of the soul with the demand to re-
> nounce a work which has been all the significance of
> its life—a significance which is to vanish as the waters
> which come and go where no man has need of them?
> But there was nothing to strike others as sublime about
> Mr. Casaubon, and Lydgate, who had some contempt
> at hand for futile scholarship, felt a little amusement
> mingling with his pity. He was at present too ill ac-
> quainted with disaster to enter into the pathos of a lot
> where everything is below the level of tragedy except
> the passionate egoism of the sufferer.'

Actually, the *pathos* that Casaubon enacts 'below the
tragic level' is not quite what this passage by itself might
suggest; egoism plays a part more like that which it plays
in Mrs. Transome's tragedy. The essential predicament in
both cases involves the insulation of the egoism from all
large or heroic ends. Not only is Casaubon's scholarship
futile; he himself inwardly knows it to be so, and is more
preoccupied with saving himself from having to recognize
the fact than with anything else. To have communicated
movingly the pathos of such a situation is the more remarkable in that Lydgate's amused contempt is clearly not
altogether unlike something that is strongly felt by the
novelist: she does more than hint at the potentialities of
comedy in Casaubon, and of a comedy more critical than
sympathetic. This, for instance, is extraordinarily like
something of the early satiric felicities of Mr. E. M. Forster:

> 'Mr. Casaubon, as might be expected, spent a great
> deal of his time at the Grange in these weeks, and the
> hindrance which courtship occasioned to the progress
> of his great work—the Key to all Mythologies—naturally

made him look forward the more eagerly to the happy termination of courtship. But he had deliberately incurred the hindrance, having made up his mind that it was now time for him to adorn his life with the graces of female companionship, to irradiate the gloom which fatigue was apt to hang over the intervals of studious labour with the play of female fancy, and to secure in this, his culminating age, the solace of female tendance for his declining years. Hence he determined to abandon himself to the stream of feeling, and perhaps was surprised to find what an exceedingly shallow rill it was. As in droughty regions baptism by immersion could only be performed symbolically, so Mr. Casaubon found that sprinkling was the utmost approach to a plunge which his stream would afford him; and he concluded that the poets had much exaggerated the force of masculine passion. Nevertheless, he observed with pleasure that Miss Brooke showed an ardent submissive affection which promised to fulfil his most agreeable previsions of marriage. It had once or twice crossed his mind that possibly there was some deficiency in Dorothea to account for the moderation of his abandonment; but he was unable to discern the deficiency, or to figure to himself a woman who would have pleased him better; so that there was clearly no reason to fall back upon but the exaggerations of human tradition.'

—Compare that with the account of Mr. Pembroke's proposal in *The Longest Journey*, and it is difficult not to suspect that this is in a different class from the general resemblances that relate Mr. Forster by way of George Eliot and Jane Austen back to Fielding, and that we have a direct relation of reminiscence here. However that may be, the point to be made regards the critical quality of George Eliot's irony. Here we have the note again:

'He had done nothing exceptional in marrying—nothing but what society sanctions and considers an occasion for wreaths and bouquets. It had occurred to him that he must not any longer defer his intention of matrimony, and he had reflected that in taking a wife, a man of good position should expect and carefully choose a blooming young lady—the younger the better, because more educable, and submissive—of a rank equal to his own, of religious principles, virtuous disposition, and good understanding. On such a young lady he would make handsome settlements, and he would neglect no arrangement for her happiness: in return, he should receive family pleasures and leave behind him that copy of himself which seemed so urgently required of a man —to the sonneteers of the sixteenth century. Times had altered since then, and no sonneteer had insisted on Mr. Casaubon's leaving a copy of himself; moreover he had not yet succeeded in issuing copies of his mythological key; but he had always intended to acquit himself by marriage, and the sense that he was fast leaving the years behind him, that the world was getting dimmer and that he felt lonely, was a reason to him for losing no more time in overtaking domestic delights before they too were left behind by the years.

'And when he had seen Dorothea he believed that he had found even more than he demanded: she might really be such a helpmate to him as would enable him to dispense with a hired secretary, an aid which Mr. Casaubon had never yet employed and had a suspicious dread of. (Mr. Casaubon was nervously conscious that he was expected to manifest a powerful mind.) Providence, in its kindness, had supplied him with the wife he needed. A wife, a modest young lady, with the purely appreciative, unambitious abilities of her sex, is sure to think her husband's mind powerful. Whether Providence had taken equal care of Miss Brooke in presenting her with Mr. Casaubon was an idea which could hardly occur to him. Society never made the preposterous demand that a man should think as much about his own qualifications for making a charming girl happy as he thinks of hers for making himself happy. As if a man could choose not only his wife but his wife's husband! Or as if he were bound to provide charms for his posterity in his own person!—When Dorothea accepted him with effusion, that was only natural; and Mr. Casaubon believed that his happiness was going to begin.'

By now the torture has begun for Mr. Casaubon, and is felt as such by us. For all the tone that has just been sampled, we feel his torment of isolation, self-distrust having, with terrible irony, been turned by his marriage into a peculiarly torturing form of solitary confinement:

'We are angered even by the full acceptance of our humiliating confessions—how much more by hearing in hard distinct syllables from the lips of a near observer, those confused murmurs which we try to call morbid, and strive against as if they were the oncoming of numbness! And this cruel outward accuser was there in the shape of a wife—nay, of a young bride, who, instead of observing his abundant pen-scratches and amplitude of paper with the uncritical awe of an elegant-minded canary-bird, seemed to present herself as a spy watching everything with a malign power of inference. Here, towards this particular point of the compass, Mr. Casaubon had a sensitiveness to match Dorothea's, and an equal quickness to imagine more than the fact. He had formerly observed with approbation her capacity for worshipping the right object; he now foresaw with sudden terror that this capacity might be re-placed by presumption, this worship by the most exasperating of all criticism—that which sees vaguely a great many fine ends, and has not the least notion what it costs to reach them.'

It is not only an intellectual, it is a spirit profoundly noble, one believing profoundly in a possible nobility to be aimed at by men, that can make us, with her, realize such a situation fully as one for compassion. Close upon the longer ironic passage quoted above she says:

'It is an uneasy lot at best, to be what we call highly taught and yet not to enjoy: to be present at this great spectacle of life and never to be liberated from a small hungry shivering self—never to be fully possessed by the glory we behold, never to have our consciousness rapturously transformed into the vividness of a thought, the ardour of a passion, the energy of an action, but always to be scholarly and uninspired, ambitious and timid, scrupulous and dim-sighted.'

Such a passage reminds us—and the prompt recognition is a wise insurance when paying tribute to George Eliot's nobility—that her nobility is not altogether a simple subject. The reminder is effected by something in the mode of expression; something adverting us that Dorothea isn't far away. George Eliot tends to identify herself with Dorothea, though Dorothea is far from being the whole of George Eliot. When 'nobility' is mentioned in connection with George Eliot it is probable that most people think of the Dorothea (or Maggie Tulliver) in her. I want at the moment to insist (postponing the consideration of Dorothea, who doesn't represent her author's strength) that what we have in the treatment of Casaubon is wholly strong.

The other character of whom pre-eminently it can be said that he could have been done only by someone who knew the intellectual life from the inside is Lydgate. He is done with complete success. 'Only those,' his creator tells us, '. . . who know the supremacy of the intellectual life—the life which has a seed of ennobling thought and purpose in it—can understand the grief of one who falls from that serene activity into the absorbing soul-wasting struggle with worldly annoyances.' Lydgate's concern with 'ennobling thought and purpose' is very different from Dorothea's. He knows what he means, and his aim is specific. It is remarkable how George Eliot makes us feel his intellectual passion as something concrete. When novelists tell us that a character is a thinker (or an artist) we have usually only their word for it, but Lydgate's 'triumphant delight in his studies' is a concrete presence: it is plain that George Eliot knows intimately what it is like, and knows what his studies are.

But intensely as she admires his intellectual idealism,[13] and horrifyingly as she evokes the paralysing torpedo-touch of Rosamond, she doesn't make him a noble martyr to the femininity she is clearly so very far from admiring —the femininity that is incapable of intellectual interests, or of idealism of any kind. He is a gentleman in a sense that immediately recommends him to Rosamond—he is 'no radical in relation to anything but medical reform and the prosecution of discovery.' That is, the 'distinction' Rosamond admires is inseparable from a 'personal pride and unreflecting egoism' that George Eliot calls 'common-ness.' In particular, his attitude towards women is such as to give a quality of poetic justice to his misalliance: 'he held it one of the prettiest attributes of the feminine mind to adore a man's pre-eminence without too precise a knowledge of what it consisted in.' This insulation of his interest in the other sex from his serious interests is emphasized by our being given the history of his earlier affair with the French actress, Laure. As a lover he is Rosamond Vincy's complement.

The element of poetic justice in the relationship is apparent here (they are now married):

'He had regarded Rosamond's cleverness as precisely of the receptive kind which became a woman. He was now beginning to find out what that cleverness was— what was the shape into which it had run as into a close network aloof and independent. No one quicker than Rosamond to see causes and effects which lay within the track of her own tastes and interests: she had seen clearly Lydgate's pre-eminence in Middlemarch society, and could go on imaginatively tracing still more agree-able social effects when his talent should have advanced him; but for her, his professional and scientific ambi-

---

[13] The medical profession, he believes, offers 'the most direct alliance between intellectual conquest and social good.'

tion had no other relation to these desirable effects than if they had been the fortunate discovery of an ill-smelling oil. And that oil apart, with which she had nothing to do, of course she believed in her own opinion more than she did in his. Lydgate was astounded to find in numberless trifling matters, as well as in this last serious case of the riding, that affection did not make her compliant.'

The fact that there is nothing else in Rosamond beside her egoism—that which corresponds (as it responded) to Lydgate's 'commonness'—gives her a tremendous advantage, and makes her invincible. She is simple ego, and the concentrated subtlety at her command is unembarrassed by any inner complexity. She always knows what she wants, and knows that it is her due. Other people usually turn out to be 'disagreeable people, who only think of themselves, and do not mind how annoying they are to her.' For herself, she is always 'convinced that no woman could behave more irreproachably than she is behaving.' No moral appeal can engage on her; she is as well defended by nature against that sort of embarrassment as she is against logic. It is of no use accusing her of mendacity, or insincerity, or any kind of failure in reciprocity:

'Every nerve and muscle in Rosamond was adjusted to the consciousness that she was being looked at. She was by nature an actress of parts that entered into her *physique*: she even acted her own character, and so well, that she did not know it to be precisely her own.'

If one judges that there is less of sympathy in George Eliot's presentment of Rosamond than in her presentment of any other of her major characters (except Grandcourt in *Daniel Deronda*), one goes on immediately to note that Rosamond gives sympathy little lodgment. It is tribute enough to George Eliot to say that the destructive and demoralizing power of Rosamond's triviality wouldn't have seemed so appalling to us if there had been any animus in the presentment. We are, from time to time, made to feel from within the circumference of Rosamond's egoism—though we can't, of course, at any time be confined to it, and, there being no potential nobility here, it is implicitly judged that this case can hardly, by any triumph of compassion, be felt as tragic.

To say that there is no animus in the presentment of Rosamond is perhaps misleading if one doesn't add that the reader certainly catches himself, from time to time, wanting to break that graceful neck, the turns of which, as George Eliot evokes them, convey both infuriating obstinacy and a sinister hint of the snake. But Rosamond ministers too to our amusement; she figures in some of the best exchanges in a book rich in masterly dialogue. There is that between her and Mary Garth in Book I, Chapter XII, where she tests her characteristic suspicion that Mary is interested in Lydgate. The honours go easily to Mary, who, her antithesis, may be said to offset her in the representation of her sex; for Mary is equally real. She is equally a woman's creation too, and equally feminine; but femininity in her is wholly admirable—something that gives her in any company a wholly admirable advantage. Her good sense, quick intelligence and fine strength of character appear as the poised liveliness, shrewd good-humoured sharpness and direct honesty of her speech. If it were not a part of her strength to lack an aptitude for emotional exaltations, she might be said to represent George Eliot's ideal of femininity—she certainly represents a great deal of George Eliot's own characteristic strength.

Rosamond, so decidedly at a disadvantage (for once) with Mary Garth, is more evenly matched with Mrs. Bulstrode, who calls in Book III, Chapter XXX, to find out whether the flirtation with Lydgate is, or is not, anything more than a flirtation. Their encounter, in which unspoken inter-appreciation of attire accompanies the verbal fence, occurs in the same chapter as that between Mrs. Bulstrode and Mrs. Plymdale, 'well-meaning women both, knowing very little of their motives.' These encounters between women give us some of George Eliot's finest comedy; only a woman could have done them. And the comedy can be of the kind in which the tragic undertone is what tells most on us, as we see in Book VIII, Chapter LXXIV, where Mrs. Bulstrode goes the round of her friends in an attempt to find out what is the matter with her husband:

> 'In Middlemarch a wife could not long remain igno-rant that the town held a bad opinion of her husband. No feminine intimate might carry her friendship so far as to make a plain statement to the wife of the unpleas-ant fact known or believed about her husband; but when a woman with her thoughts much at leisure got them suddenly employed on something grievously dis-advantageous to her neighbours, various moral im-pulses were called into play which tended to stimulate utterance. Candour was one. To be candid, in Middle-march phraseology, meant, to use an early opportunity of letting your friends know that you did not take a cheerful view of their capacity, their conduct, or their position; and a robust candour never waited to be asked for its opinion. Then, again, there was the love of truth. . . . Stronger than all, there was the regard for a friend's moral improvement, sometimes called her soul, which was likely to be benefited by remarks tending to gloom, uttered with the accompaniment of pensive staring at the furniture and a manner implying that the speaker would not tell what was on her mind, from regard to the feelings of her hearer.'

The treatment of Bulstrode himself is a triumph in which the part of a magnificent intelligence in the novel-ist's art is manifested in some of the finest analysis any novel can show. The peculiar religious world to which Bulstrode belongs, its ethos and idiom, George Eliot knows from the inside—we remember the Evangelicalism of her youth. The analysis is a creative process; it is penetrating imagination, masterly and vivid in understanding, bring-ing the concrete before us in all its reality. Bulstrode is not an attractive figure:

> 'His private minor loans were numerous, but he

would inquire strictly into the circumstances both before and after. In this way a man gathers a domain in his neighbours' hope and fear as well as gratitude; and power, when once it has got into that subtle region, propagates itself, spreading out of all proportion to its external means. It was a principle with Mr. Bulstrode to gain as much power as possible, that he might use it for the glory of God. He went through a great deal of spiritual conflict and inward argument in order to adjust his motives, and make clear to himself what God's glory required.'

This looks like a promise of satire. But George Eliot's is no satiric art; the perceptions that make the satirist are there right enough, but she sees too much, and has too much the humility of the supremely intelligent whose intelligence involves self-knowledge, to be more than incidentally ironical. Unengaging as Bulstrode is, we are not allowed to forget that he is a highly developed member of the species to which we ourselves belong, and so capable of acute suffering; and that his case is not as remote from what might be ours as the particulars of it encourage our complacency to assume.[14] When his Nemesis closes in on him we feel his agonized twists and turns too much from within—that is the effect of George Eliot's kind

---

[14] 'His doubts did not arise from the possible relations of the event to Joshua Rigg's destiny, which belonged to the unmapped regions not taken under the providential government, except perhaps in an imperfect colonial way; but they arose from reflecting that this dispensation too might be a chastisement for himself, as Mr. Farebrother's induction to the living clearly was.

'This was not what Mr. Bulstrode said to any man for the sake of deceiving him; it was what he said to himself—it was as genuinely his mode of explaining events as any theory of yours may be, if you happen to disagree with him. For the egoism which enters into our theories does not affect their sincerity; rather the more our egoism is satisfied the more robust is our belief.'

of analysis—not to regard him with more compassion than contempt:

'Strange, piteous conflict in the soul of this unhappy man who had longed for years to be better than he was—who had taken his selfish passions into discipline and clad them in severe robes, so that he had walked with them as a devout quire, till now that a terror had risen among them, and they could chant no longer, but threw out their common cries for safety.'

George Eliot's analysis is of the 'merciless' kind that only an intelligence lighted by compassion can attain:

'At six o'clock he had already been long dressed, and had spent some of his wretchedness in prayer, pleading his motives for averting the worst evil if in anything he had used falsity and spoken what was not true before God. For Bulstrode shrank from the direct lie with an intensity disproportionate to the numbers of his more indirect misdeeds. But many of these misdeeds were like the subtle muscular movements which are not taken account of in the consciousness, though they bring about the end that we fix our mind on and desire. And it is only what we are vividly conscious of that we can vividly imagine to be seen by Omniscience.'

Here he is, struggling with hope and temptation, by the bedside of his helpless tormentor:

'Bulstrode's native imperiousness and strength of determination served him well. This delicate-looking man, himself nervously perturbed, found the needed stimulus in his strenuous circumstances, and through that difficult night and morning, while he had the air of an animated corpse returned to movement without warmth, holding the mastery by its chill impassibility, his mind was intensely at work thinking of what he had to guard against and what would win him security. Whatever prayers he might lift up, whatever statements he might inwardly make of this man's wretched spiritual condi-

tion, and the duty he himself was under to submit
to the punishment divinely appointed for him rather
than to wish for evil to another—through all this effort
to condense words into a solid mental state, there pierced
and spread with irresistible vividness the images of the
events he desired. And in the train of those images came
their apology. He could not but see the death of Raffles,
and see in it his own deliverance. What was the removal
of this wretched creature? He was impenitent—but were
not public criminals impenitent?—yet the law decided
on their fate. Should Providence in this case award
death, there was no sin in contemplating death as the
desirable issue—if he kept his hands from hastening it
—if he scrupulously did what was prescribed. Even here
there might be a mistake: human prescriptions were
fallible things: Lydgate had said that treatment had
hastened death—why not his own method of treatment?
But, of course, intention was everything in the question
of right and wrong.

'And Bulstrode set himself to keep his intention separate from his desire. He inwardly declared that he intended to obey orders. Why should he have got into any
argument about the validity of these orders? It was
only the common trick of desire—which avails itself of
any irrelevant scepticism, finding larger room for itself
in all uncertainty about effects, in every obscurity that
looks like the absence of law. Still, he did obey the orders.'

Here is the commentary on his move to square Lydgate:

'The banker felt that he had done something to nul-
lify one cause of uneasiness, and yet he was scarcely the
easier. He did not measure the quantity of diseased motive which had made him wish for Lydgate's goodwill,
but the quantity was none the less actively there, like
an irritating agent in his blood. A man vows, and yet
will not cast away the means of breaking his vow. Is it
that he distinctly means to break it? Not at all; but the
desires which tend to break it are at work in him dimly,

and make their way into his imagination, and relax his muscles in the very moments when he is telling himself over again the reasons for his vow. Raffles, recovering quickly, returning to the free use of his odious powers —how could Bulstrode wish for that?'

It is a mark of the quality of George Eliot's presentment of Bulstrode that we should feel that the essential aspect of Nemesis for him is what confronts him here, in the guise of salvation, as he waits for the death he has ensured —ensured by disobeying, with an intention that works through dark indirections and tormented inner casuistries, Lydgate's strict 'doctor's orders':

'In that way the moments passed, until a change in the stertorous breathing was marked enough to draw his attention wholly to the bed, and forced him to think of the departing life, which had once been subservient to his own—which he had once been glad to find base enough for him to act on as he would. It was his gladness then which impelled him now to be glad that the life was at an end.

'And who could say that the death of Raffles had been hastened? Who knew what would have saved him?'

Raffles himself is Dickensian, and so is Mr. Borthrop Trumbull, the auctioneer, to say which is to suggest that, while adequate to their functions, they don't exhibit that peculiar quality of life which distinguishes George Eliot's own creativeness. There is abundance of this quality in the book as a whole; we have it in the Garths, father, mother and daughter, the Vincy family, Mr. Farebrother, the Cadwalladers, and also in the grotesquerie of Peter Featherstone and his kin, which is so decidedly George Eliot and not Dickens.

The weakness of the book, as already intimated, is in Dorothea. We have the danger-signal in the very outset, in the brief Prelude, with its reference to St. Theresa, whose 'flame . . . fed from within, soared after some il-limitable satisfaction, some object which would never justify weakness, which would reconcile self-despair with the rapturous consciousness of life beyond self.' 'Many Theresas,' we are told, 'have been born who found for themselves no epic life wherein there was a constant unfolding of far-resonant action. . . .' In the absence of a 'coherent social faith and order which could perform the function of knowledge for the ardently willing soul' they failed to realize their aspiration: 'Their ardour alternated between a vague ideal and the common yearning of womanhood . . .' Their failure, we gather, was a case of 'a certain spiritual grandeur ill-matched with the meanness of opportunity. . . .' It is a dangerous theme for George Eliot, and we recognize a far from reassuring accent. And our misgivings are not quieted when we find, in the close of the Prelude, so marked a reminder of Maggie Tulliver as this:

> 'Here and there a cygnet is reared uneasily among the ducklings in the brown pond, and never finds the living stream in fellowship with its own oary-footed kind. Here and there is born a Saint Theresa, foundress of nothing, whose loving heartbeats and sobs after an unattained goodness tremble off and are dispersed among hindrances, instead of centring in some long-recognisable deed.'

All the same, the first two chapters make us forget these alarms, the poise is so sure and the tone so right. When we are told of Dorothea Brooke that 'her mind was theoretic, and yearned by its nature after some lofty conception of the world which might fairly include the parish of Tipton, and her own rule of conduct there,' we give that 'parish of Tipton' its full weight. The provinciality of the provincial scene that George Eliot presents is not a mere foil for a heroine; we see it in Dorothea herself as a callowness confirmed by culture: she and her sister had 'both been educated . . . on plans at once narrow and promiscuous, first in an English family and afterwards in a Swiss family at Lausanne. . . .' This is an education that makes little difference to Maggie Tulliver—who is now, we feel, seen by the novelist from the outside as well as felt from within. Dorothea, that is to say, is not exempted from the irony that informs our vision of the other characters in these opening chapters—Celia, Mr. Brooke, Sir James Chetham and Mr. Casaubon. It looks as if George Eliot had succeeded in bringing within her achieved maturity this most resistant and incorrigible self.

Unhappily, we can't go on in that belief for long. Already in the third chapter we find reasons for recalling the Prelude. In the description of the 'soul-hunger' that leads Dorothea to see Casaubon so fantastically as a 'winged messenger' we miss the poise that had characterized the presentment of her at her introduction:

'For a long while she had been oppressed by the indefiniteness which hung in her mind, like a thick summer haze, over all her desire to make her life greatly effective. What could she do, what ought she to do? . . . The intensity of her religious disposition, the coercion it exercised over her life, was but one aspect of a nature altogether ardent, theoretic, and intellectually consequent: and with such a nature struggling in the bands of a narrow teaching, hemmed in by a social life which seemed nothing but a labyrinth of petty courses, a walled-in maze of small paths that led no whither, the outcome was sure to strike others as at once exaggeration and inconsistency.'

Aren't we here, we wonder, in sight of an unqualified self-identification? Isn't there something dangerous in the way the irony seems to be reserved for the provincial background and circumstances, leaving the heroine immune? The doubt has very soon become more than a doubt. When (in Chapter VII) Dorothea, by way of illustrating the kind of music she enjoys, says that the great organ at Freiberg, which she heard on her way home from Lausanne, made her sob, we can't help noting that it is the fatuous Mr. Brooke, a figure consistently presented for our ironic contemplation, who comments: 'That kind of thing is not healthy, my dear.' By the time we see her by the 'reclining Ariadne' in the Vatican, as Will Ladislaw sees her—

'a breathing, blooming girl, whose form, not shamed by the Ariadne, was clad in Quakerish grey drapery; her long cloak, fastened at the neck, was thrown backward from the arms, and one beautiful ungloved hand pillowed her cheek, pushing somewhat backward the white beaver bonnet which made a sort of halo to her face around the simply braided dark-brown hair'

—we are in a position to say that seeing her here through Will's eyes involves for us no adjustment of vision: this is how we *have* been seeing her—or been aware that we are meant to see her. And in general, in so far as we respond to the novelist's intention, our vision goes on being Will's.

The idealization is overt at the moment, finding its licence in the surrounding statuary and in Will's rôle of artist (he is with his German artist friend). But Will's idealizing faculty clearly doesn't confine itself to her outward form even here, and when, thirty or so pages further on, talking with her and Casaubon, he reflects, 'She was an angel beguiled,' we are clearly not meant to dissociate ourselves or the novelist. In fact, he has no independent status of his own—he can't be said to exist; he merely represents, not a dramatically real point of view, but certain of George Eliot's intentions—intentions she has failed to realize creatively. The most important of these is to impose on the reader her own vision and valuation of Dorothea.

Will, of course, is also intended—it is not really a separate matter—to be, in contrast to Casaubon, a fitting soulmate for Dorothea. He is not substantially (everyone agrees) 'there,' but we can see well enough what kind of qualities and attractions are intended, and we can see equally well that we are expected to share a valuation of them extravagantly higher than any we can for a moment countenance. George Eliot's valuation of Will Ladislaw, in short, is Dorothea's, just as Will's of Dorothea is George Eliot's. Dorothea, to put it another way, is a product of

George Eliot's own 'soul-hunger'—another day-dream ideal self. This persistence, in the midst of so much that is so other, of an unreduced enclave of the old immaturity is disconcerting in the extreme. We have an alternation between the poised impersonal insight of a finely tempered wisdom and something like the emotional confusions and self-importances of adolescence.

It is given us, of course, at the outset, as of the essence of Dorothea's case, that she is vague in her exaltations, that she 'was oppressed by the indefiniteness which hung in her mind, like a thick summer haze, over all her desire to make her life greatly effective.' But the show of presenting this haze from the outside soon lapses; George Eliot herself, so far as Dorothea is concerned, is clearly in it too. That is peculiarly apparent in the presentment of those impossibly high-falutin' *tête-à-tête*—or soul to soul—exchanges between Dorothea and Will, which is utterly without irony or criticism. Their tone and quality is given fairly enough in this retrospective summary (it occurs at the end of Chapter LXXXII): 'all their vision, all their thought of each other, had been in a world apart, where the sunshine fell on tall white lilies, where no evil lurked, and no other soul entered.' It is Will who is supposed to be reflecting to this effect, but Will here—as everywhere in his attitude towards Dorothea—is unmistakably not to be distinguished from the novelist (as we have noted, he hardly exists).[15]

There is, as a matter of fact, one place where for a moment George Eliot dissociates herself from him (Chapter XXXIX):

'For the moment Will's admiration was accompanied with a chilling sense of remoteness. A man is seldom ashamed of feeling that he cannot love a woman so well

---

[15] Though, significantly, it is he alone who is adequate to treating Rosamond with appropriate ruthlessness—see the episode (Chapter LXXVIII) in which he 'tells her straight' what his author feels about her.

when he sees a certain greatness in her; nature having
intended greatness for men.'

What she dissociates herself from, it will be noted, is not
the valuation; the irony is not directed against that, but, on
the contrary, implicitly endorses it. To point out that
George Eliot identifies herself with Will's sense of Dorothea's 'subduing power, the sweet dignity, of her noble
unsuspicious inexperience,' doesn't, perhaps, seem a very
damaging criticism. But when it becomes plain that in
this self-identification such significant matters of valuation are involved the criticism takes on a different look.

'Men and women make such sad mistakes about their
own symptoms, taking their vague uneasy longings,
sometimes for genius, sometimes for religion, and of-
tener still for a mighty love.'

—The genius of George Eliot is not questioned, but what
she observes here in respect of Rosamond Vincy has obvious bearings on her own immature self, the self persisting so extraordinarily in company with the genius that is
self-knowledge and a rare order of maturity.

Dorothea, with her 'genius for feeling nobly,' that 'current' in her mind 'into which all thought and feeling were
apt sooner or later to flow—the reaching forward of the
whole consciousness towards the fullest truth, the least
partial good' (end of Chapter XX), and with her ability
to turn that current into a passion for Will Ladislaw, gives
us Maggie's case again, and Maggie's significance: again
we have the confusions represented by the exalted vagueness of Maggie's 'soul-hunger'; we have the unacceptable
valuations and the daydream self-indulgence.

The aspect of self-indulgence is most embarrassingly
apparent in Dorothea's relations (as we are invited to see
them) with Lydgate, who, unlike Ladislaw, is real and a
man. Lydgate's reality makes the unreality of the great
scene intended by George Eliot (or by the Dorothea in
her) the more disconcerting: the scene in which to Lydgate, misunderstood, isolated, ostracized, there appears,

an unhoped-for angelic visitation, Dorothea, all-comprehending and irresistibly good (Chapter LXXVI):

'"Oh, it is hard!" said Dorothea. "I understand the difficulty there is in your vindicating yourself. And that all this should have come to you who had meant to lead a higher life than the common, and to find out better ways—I cannot bear to rest in this as unchangeable. I know you meant that. I remember what you said to me when you first spoke to me about the hospital. There is no sorrow I have thought more about than that—to love what is great, and try to reach it, and yet to fail."

'"Yes," said Lydgate, feeling that here he had found room for the full meaning of his grief. . . .

'"Suppose," said Dorothea meditatively. "Suppose we kept on the hospital according to the present plan, and you stayed here though only with the friendship and support of the few, the evil feeling towards you would gradually die out; there would come opportunities in which people would be forced to acknowledge that they had been unjust to you, because they would see that your purposes were pure. You may still win a great fame like the Louis and Laennec I have heard you speak of, and we shall all be proud of you," she ended, with a smile.'

We are given a good deal in the same vein of winning simplicity. Such a failure in touch, in so intelligent a novelist, is more than a surface matter; it betrays a radical disorder. For Lydgate, we are told, the 'childlike grave-eyed earnestness with which Dorothea said all this was irresistible—blent into an adorable whole with her ready understanding of high experience.' And lest we shouldn't have appreciated her to the full, we are told that

'As Lydgate rode away, he thought, "This young creature has a heart large enough for the Virgin Mary. She evidently thinks nothing of her own future, and would pledge away half her income at once, as if she wanted nothing for herself but a chair to sit in from which she can look down with those clear eyes at the poor mortals who pray to her. She seems to have what I never saw in any woman before—a fountain of friendship towards men—a man can make a friend of her."'

What we have here is unmistakably something of the same order as Romola's epiphany in the plague-stricken village; but worse—or, at any rate, more painfully significant. Offered as it is in a context of George Eliot's maturest art, it not only matters more; it forces us to recognize how intimately her weakness attends upon her strength. Stressing the intended significance of the scene she says, in the course of it:

'The presence of a noble nature, generous in its wishes, ardent in its charity, changes the lights for us: we begin to see things again in their larger, quieter masses, and to believe that we too can be seen and judged in the wholeness of our character.'

This is a characteristic utterance, and, but for the illustration we are being offered, we should say it came from her strength—the strength exhibited in her presentment of Casaubon, Rosamond, Lydgate and Bulstrode. It is certainly her strength as a novelist to have a noble and ardent nature—it is a condition of that maturity which makes her so much greater an artist than Flaubert. What she says of Dorothea might have been said of herself:

'Permanent rebellion, the disorder of a life without some loving reverent resolve, was not possible to her.'

But that she says it of Dorothea must make us aware how far from a simple trait it is we are considering, and how readily the proposition can slide into such another as this:

'No life would have been possible for Dorothea that was not filled with emotion.'

Strength, and complacent readiness to yield to temptation—they are not at all the same thing; but we see how

insidiously, in George Eliot, they are related. Intensely
alive with intelligence and imaginative sympathy, quick
and vivid in her realizaton of the 'equivalent centre of
self' in others—even in a Casaubon or a Rosamond, she is
incapable of morose indifference or the normal routine
obtuseness, and it may be said in a wholly laudatory sense,
by way of characterizing her at her highest level, that no
life would have been possible for her that was not filled
with emotion: her sensibility is directed outward, and
she responds from deep within. At this level, 'emotion'
is a disinterested response defined by its object, and hardly
distinguishable from the play of the intelligence and self-
knowledge that give it impersonality. But the emotional
'fulness' represented by Dorothea depends for its exalting
potency on an abeyance of intelligence and self-knowledge, and the situations offered by way of 'objective correlative' have the daydream relation to experience; they
are generated by a need to soar above the indocile facts
and conditions of the real world. They don't, indeed, strike
us as real in any sense; they have no objectivity, no vigour
of illusion. In this kind of indulgence, complaisantly as
she abandons herself to the current that is loosed, George
Eliot's creative vitality has no part.

(iii) 'Daniel Deronda' and 'The Portrait of a Lady'

In no other of her works is the association of the
strength with the weakness so remarkable or so unfortunate as in *Daniel Deronda*. It is so peculiarly unfortunate, not because the weakness spoils the strength—the
two stand apart, on a large scale, in fairly neatly separable
masses—but because the mass of fervid and wordy unreality seems to have absorbed most of the attention the book
has ever had, and to be all that is remembered of it. That
this should be so shows, I think, how little George Eliot's

acceptance has rested upon a critical recognition of her real strength and distinction, and how unfair to her, in effect, is the conventional overvaluing of her early work. For if the nature of her real strength had been appreciated for what it is, so magnificent an achievement as the good half of *Daniel Deronda* could not have failed to compel an admiration that would have established it, not the less for the astonishing badness of the bad half, among the great things in fiction.

It will be best to get the bad half out of the way first. This can be quickly done, since the weakness doesn't require any sustained attention, being of a kind that has already been thoroughly discussed. It is represented by Deronda himself, and by what may be called in general the Zionist inspiration. And this is the point at which to mention a work of George Eliot's that preceded *Middlemarch—The Spanish Gypsy*. It is a drama in verse, the action of which is placed in mediaeval Spain. The heroine, when on the eve of marriage to her lover, a Spanish noble, is plunged into a conflict between love and duty by the appearance of a gypsy who (to quote Leslie Stephen's summary) 'explains without loss of time that he is her father; that he is about to be the Moses or Mahomet of a gypsy nation; and orders her to give up her country, her religion, and her lover to join him in this hopeful enterprise.' The conflict is resolved by her embracing this duty with ardour, and feeling it as an exalted and exalting passion or Cause:

> Father, my soul is not too base to ring
> At touch of your great thoughts; nay, in my blood
> There streams the sense unspeakable of kind,
> As leopard feels at ease with leopard.
>
> . . . I will wed
> The curse that blights my people.

'Why place the heroine among conditions so hard to

imagine?' asks Leslie Stephen. He gives no answer, but the analysis we have arrived at of her weakness points us to one—and a more interesting one than that which his smile at a great novelist's bluestocking caprice seems to suggest.

George Eliot was too intelligent to be able to offer herself the promptings of Comtism, or of the Victorian interest in race and heredity, as providing the religious exaltations she craved—too intelligent, that is, to offer them directly as such. But imaginative art provided her with opportunities for confusion; she found herself licensed to play with daydream unrealities so strenuously as not to recognize them for such. Author-martyr of *Romola*, she pretends, with painful and scholarly earnestness, that they are historical and real; but the essential function of the quasi-historical setting is one with that of the verse form: it is to evade any serious test for reality (poetry, we know, idealizes and seeks a higher truth).

We see how incomparably better were the opportunities offered her by Zionism. She didn't need to reconstruct Anti-Semitism or its opposite: the Jews were there in the contemporary world of fact, and represented real, active and poignant issues. All her generous moral fervour was quite naturally and spontaneously engaged on their behalf, and, on the other hand, her religious bent and her piety, as well as her intellectual energies and interests, found a congenial field in Jewish culture, history and tradition. Advantages which, once felt, were irresistible temptations. Henry James in his 'Conversation' on *Daniel Deronda* speaks (through Constantius) of the difference between the strong and the weak in George Eliot as one between 'what she is by inspiration and what she is because it is expected of her.' But it is the reverse of a 'sense of the author writing under a sort of external pressure' (Constantius) that I myself have in reading the bad part of *Daniel Deronda*. Here, if anywhere, we have the marks of 'inspiration': George Eliot clearly feels herself swept along on a warm emotional flow. If there is anything at all to be said for the proposition (*via* Constantius again) that 'all the Jewish part is at bottom cold,' it must be that it can be made to point to a certain quality in that part which relates it to the novel in which D. H. Lawrence tries, in imaginative creation, to believe that the pre-Christian Mexican religion might be revived—*The Plumed Serpent,* the one book in which Lawrence falls into insincerity. The insincerity, of the kind he was so good at diagnosing and defining, lies, of course, in the quality that leads one to say 'tries'—though it is flow rather than effort one is conscious of. And there is certainly something of that quality in *Daniel Deronda*—something to provoke the judgment that so intelligent a writer couldn't, at that level, have been so self-convinced of inspiration without some inner connivance or complicity: there is an element of the tacitly *voulu.*

But this is not to say that George Eliot's intellect here prevails over the spontaneities, or that there isn't a determining drive from within, a triumphant pressure of emotion; there is, and that is the trouble. The Victorian intellectual certainly has a large part in her Zionist inspirations, but that doesn't make these the less fervidly emotional; the part is one of happy subordinate alliance with her immaturity. We have already seen that this alliance comes very naturally (for the relation between the Victorian intellectual and the very feminine woman in her is not the simple antithesis her critics seem commonly to suppose); it comes very naturally and insidiously, establishing the conditions in which her mature intelligence lapses and ceases to inhibit her flights—flights not deriving their impulsion from any external pressure. A distinguished mind and a noble nature are unquestionably present in the bad part of *Daniel Deronda,* but it *is* bad; and the nobility, generosity, and moral idealism are at the same time modes of self-indulgence.

The kind of satisfaction she finds in imagining her hero, Deronda (if he can be said to be imagined), doesn't need analysis. He, decidedly, is a woman's creation[16]:

> 'Persons attracted him . . . in proportion to the pos-
> sibility of his defending them, rescuing them, telling
> upon their lives with some sort of redeeming influence;
> and he had to resist an inclination to withdraw coldly
> from the fortunate.' (Chapter XXVIII.)

He has all the personal advantages imagined by Mordecai,
the consumptive prophet, for the fulfiller of his dream, the
new Moses:

> 'he must be a Jew, intellectually cultured, morally fervid
> —in all this a nature ready to be plenished from Mor-
> decai's; but his face and frame must be beautiful and
> strong, he must have been used to all the refinements of
> social life, his life must flow with a full and easy current,
> his circumstances must be free from sordid need: he
> must glorify the possibilities of the Jew. . . .' (Chap-
> ter XXXVIII.)

---

[16] But this about his experience at Cambridge is characteristic
of the innumerable things by the way that even in George
Eliot's weaker places remind us we are dealing with an extremely vigorous and distinguished mind, and one in no
respect disabled by being a woman's:

> 'He found the inward bent towards comprehension and
> thoroughness diverging more and more from the track
> marked out by the standards of examination: he felt a
> heightening discontent with the wearing futility and en-
> feebling strain of a demand for excessive retention and
> dexterity without any insight into the principles which form
> the vital connections of knowledge.'

This goes well with her note on Lydgate's education:

> 'A liberal education had of course left him free to read the
> indecent passages in the school classics, but beyond a gen-
> eral sense of secrecy and obscenity in connection with his
> internal structure, had left his imagination quite unbiassed,
> so that for anything he knew his brains lay in small bags
> at his temples, and he had no more thought of representing
> to himself how his blood circulated than how paper served
> instead of gold.'

We feel, in fact, that Deronda was conceived in terms of general specifications, George Eliot's relation to him being pretty much that shown here as Mordecai's, whose own show of dramatic existence is merely a licence for the author to abound copiously in such exaltations and fervours as the Dorothea in her craves.

Her own misgivings about the degree of concrete presence she has succeeded in bestowing upon Deronda is betrayed, as Henry James points out, in the way she reminds us again and again of the otherwise non-significant trick she attributes to him—the trick of holding the lapels of his coat as he talks. And when he talks, this is his style:

> ' "Turn your fear into a safeguard. Keep your dread fixed on the idea of increasing that remorse which is so bitter to you. Fixed meditaton may do a great deal towards defining our longing or dread. We are not always in a state of strong emotion, and when we are calm we can use our memories and gradually change the bias of our fear, as we do our tastes. Take your fear as a safeguard. It is like quickness of hearing. It may make consequences passionately present to you. Try to take hold of your sensibility, and use it as if it were a faculty, like vision." ' (Chapter XXXVI.)

It is true that he is here speaking as lay-confessor to Gwendolen Harleth ('her feeling had turned this man into a priest'), but that, in George Eliot's conception, is for him the most natural and self-expressive of rôles.[17] And the style of talk sorts happily (if that is the word) with the

---

[17] Here he is in ordinary drawing-room conversation: ' "For my part," said Deronda, "people who do anything finely always inspirit me to try. I don't mean that they make me believe I can do it as well. But they make the thing, whatever it may be, seem worthy to be done. I can bear to think my own music not good for much, but the world would be more dismal if I thought music itself not good for much. Excellence encourages one about life generally; it shows the spiritual wealth of the world." ' (Chapter XXXVI.)

style in general of the weak half of the book—though one would hardly guess from this specimen of Deronda's speech alone how diffusely ponderous and abstract George Eliot can be, and for pages on end (pages among her most embarrassingly fervid, for the wordiness and the emotionality go together). A juxtaposition of specimens of the worst dialogue and the worst prose with specimens of the best (of which there is great abundance in the book) would offer some astonishing contrasts. But it would take up more room than can be spared, and an interested reader will very easily choose representative specimens for himself.

The kind of satisfaction George Eliot finds in Deronda's Zionism is plain. '"The refuge you are needing from personal trouble is the higher, the religious life, which holds an enthusiasm for something more than our own appetites and vanities."' But since poor Gwendolen is not in a position to discover herself a Jewess, and so to find her salvation in Deronda's way, she might in time— when Deronda has gone off to Palestine with Mirah— come to reflect critically upon the depth and general validity of his wisdom. We, at any rate, are obliged to be critical of the George Eliot who can so unreservedly endorse the account of the 'higher, the religious life' represented by Deronda. A paragon of virtue, generosity, intelligence and disinterestedness, he has no 'troubles' he needs a refuge from; what he feels he needs, and what he yearns after, is an 'enthusiasm'—an enthusiasm which shall be at the same time a 'duty.' Whether or not such a desire is necessarily one to have it both ways needn't be discussed; but it is quite plain that the 'duty' that Deronda embraces— '"I considered it my duty—it is the impulse of my feeling— to identify myself . . . with my hereditary people"'—combines moral enthusiasm and the feeling of emotional intensity with essential relaxation in such a way that, for any 'higher life' promoted, we may fairly find an analogy in the exalting effects of alcohol. The element of self-indulgence is patent. And so are the confusions. There is no equivalent of Zionism for Gwendolen, and even if there were—: the religion of heredity or race is not, as a generalizable solution of the problem, one that George Eliot herself, directly challenged, could have stood by. In these inspirations her intelligence and real moral insight are not engaged. But she is otherwise wholly engaged— how wholly and how significantly being brought further home to us when we note that Deronda's racial mission finds itself identified with his love for Mirah, so that he is eventually justified in the 'sweet irresistible hopefulness that the best of human possibilities might befall him—the blending of a complete personal love in one current with a larger duty. . . .'

All in the book that issues from this inspiration is un-real and impotently wordy in the way discussed earlier in connexion with Dorothea—though *Middlemarch* can show nothing to match the wastes of biblicality and fervid idealism ('Revelations') devoted to Mordecai, or the co-pious and drearily comic impossibility of the working-men's club (Chapter CXLII), or the utterly routing Shakespearean sprightliness of Hans Meyrick's letter in Chapter LII. The Meyricks who, while not being direct products of the prophetic afflatus, are subordinate min-isters to it, are among those elements in George Eliot that seem to come from Dickens rather than from life, and so is the pawnbroker's family: the humour and tenderness are painfully trying, with that quality they have, that ob-viousness of intention, which relates them so intimately to the presiding solemnity they subserve.

No more need be said about the weak and bad side of *Daniel Deronda.* By way of laying due stress upon the astonishingly contrasting strength and fineness of the large remainder, the way in which George Eliot transcends in it not only her weakness, but what are commonly thought to be her limitations, I will make an assertion of fact and a critical comparison: Henry James wouldn't have written *The Portrait of a Lady* if he hadn't read *Gwendolen Harleth* (as I shall call the good part of *Dan-iel Deronda*), and, of the pair of closely comparable works, George Eliot's has not only the distinction of having come first; it is decidedly the greater. The fact, once asserted, can hardly be questioned. Henry James wrote his 'Conversation' on *Daniel Deronda* in 1876, and he began *The Portrait of a Lady* 'in the spring of 1879.' No one who considers both the intense appreciative interest he shows in *Gwendolen Harleth* and the extraordinary resemblance of his own theme to George Eliot's (so that *The Portrait of a Lady* might fairly be called a variation) is likely to suggest that this resemblance is accidental and non-significant.

Isabel Archer is Gwendolen and Osmond is Grandcourt —the parallel, in scheme, at any rate, is very close and very obvious. As for the individual characters, that Osmond is Grandcourt is a proposition less likely to evoke protest than the other. And there are certainly more important differences between Isabel and Gwendolen than between Osmond and Grandcourt—a concession that, since the woman is the protagonist and the centre of interest, may seem to be a very favourably significant one in respect of James's originality. The differences, however, as I see them are fairly suggested by saying that Isabel Archer is Gwendolen Harleth seen by a man. And it has to be added that, in presenting such a type, George Eliot has a woman's advantage.

To say that, in the comparison, James's presentment is seen to be sentimental won't, perhaps, quite do; but it is, I think, seen to be partial in both senses of the word—controlled, that is, by a vision that is both incomplete and indulgent; so that we have to grant George Eliot's presentment an advantage in reality. Here it may be protested that James is *not* presenting Gwendolen Harleth, but another girl, and that he is perfectly within his rights in choosing a type that is more wholly sympathetic. That, no doubt, is what James intended to do in so far as he had Gwendolen Harleth in mind. But that he had her in mind at all consciously, so that he thought of himself as attempting a variation on George Eliot's theme, seems to me very unlikely. The inspiration, or challenge, he was conscious of was some girl encountered in actual life:

'a perfect picture of youthfulness—its eagerness, its presumption, its preoccupation with itself, its vanity and silliness, its sense of its own absoluteness. But she is extremely intelligent and clever, and therefore tragedy *can* have a hold on her.'

This, as a matter of fact, is James's description of Gwendolen (given through Theodora, the most sympathetic of the three *personae* of the 'Conversation,' who is here—as the style itself shows—endorsed by the judicially central Constantius): there seems no need to insist further that there is point in saying that Isabel Archer is Gwendolen Harleth seen by a man—or that Gwendolen is Isabel seen by a woman. For clearly, in the girl so described there must have been (even if we think of her as Isabel Archer—in whom James doesn't *see* vanity or silliness) expressions of her 'preoccupation with self' and her 'sense of her own absoluteness' justifying observations and responses more critical and unsympathetic than any offered by James. It isn't that George Eliot shows any animus towards Gwendolen; simply, as a very intelligent woman she is able, unlimited by masculine partiality of vision, and only the more perceptive because a woman, to achieve a much *completer* presentment of her subject than James of his. This strength which manifests itself in sum as completeness affects us locally as a greater specificity, an advantage which, when considered, turns out to be also an advantage over James in consistency. And, as a matter of fact, a notable specificity marks the strength of her mature art in general.

This strength appears in her rendering of country-house and 'county' society compared with James's. Here we have something that is commonly supposed to lie outside her scope. Her earlier life having been what it was, and her life as a practising novelist having been spent with G. H. Lewes, 'cut off from the world' ('the loss for a novelist was serious,' says Mrs. Woolf), what can she have known of the 'best society where no one makes an invidious display of anything in particular, and the advantages of the world are taken with that high-bred depreciation which follows from being accustomed to them' (her own words)? The answer is that, however she came by her knowledge, she can, on the showing of *Daniel Deronda*, present that world with such fulness and reality as to suggest that she knows it as completely and inwardly as she knows Middlemarch. James himself was much impressed by this aspect of her strength. Of the early part of George Eliot's book he says (through Constantius): 'I delighted in its deep, rich English tone, in which so many notes seemed melted together.'

The stress should fall on the 'many notes' rather than on the 'melted,' for what James is responding to is the specificity and completeness of the rendering, whereas 'melted' suggests an assimilating mellowness, charming and conciliating the perceptions; a suffusing richness, bland and emollient. George Eliot's richness is not of that kind; she has too full and strong a sense of the reality, she sees too clearly and understandingly, sees with a judging vision that relates everything to her profoundest moral experience: her full living sense of value is engaged, and sensitively responsive. It isn't that she doesn't appreciate the qualities that so appeal to Henry James: she renders them at least as well as he—renders them better, in the sense that she 'places' them (a point very intimately related to the other, that her range of 'notes' is much wider than his). It is true that, as Virginia Woolf says, 'She is no satirist.' But the reason given, 'The movement of her mind was too slow and cumbersome to lend itself to comedy,' shows that Mrs. Woolf hadn't read *Daniel Deronda*—and can't have read other things at all perceptively. If George Eliot is no satirist it is not because she hasn't the quickness, the delicacy of touch and the precision. And it certainly is not that she hasn't the perceptions and responses that go to make satire. Consider, for instance, the interview between Gwendolen and her uncle, the Reverend Mr. Gascoigne ('man of the world turned clergyman'), in Chapter XIII:

'This match with Grandcourt presented itself to him

as a sort of public affair; perhaps there were ways in which it might even strengthen the Establishment. To the Rector, whose father (nobody would have suspected it, and nobody was told) had risen to be a provincial corn-dealer, aristocratic heirship resembled regal heirship in excepting its possessor from the ordinary standard of moral judgments, Grandcourt, the almost certain baronet, the probable peer, was to be ranged with public personages, and was a match to be accepted on broad general grounds national and ecclesiastical. . . . But if Grandcourt had really made any deeper or more unfortunate experiments in folly than were common in young men of high prospects, he was of an age to have finished them. All accounts can be suitably wound up when a man has not ruined himself, and the expense may be taken as an insurance against future error. This was the view of practical wisdom; with reference to higher views, repentance had a supreme moral and religious value. There was every reason to believe that a woman of well-regulated mind would be happy with Grandcourt.'

* * * * * *

' "Is he disagreeable to you personally?"
' "No."
' "Have you heard anything of him which has affected you disagreeably?" The Rector thought it impossible that Gwendolen could have heard the gossip he had heard, but in any case he must endeavour to put all things in the right light for her.

' "I have heard nothing about him except that he is a great match," said Gwendolen, with some sauciness; "and that affects me very agreeably."

' "Then, my dear Gwendolen, I have nothing further to say than this: you hold your fortune in your own hands—a fortune such as rarely happens to a girl in your circumstances—a fortune in fact which almost takes the question out of the range of mere personal feeling, and makes your acceptance of it a duty. If Providence offers you power and position—especially when unclogged by any conditions that are repugnant to you—your course is one of responsibility, into which caprice must not enter. A man does not like to have his attachment trifled with: he may not be at once repelled—these things are matters of individual disposition. But the trifling may be carried too far. And I must point out to you that in case Mr. Grandcourt were repelled without your having refused him—without your having intended ultimately to refuse him, your situation would be a humiliating and painful one. I, for my part, should regard you with severe disapprobation, as the victim of nothing else than your own coquetry and folly."

'Gwendolen became pallid as she listened to this admonitory speech. The ideas it raised had the force of sensations. Her resistant courage would not help her here, because her uncle was not urging her against her own resolve; he was pressing upon her the motives of dread which she already felt; he was making her more conscious of the risks that lay within herself. She was silent, and the Rector observed that he had produced some strong effect.

' "I mean this in kindness, my dear." His tone had softened.

' "I am aware of that, uncle," said Gwendolen, rising and shaking her head back, as if to rouse herself out of painful passivity. "I am not foolish. I know that I must be married some time—before it is too late. And I don't see how I could do better than marry Mr. Grandcourt. I mean to accept him, if possible." She felt as if she were reinforcing herself by speaking with this decisiveness to her uncle.

'But the Rector was a little startled by so bare a version of his own meaning from those young lips. He wished that in her mind his advice should be taken in an infusion of sentiments proper to a girl, and such as are presupposed in the advice of a clergyman, although he may not consider them always appropriate to be put forward. He wished his niece parks, carriages, a title—

everything that would make this world a pleasant abode; but he wished her not to be cynical—to be, on the contrary, religiously dutiful, and have warm domestic affections.

'"My dear Gwendolen," he said, rising also, and speaking with benignant gravity. "I trust that you will find in marriage a new fountain of duty and affection. Marriage is the only true and satisfactory sphere of a woman, and if your marriage with Mr. Grandcourt should be happily decided upon, you will have probably an increasing power, both of rank and wealth, which may be used for the benefit of others. These considerations are something higher than romance. You are fitted by natural gifts for a position which, considering your birth and early prospects, could hardly be looked forward to as in the ordinary course of things; and I trust that you will grace it not only by those personal gifts, but by a good and consistent life."

'"I hope mamma will be the happier," said Gwendolen, in a more cheerful way, lifting her hands backward to her neck, and moving towards the door. She wanted to waive those higher considerations.'

This is Samuel Butler's matter, and taken by itself, not, in effect, altogether remote from Samuel Butler's mode. The presentment of the Rector here is directly satirical—at any rate, it might very well have come from a satirical novel. But even within the passage quoted there are signs (notably in the short narrative passage describing Gwendolen's state of mind) adverting us that the author isn't a satirist. And we know from his appearances elsewhere that her total attitude towards Mr. Gascoigne is very far from being satirical; she shows him as an impressive and, on the whole, admirable figure: 'cheerful, successful worldliness,' she tells us, 'has a false air of being more selfish than the acrid, unsuccessful kind, whose secret history is summed up in the terrible words, "Sold, but not paid for."' And Mr. Gascoigne not only has strong family feeling and a generous sense of duty, but shows himself in adversity not only admirably practical, but admirably unselfish. George Eliot sees too much and has too strong a sense of the real (as well as too much self-knowledge and too adequate and constant a sense of her own humanity) to be a satirist.

The kind of complexity and completeness, the fulness of vision and response, represented by her Mr. Gascoigne characterizes her rendering in general of the world to which he belongs. Henry James's presentment of what is essentially the same world is seen, in the comparison, to have entailed much excluding and simplifying. His is a subtle art, and he has his irony; but the irony doesn't mean inclusiveness—an adequacy to the complexities of the real in its concrete fulness; it doesn't mark a complex valuing process that has for upshot a total attitude in which all the elements of a full response are brought together. His art (in presenting this world in *The Portrait of a Lady,* I mean) seems to leave out all such perceptions as evoke the tones and facial expressions with which we register the astringent and the unpalatable. The irony is part of the subtlety of the art by which, while being so warmly concrete in effect, he can, without challenge, be so limited and selective, and, what is an essential condition of his selectiveness, so lacking in specificity compared with George Eliot. His world of 'best society' and country-house is, for all its life and charm, immeasurably less real (the word has a plain enough force here, and will bear pondering) than George Eliot's. He idealizes, and his idealizing is a matter of not seeing, and not knowing (or not taking into account), a great deal of the reality. And it seems to me that we have essentially this kind of idealizing in his Isabel Archer; she stands to Gwendolen Harleth as James's 'best society' does to George Eliot's.

In saying this, of course, I am insisting on the point of comparing Gwendolen with Isabel. The point is to bring out the force of James's own tribute (paid through Constantius) to the characteristic strength of George Eliot's art as exhibited in her protagonist:

'And see how the girl is known, inside out, how thoroughly she is felt and understood. It is the most *intelligent* thing in all George Eliot's writing; and that is saying much. It is so deep, so true, so complete, it holds such a wealth of psychological detail, it is more than masterly.'

It would hardly be said of Isabel Archer that the presentment of her is complete; it is characteristic of James's art to have made her an effective enough presence for his purpose without anything approaching a 'wealth of psychological detail.' Her peculiar kind of impressiveness, in fact, is conditioned by her *not* being known inside out, and—we have to confess it—could *not* have been achieved by George Eliot: she knows too much about that kind of girl. For it is fair to say that if James had met a Gwendolen Harleth (at any rate, an American one) he would have seen Isabel Archer; he immensely admired George Eliot's inwardness and completeness of rendering, but when he met the type in actual life and was prompted to the conception of *The Portrait of a Lady*, he saw her with the eyes of an American gentleman. One must add—an essential point—that he saw *her* as American.

It is, of course, possible to imagine a beautiful, clever and vital girl, with 'that sense of superior claims which made a large part of her consciousness' (George Eliot's phrase for Gwendolen, but it applies equally to Isabel), whose egoism yet shouldn't be as much open to the criticism of an intelligent woman as Gwendolen's. But it is hard to believe that, in life, she could be as free from qualities inviting a critical response as the Isabel Archer seen by James. Asking of Gwendolen, why, though a mere girl, she should be everywhere a centre of deferential attention, George Eliot says (Chapter IV): 'The answer may seem to lie quite on the surface:—in her beauty, a certain unusualness about her, a decision of will which made itself felt in her graceful movements and clear unhesitating tones, so that if she came into the room on a rainy day when everybody else was flaccid and the use of things in general was not apparent to them, there seemed to be a sudden reason for keeping up the forms of life.' James might very well have been glad to have found these phrases for his heroine. But George Eliot isn't satisfied with the answer: she not only goes on, as James would hardly have done, to talk about the girl's 'inborn energy of egoistic desire,' she is very specific and concrete in exhibiting the play of that energy—the ways in which it imposes her claims on the people around her. And it is not enough to reply that James doesn't need to be specific to this effect—even granting, as we may, that the two authors are dealing with different girls: it is so plain that George Eliot knows more about hers than he about his, and that this accounts for an important part of the ostensible difference.

And in so far as the ostensible difference does, as we have to grant it does, go back to an actual difference in the object of the novelist's interest, then we must recognize, I think, that George Eliot's choice—one determined by the nature of her interests and the quality of her interestedness—of a Gwendolen rather than an Isabel is that of someone who knows and sees more and has a completer grasp of the real; and that it is one that enables the novelist to explore more thoroughly and profoundly the distinctive field of human nature, to be representative of which is the essential interest offered by both girls—though the one offers a fuller and richer development than the other. Difference of actual type chosen for presentment, difference of specificity and depth in presenting—it isn't possible, as a matter of fact, to distinguish with any decision and say which mainly we have to do with. Isabel, a beautiful and impressive American girl, is in the habit of receiving deferential masculine attention; she would certainly be very extraordinary if she were not in the habit of expecting something in the nature of homage. Here is George Eliot on Gwendolen (Chapter XI):

'In the ladies' dining-room it was evident that Gwendolen was not a general favourite with her own sex;

there were no beginnings of intimacy between her and
the other girls, and in conversation they rather noted
what she said than spoke to her in free exchange. Perhaps it was that she was not much interested in them,
and when left alone in their company had a sense of
empty benches. Mrs. Vulcany once remarked that Miss
Harleth was too fond of the gentlemen; but we know
that she was not in the least fond of them—she was
only fond of their homage—and women did not give her
homage.'

James *tells* us nothing like this about Isabel; in fact, he
shows us her receiving homage from women as well. But
we can't help remembering that James himself is a gentleman—and remembering also as relevant (without, of
course, imputing silliness to James) George Eliot's description of Herr Klesmer being introduced, by Mrs. Arrowpoint, to Gwendolen (Chapter V): 'his alarming
cleverness was made less formidable just then by a certain
softening air of silliness which will sometimes befall even
Genius in the desire of being agreeable to Beauty.'

George Eliot's genius appears in the specificity with
which she exhibits the accompaniments in Gwendolen of
the kind of conscious advantage she resembles Isabel in
enjoying. There is the conversation with Mrs. Arrowpoint
that comes just before Herr Klesmer has the opportunity
to produce that 'softening air of silliness,' a conversation
that illustrates one of the disabilities of egoism: 'self-con-
fidence is apt to address itself to an imaginary dulness in
others; as people who are well off speak in a cajoling tone
to the poor, and those who are in the prime of life raise
their voice and speak artificially to seniors, hastily conceiv-
ing them to be deaf and rather imbecile.' We have hardly
here a writer the movement of whose mind is 'too slow and
cumbersome for comedy' and whose 'hold upon dialogue is
slack.' When she is at her best, as she is on so large a scale
in *Gwendolen Harleth,* there is no writer of whom these
criticisms are less true. Nowhere is her genius more apparent than in the sensitive precision of her 'hold on dialogue';

a hold which, with the variety of living tension she can create with it, is illustrated below (see page 125) in the scene between Gwendolen and her mother that follows on the arrival of Grandcourt's self-committing note, and (see page 129) in the decisive *tête-à-tête* with Grandcourt. It is essentially in her speech that Gwendolen is made a concrete presence—Gwendolen, whose 'ideal it was to be daring in speech and reckless in braving danger, both moral and physical'; of whom it is hard to say whether she is more fitly described as tending to act herself or her ideal of herself; 'whose lively venturesomeness of talk has the effect of wit' ('it was never her aspiration to express herself virtuously so much as cleverly—a point to be remembered in extenuation of her words, which were usually worse than she was'). Here she is with her mother before the anticipated first meeting with Grandcourt:

'Mrs. Davilow felt her ears tingle when Gwendolen, suddenly throwing herself into the attitude of drawing her bow, said with a look of comic enjoyment—

' "How I pity all the other girls at the Archery Meeting—all thinking of Mr. Grandcourt! And they have not a shadow of a chance."

'Mrs. Davilow had not presence of mind to answer immediately, and Gwendolen turned quickly round towards her, saying, wickedly, "Now you know they have not, mamma. You and my uncle and aunt—you all intend him to fall in love with me."

'Mrs. Davilow, piqued into a little stratagem, said, "Oh, my dear, that is not so certain. Miss Arrowpoint has charms which you have not."

' "I know; but they demand thought. My arrow will pierce him before he has time for thought. He will declare himself my slave—I shall send him round the world to bring me back the wedding-ring of a happy woman—in the meantime all the men who are between him and the title will die of different diseases—he will come back Lord Grandcourt—but without the ring—and fall at my feet. I shall laugh at him—he will rise in resentment—

I shall laugh more—he will call for his steed and ride to Quetcham, where he will find Miss Arrowpoint just married to a needy musician, Mrs. Arrowpoint tearing her cap off, and Mr. Arrowpoint standing by. Exit Lord Grandcourt, who returns to Diplow, and, like M. Jabot, *change de linge*."

'Was ever any young witch like this? You thought of hiding things from her—sat upon the secret and looked innocent, and all the while she knew by the corner of your eye that it was exactly five pounds ten you were sitting on! As well turn the key to keep out the damp! It was probably that by dint of divination she already knew more than any one else did of Mr. Grandcourt. That idea in Mrs. Davilow's mind prompted the sort of question which often comes without any other apparent reason than the faculty of speech and the not knowing what to do with it.

' "Why, what kind of man do you imagine him to be, Gwendolen?"

' "Let me see!" said the witch, putting her forefinger to her lips with a little frown, and then stretching out the finger with decision. "Short—just above my shoulder—trying to make himself tall by turning up his mustache and keeping his beard long—a glass in his right eye to give him an air of distinction—a strong opinion about his waistcoat, but uncertain and trimming about the weather, on which he will try to draw me out. He will stare at me all the while, and the glass in his eye will cause him to make horrible faces, especially when he smiles in a flattering way. I shall cast down my eyes in consequence, and he will perceive that I am not indifferent to his attentions. I shall dream at night that I am looking at the extraordinary face of a magnified insect—and the next morning he will make me the offer of his hand; the sequel as before." '

With such sureness of touch does George Eliot render the kind of lively, 'venturesome' lightness it is something more than a second nature in Gwendolen to affect that one's mind reverts again and again to the peculiar reputation enjoyed by Congreve. That kind of praise applies more reasonably to the perfection achieved by George Eliot; to the unfailing rightness with which she gets, in all its turns and moods, her protagonist's airy self-dramatizing sophistication—in which there is a great deal more point than in the alleged 'perfection of style' Congreve gives to Millamant, since Gwendolen's talk is really dramatic, correspondingly significant, and duly 'placed.' We are not offered wit and phrasing for our admiration and the delight of our palates.

It is in the scene between Gwendolen and Grandcourt that George Eliot's mastery of dialogue is most strikingly exhibited. We have it in the brush that follows, in Chapter XI, on their being introduced to each other. It is shown in the rendering of high dramatic tension in Chapter XIII, where Gwendolen takes evasive action in the face of Grandcourt's clear intent to propose. I will save quotation for the marvellously economical passage (reference to it will be in place later) in which she finds that she has placed herself in a position in which she can't not accept, and acceptance seems to determine itself without an act of will. There is a good example of light exchange between them in the following Chapter (XXVIII).

At the moment, what has to be noted is that, though James's Pulcheria of the 'Conversation' says 'they are very much alike' ('it proves how common a type the worldly, *pincée*, selfish young woman seemed to her'), Gwendolen is decidedly not another Rosamond Vincy: her talk is enough to establish that; as Theodora says, she is intelligent. It is with Mrs. Transome that she belongs, being qualified in the same kind of way as Mrs. Transome had been in youth to enact the rôle of daringly brilliant beauty: 'she had never dissociated happiness from personal preeminence and *éclat*.' [18] She is intelligent—in Mrs. Transome's way:

---

[18] 'Church was not markedly distinguished in her mind from the other forms of self-presentation. . . .' (Chapter XLVIII.)

'In the schoolroom her quick mind had taken readily that strong starch of unexplained rules and disconnected facts which saves ignorance from any painful sense of limpness; and what remained of all things knowable, she was conscious of being sufficiently acquainted with through novels, plays and poems. About her French and music, the two justifying accomplishments of a young lady, she felt no ground for uneasiness; and when to all these qualifications, negative and positive, we add the spontaneous sense of capability some happy persons are born with, so that any subject they turn attention to impresses them with their own power of forming a correct judgment on it, who can wonder if Gwendolen felt ready to manage her own destiny.' (Chapter IV.)

It is only when compared with George Eliot herself that she is (like Mrs. Transome) to be classed with Rosamond Vincy: none of these three *personae* is at all like Dorothea, or represents any possibility of the Dorothea relation to the novelist. As James's Theodora says, she is intelligent, 'and therefore tragedy *can* have a hold on her.' She is a young Mrs. Transome, in whom disaster forces a development of conscience; for, in George Eliot's phrase, 'she has a root of conscience in her.' It is there from the beginning in her dread of 'the unpleasant sense of compunction towards her mother, which was the nearest approach to self-condemnation and self-distrust she had known.' We are told also: 'Hers was one of the natures in which exultation invariably carries an infusion of dread ready to curdle and declare itself.' This, which is dramatically exemplified in the episode of the suddenly revealed picture of the dead face during the charades (in Chapter VI), may seem a merely arbitrary *donnée*. Actually, in a youthful egoist, dreading compunction and intelligent enough to dread also the unknown within—the anarchic movement of impulse with its irrevocable consequences, it can be seen to be part of the essential case; especially when the trait is associated with an uneasy sense of the precarious status of egoistic 'exultation' and egoistic claims—a sense natural to an imaginative young egoist in the painful impression-ableness of immaturity. 'Solitude in any wide scene,' we are told, 'impressed her with an undefined feeling of im-measurable existence aloof from her, in the midst of which she was helplessly incapable of asserting herself.' It all seems to me imagined with truth and subtlety, and ad-mirably analysed. So that when we are told, 'Whatever was accepted as consistent with being a lady she had no scruple about; but from the dim region of what was called disgraceful, wrong, guilty, she shrank with mingled pride and terror,' then a whole concrete case is focussed in the summary. The potentiality in Gwendolen of a seismic re-morse is concretely established for us.

Here, of course, we have a difference between her and Isabel Archer: remorse—it doesn't belong to James's con-ception of his young woman that she shall have any need for that. She is merely to make a wrong choice, the wrong-ness of which is a matter of an error in judgment involving no guilt on her part, though it involves tragic conse-quences for her. As Mr. Yvor Winters sees it in his essay on him in *Maule's Curse*, James is concerned, characteris-tically, to present the choice as free—to present it as pure choice. 'The moral issue, then, since it is primarily an American affair, is freed in most of the Jamesian novels, and in all of the greatest, from the compulsion of a code of manners.' This certainly has a bearing on the difference between Gwendolen and Isabel; between the English young lady in her proper setting of mid-Victorian English 'best society,' one who in her 'venturesomeness' 'cannot conceive herself as anything else than a lady,' [19] and the 'free' American girl, who moves on the Old World stage as an indefinitely licensed and privileged interloper. But

---

[19] 'She rejoiced to feel herself exceptional; but her horizon was that of a genteel romance where the heroine's soul poured out in her journal is full of vague power, originality and general rebellion, while her life moves strictly in the sphere of fashion; and if she wanders into a swamp, the pathos lies partly, so to speak, in her having on satin shoes.' (Chapter VI.)

there is a more obviously important difference: 'The moral issue is also freed from economic necessity . . . Isabel Archer is benevolently provided with funds after her story opens, with the express purpose that her action shall thereafter be unhampered.'

The contrast offered by George Eliot's preoccupation is extreme. All her creative power works to the evoking of a system of pressures so intolerable to Gwendolen, and so enclosing, that her final acceptance of Grandcourt seems to issue, not from her will, but from them; if she acts, it is certainly not in freedom, and she hasn't even the sense of exercising choice. Economic necessity plays a determining part. In the earlier phase of the history she has, as much as Isabel Archer in respect of Lord Warburton and Gilbert Osmond, a free choice in front of her: does she, or does she not, want to marry Grandcourt? But after the meeting with Mrs. Glasher and Grandcourt's children she recoils in disgust and horror from the idea of marriage with him; she recoils from the wrong to others, and from the insult (she feels) offered herself. Then comes the financial disaster, engulfing her family. The effect on Gwendolen, with her indocile egoism and her spoilt child's ignorance of practical realities, and the consequences for her—these are evoked with vivid particularity. There is, pressed on her by the kind and efficient Rector, her uncle, as a duty that is at the same time a gift of fortune she can't fail to accept with grateful gladness, the situation of governess with Mrs. Mompert, the Bishop's wife—who, as a woman of 'strict principle' such as precludes her from 'having a French person in the house,' will want to inspect even the Rector's nominee before appointing her: the sheer impossibility of such a 'situation' for Gwendolen is something we are made to feel from the inside. The complementary kind of impossibility, the impossibility of her own plan of exploiting with *èclat* her talents and advantages and becoming a great actress or singer, is brought home to her with crushing and humiliating finality by Herr Klesmer (Chapter XXIII). It is immediately after this interview, which leaves her with no hope of an alternative to Mrs.

Mompert and the 'episcopal penitentiary,' that Grandcourt's note arrives, asking if he may call. No better illustration of George Eliot's peculiar genius as a novelist—a kind of genius so different from that she is commonly credited with—can be found for quoting than the presentment of Gwendolen's reactions. Here we have the most subtle and convincing analysis rendered, with extraordinary vividness and economy, in the concrete; the shifting tensions in Gwendolen are registered in her speech and outward movements, and the whole is (in an essentially novelistic way) so dramatic that we don't distinguish the elements of description and commentary as such:

'Gwendolen let it fall on the floor, and turned away.
'"It must be answered, darling," said Mrs. Davilow, timidly. "The man waits."
'Gwendolen sank on the settee, clasped her hands, and looked straight before her, not at her mother. She had the expression of one who had been startled by a sound and was listening to know what would come of it. The sudden change of the situation was bewildering. A few minutes before she was looking along an inescapable path of repulsive monotony, with hopeless inward rebellion against the imperious lot which left her no choice: and lo, now, a moment of choice was come. Yet —was it triumph she felt most or terror? Impossible for Gwendolen not to feel some triumph in a tribute to her power at a time when she was first tasting the bitterness of insignificance: again she seemed to be getting a sort of empire over her own life. But how to use it? Here came the terror. Quick, quick, like pictures in a book beaten open with a sense of hurry, came back vividly, yet in fragments, all that she had gone through in relation to Grandcourt—the allurements, the vacillations, the resolve to accede, the final repulsion; the incisive face of that dark-eyed lady with the lovely boy; her own pledge (was it a pledge not to marry him?)—the new disbelief in the worth of men and things for which that scene of disclosure had become a symbol. That unalter-

able experience made a vision at which in the first agitated moment, before tempering reflections could suggest themselves, her native terror shrank.

'Where was the good of choice coming again? What did she wish? Anything different? No! and yet in the dark seed-growths of consciousness a new wish was forming itself—"I wish I had never known it!" Something, anything she wished for that would have saved her from the dread to let Grandcourt come.

'It was no long while—yet it seemed long to Mrs. Davilow, before she thought it well to say, gently—

' "It will be necessary for you to write, dear. Or shall I write an answer for you—which you will dictate?"

' "No, mamma," said Gwendolen, drawing a deep breath. "But please lay me out the pen and paper."

'That was gaining time. Was she to decline Grandcourt's visit—close the shutters—not even look out on what would happen?—though with the assurance that she should remain just where she was? The young activity within her made a warm current through her terror and stirred towards something that would be an event—towards an opportunity in which she could look and speak with the former effectiveness. The interest of the morrow was no longer at a deadlock.

' "There is really no reason on earth why you should be so alarmed at the man's waiting for a few minutes, mamma," said Gwendolen, remonstrantly, as Mrs. Davilow, having prepared the writing materials, looked towards her expectantly. "Servants expect nothing else than to wait. It is not to be supposed that I must write on the instant."

' "No, dear," said Mrs. Davilow, in the tone of one corrected, turning to sit down and take up a bit of work that lay at hand; "he can wait another quarter of an hour, if you like."

'It was a very simple speech and action on her part, but it was what might have been subtly calculated. Gwendolen felt a contradictory desire to be hastened: hurry would save her from deliberate choice.

' "I did not mean him to wait long enough for that needlework to be finished," she said, lifting her hands to stroke the backward curves of her hair, while she rose from her seat and stood still.

' "But if you don't feel able to decide?" said Mrs. Davilow, sympathizingly.

' "I *must* decide," said Gwendolen, walking to the writing-table and seating herself. All the while there was a busy undercurrent in her, like the thought of a man who keeps up a dialogue while he is considering how he can slip away. Why should she not let him come? It bound her to nothing. He had been to Leubronn after her: of course he meant a direct unmistakable renewal of the suit which before had been only implied. What then? She could reject him. Why was she to deny herself the freedom of doing this—which she would like to do?

' "If Mr. Grandcourt has only just returned from Leubronn," said Mrs. Davilow, observing that Gwendolen leaned back in her chair after taking the pen in her hand—"I wonder whether he has heard of our misfortunes."

' "That could make no difference to a man in his position," said Gwendolen, rather contemptuously.

' "It would, to some men," said Mrs. Davilow. "They would not like to take a wife from a family in a state of beggary almost, as we are. Here we are at Offendene, with a great shell over us as usual. But just imagine his finding us at Sawyer's Cottage. Most men are afraid of being bored or taxed by a wife's family. If Mr. Grandcourt did know, I think it a strong proof of his attachment to you."

'Mrs. Davilow spoke with unusual emphasis: it was the first time she had ventured to say anything about Grandcourt which would necessarily seem intended as an argument in favour of him, her habitual impression being that such arguments would certainly be useless and might be worse. The effect of her words now was stronger than she could imagine: they raised a new set

of possibilities in Gwendolen's mind—a vision of what
Grandcourt might do for her mother if she, Gwendolen,
did—what she was not going to do. She was so moved
by a new rush of ideas, that like one conscious of being
urgently called away, she felt that the immediate task
must be hastened: the letter must be written, else it
might be endlessly deferred. After all, she acted in a
hurry as she had wished to do. To act in a hurry was to
have a reason for keeping away from an absolute decision, and to leave open as many issues as possible.

'She wrote: "Miss Harleth presents her compliments
to Mr. Grandcourt. She will be at home after two
o'clock to-morrow."'

Reading this, it is hard to remember that George Eliot
was contemporary with Trollope. What later novelist has
rendered the inner movement of impulse, the play of motive that issues in speech and act and underlies formed
thought and conscious will, with more penetrating subtlety than she? It is partly done *through* speech and action.
But there is also, co-operating with these, a kind of psychological notation that is well represented in the passage quoted above, and is exemplified in 'Quick, quick,
like pictures in a book beaten open with a sense of hurry
. . .', and 'yet in the dark seed-growths of consciousness
a new wish was forming itself . . .' and 'The young activity within her made a warm current through her terror
. . .', and 'All the while there was a busy under-current
in her, like the thought of a man who keeps up a dialogue
while he is considering how he can slip away'—and so
much else. This notation is one of the distinctive characteristics of her mature style,[20] doing its work always with

---

[20] The record of Gwendolen's later days of desperation is rich
in quotable instances, e.g.: 'The thought of his dying would
not subsist: it turned as with a dream-change into the terror
that she should die with his throttling fingers on her neck
avenging that thought. Fantasies moved within her like ghosts,
making no break in her more acknowledged consciousness

an inevitable rightness—and *Daniel Deronda* (with *Middlemarch*) was written in the earlier 'seventies. But remarkable as it is, and impressive as would be the assemblage of instances that could be quickly brought together, it is better not to stress it without adding that, as she uses it, it is inseparable from her rendering of 'psychology' in speech and action. It doesn't seem to me that her genius as exhibited in these ways has been anything like duly recognized.

The passage last quoted is not the work of a 'slow and cumbersome mind.' As for the 'hold on dialogue,' here is the proposal scene (Chapter XXVII—again quotation must be at length):

> 'In eluding a direct appeal Gwendolen recovered some of her self-possession. She spoke with dignity and looked straight at Grandcourt, whose long, narrow, impenetrable eyes met hers, and mysteriously arrested

and finding no obstruction in it: dark rays doing their work invisibly in the broad light.' (Chapter XLVIII.)

And here is Grandcourt (Chapter XXVIII): 'Grandcourt's thoughts this evening were like the circlets one sees in a dark pool continually dying out and continually started again by some impulses from below the surface. The deeper central impulse came from the image of Gwendolen. . . .'

Or take this from *Middlemarch* (Vol. I, Chapter XXI—the end):

'We are all of us born in moral stupidity, taking the world as an udder to feed our supreme selves: Dorothea had early begun to emerge from that stupidity, but yet it had been easier to her to imagine how she would devote herself to Mr. Casaubon, and become wise and strong in his strength and wisdom, than to conceive with that distinctness which is no longer reflection but feeling—an idea wrought back to the directness of sense, like the solidity of objects—that he had an equivalent centre of self, whence the lights and shadows must always fall with a certain difference.'

The reader will have noted a phrase for which Mr. T. S. Eliot might have been grateful in the days when he was calling attention to the 'felt thought' in seventeenth-century poetry.

them: mysteriously; for the subtly-varied drama between
man and woman is often such as can hardly be rendered
in words put together like dominoes, according to obvious fixed marks. The word of all work, Love, will no
more express the myriad modes of mutual attraction,
than the word Thought can inform you what is passing
through your neighbour's mind. It would be hard to
tell on which side—Gwendolen's or Grandcourt's—the
influence was more mixed. At that moment his strongest
wish was to be completely master of this creature—this
piquant combination of maidenliness and mischief:
that she knew things which had made her start away
from him, spurred him to triumph over that repugnance;
and he was believing that he should triumph. And she
—ah! piteous equality in the need to dominate!—she was
overcome like the thirsty one who is drawn towards the
seeming water in the desert, overcome by the suffused
sense that here in this man's homage to her lay the rescue from helpless subjection to an oppressive lot.

'All the while they were looking at each other; and
Grandcourt said, slowly and languidly, as if it were of
no importance, other things having been settled—

'"You will tell me now, I hope, that Mrs. Davilow's
loss of fortune will not trouble you further. You will
trust me to prevent it from weighing upon her. You
will give me the claim to provide against that."

'The little pauses and refined drawlings with which
this speech was uttered, gave time for Gwendolen to
go through the dream of a life. As the words penetrated
her, they had the effect of a draught of wine, which
suddenly makes all things easier, desirable things not so
wrong, and people in general less disagreeable. She had
a momentary phantasmal love for this man who chose
his words so well, and who was a mere incarnation of
delicate homage. Repugnance, dread, scruples—these
were dim as remembered pains, while she was already
tasting relief under the immediate pain of hopelessness.
She imagined herself already springing to her mother,
and being playful again. Yet when Grandcourt had

ceased to speak, there was an instant in which she was conscious of being at the turning of the ways.

'"You are very generous," she said, not moving her eyes, and speaking with a gentle intonation.

'"You accept what will make such things a matter of course?" said Grandcourt, without any new eagerness. "You consent to become my wife?"

'This time Gwendolen remained quite pale. Something made her rise from her seat in spite of herself and walk to a little distance. Then she turned and with her hands folded before her stood in silence.

'Grandcourt immediately rose too, resting his hat on the chair, but still keeping hold of it. The evident hesitation of this destitute girl to take his splendid offer stung him into a keenness of interest such as he had not known for years. None the less because he attributed her hesitation entirely to her knowledge about Mrs. Glasher. In that attitude of preparation, he said—

'"Do you command me to go?" No familiar spirit could have suggested to him more effective words.

'"No," said Gwendolen. She could not let him go: that negative was a clutch. She seemed to herself to be, after all, only drifted towards the tremendous decision: —but drifting depends on something besides the currents, when the sails have been set beforehand.

'"You accept my devotion?" said Grandcourt, holding his hat by his side and looking straight into her eyes, without other movement. Their eyes meeting in that way seemed to allow any length of pause; but wait as long as she would, how could she contradict herself? What had she detained him for? He had shut out any explanation.

'"Yes," came as gravely from Gwendolen's lips as if she had been answering to her name in a court of justice. He received it gravely, and they still looked at each other in the same attitude. Was there ever before such a way of accepting the bliss-giving "Yes?" Grandcourt liked better to be at that distance from her, and to feel under a ceremony imposed by an indefinable prohibition that breathed from Gwendolen's bearing.

'But he did at length lay down his hat and advance to take her hand, just pressing his lips upon it and letting it go again. She thought his behaviour perfect, and gained a sense of freedom which made her almost ready to be mischievous. Her "Yes" entailed so little at this moment, that there was nothing to screen the reversal of her gloomy prospects: her vision was filled by her own release from the Momperts, and her mother's release from Sawyer's Cottage. With a happy curl of the lips, she said—

'"Will you not see mamma? I will fetch her."

'"Let us wait a little," said Grandcourt, in his favourite attitude, having his left forefinger and thumb in his waistcoat-pocket, and with his right caressing his whisker, while he stood near Gwendolen and looked at her—not unlike a gentleman who has a felicitous introduction at an evening party.

'"Have you anything else to say to me?" said Gwendolen, playfully.

'"Yes—I know having things said to you is a great bore," said Grandcourt, rather sympathetically.

'"Not when they are things I like to hear."

'"Will it bother you to be asked how soon we can be married?"

'"I think it will, to-day," said Gwendolen, putting up her chin saucily.

'"Not to-day, then, but to-morrow. Think of it before I come to-morrow. In a fortnight—or three weeks—as soon as possible."

'"Ah, you think you will be tired of my company," said Gwendolen. "I notice when people are married the husband is not so much with his wife as when they are engaged. But perhaps I shall like that better too."

'She laughed charmingly.

'"You shall have whatever you like," said Grandcourt.

'"And nothing that I don't like?—please say that, because I think I dislike what I don't like more than I like what I like," said Gwendolen, finding herself in the woman's paradise where all her nonsense is adorable.'

It will be noted how beautifully the status of Gwendolen's spontaneously acted self is defined by her relieved and easy assumption of it once the phase of tense negativity has issued in 'Yes.' And it was clearly not this self that pronounced the 'Yes'; nor does it come from a profound integrated self. George Eliot's way of putting it is significant: '"Yes" came as gravely from Gwendolen's lips as if she had been answering to her name in a court of justice.' This is a response that issues out of something like an abeyance of will; it is determined for her. No acquiescence could look less like an expression of free choice. Yet we don't feel that Gwendolen is therefore not to be judged as a moral agent. The 'Yes' is a true expression of her moral economy; that the play of tensions should have as its upshot this response has been established by habits of valuation and by essential choices lived. 'She seemed to herself to be, after all, only drifted towards the tremendous decision:—but drifting depends on something besides the currents, when the sails have been set beforehand.' Even before what she saw as a moral objection arose to confront her, she had had no sense of herself as able to settle her relations with Grandcourt by a clear and free act of choice:

'Even in Gwendolen's mind that result was one of two likelihoods that presented themselves alternately, one of two decisions towards which she was being precipitated, as if they were two sides of a boundary-line, and she did not know on which she should fall. This subjection to a possible self, a self not to be absolutely predicted about, caused her some astonishment and terror: her favourite key of life—doing as she liked—seemed to fail her, and she could not foresee what at a given moment she might like to do.' (Chapter XIII.)

But we aren't inclined to think of her as being then any the less a subject for moral evaluation. We note rather, as entering into the account, that she gets a thrill out of the surrender to tense uncertainty, and that it is not for nothing that at her first introduction to us, in the opening, she figures as the gambler, lost in the intoxication of hazard. The situation, in respect of Gwendolen's status as a moral agent, isn't essentially altered by the reinforcement, in conflicting senses, of the pulls and pressures bearing on the act of choice: the supervention of a powerful force, represented by Mrs. Glasher, carrying Gwendolen in recoil from Grandcourt, which is countered by a new pressure towards acceptance—the economic one (translatable by Gwendolen into terms of duty towards her mother).[21]

We note, with regard to Gwendolen's attitude towards what she sees as the strong moral ground for refusing Grandcourt, that 'in the dark seed-growths of consciousness a new wish was forming itself—"I wish I had never known it."' There is much concrete psychological notation to this effect, deriving from the insight of a great novelist; that it has a moral significance, a relation to that ostensibly mechanical and unwilled 'Yes,' is plain. But it is possible to overstress Gwendolen's guilt in the matter of Mrs. Glasher, a guilt that is so very conscious. George Eliot's appreciation of the moral issues doesn't coincide with that of her protagonist—or of the conventional Victorian moralist. For George Eliot the essential significance of Gwendolen's case lies in the egoism expressed here (the

---

[21] 'The cheque was for five hundred pounds, and Gwendolen turned it towards her mother, with the letter.

'"How very kind and delicate!" said Mrs. Davilow, with much feeling. "But I really should like better not to be dependent on a son-in-law. I and the girls could get along very well."

'"Mamma, if you say that again, I will not marry him," said Gwendolen, angrily.

'"My dear child, I trust you are not going to marry only for my sake," said Mrs. Davilow deprecatingly.

'Gwendolen tossed her head on the pillow away from her mother, and let the ring lie. She was irritated at this attempt to take away a motive.' (Chapter XXVIII.)

passage follows immediately on that last quoted, in which she 'could not foresee what at a given moment she might like to do'):

'The prospect of marrying Grandcourt really seemed more attractive to her than she had believed beforehand that any marriage could be: the dignities, the luxuries, the power of doing a great deal of what she liked to, which had now come close to her, and within her power to secure or to lose, took hold of her nature as if it had been the strong odour of what she had only imagined and longed for before. And Grandcourt himself? He seemed as little of a flaw in his fortunes as a lover and husband could possibly be. Gwendolen wished to mount the chariot and drive the plunging horses herself, with a spouse by her side who would fold his arms and give her his countenance without looking ridiculous.'

It is again a case of Hubris with its appropriate Nemesis. What first piqued her into turning on 'this Mr. Grandcourt's a quality of intention no other man had exacted from her was that 'he seemed to feel his own importance more than he did hers—a sort of unreasonableness few of us can tolerate.' She had a similar attraction for him. When, too late, she knows to the full the mistakenness of her assumptions and finds herself beaten at her own game, the great hold Grandcourt has over her lies in her moral similarity to him: 'For she too, with her melancholy distaste for things, preferred that her distaste should include admirers.' And the best she can do is 'to bear this last great gambling loss with perfect self-possession.' 'True, she still saw that she "would manage differently from mamma"; but her management now only meant that she would carry her troubles with an air of perfect self-possession, and let none suspect them.' As for what she takes to be her guilt, pride in her overrides remorse: what she most cares about is that Grandcourt shall not know that she knew of Mrs. Glasher before accepting him (though, ironically, he has, all along, known, and his knowledge had added to Gwendolen's attractiveness for him). The consequent torment reminds us closely of Mrs. Transome's Nemesis: 'now that she was a wife, the sense that Grandcourt was gone to Gadsmere [his home for Mrs. Glasher and his children] was like red heat near a burn. She had brought on herself this indignity in her own eyes—this humiliation of being doomed to a terrified silence lest her husband should discover with what sort of consciousness she had married him; and as she had said to Deronda, she "must go on."' And 'in spite of remorse, it still seemed the worse result of her marriage that she should in any way make a spectacle of herself; and her humiliation was lightened by her thinking that only Mrs. Glasher was aware of the fact that caused it.'

So much pride and courage and sensitiveness and intelligence fixed in a destructive deadlock through false valuation and self-ignorance—this is what makes Gwendolen a tragic figure. And as George Eliot establishes for our contemplation the complexities of inner constitution and outer conditions that make Gwendolen look so different from Isabel Archer, she is exhibiting what we recognize from our own most intimate experience to be as much the behaviour of a responsible moral agent, and so as much amenable to moral judgment, as any human behaviour can be. Not, of course, that our attitude is that of the judge towards the prisoner in the dock; but neither is it that of *tout comprendre, c'est tout pardonner*. It is, or should be (with George Eliot's help), George Eliot's own, which is that of a great novelist, concerned with human and moral valuation in a way proper to her art—it is a way that doesn't let us forget that what is being lit up for us lies within.

And turning once more to Isabel Archer, we may ask whether, in this matter of choice, she is as different from Gwendolen as Mr. Winters' account suggests: isn't her appearance of being so much more free to choose with her 'ethical sensibility' largely illusion? She herself must look back on her treasured freedom of choice with some irony when, after her marriage, she has learnt of the relations between her husband and Madame Merle, and of the part played by Madame Merle in her 'choosing' to marry Osmond. But for us it is the wider significance of the revelation that needs dwelling on. It is not surprising that so young a girl, and one so new to this social climate, should have been unable to value at their true worth either Madame Merle or Osmond; and how could, in any case, anyone so little experienced in life, knowing so little about herself, and (inevitably) so vague about what in concrete terms the 'fineness' she means to achieve in life might amount to—how could such a girl exercise a choice that should be essentially more than Gwendolen's a free expression of ethical sensibility?

And isn't this (comes the comment on Mr. Winters' account) just James's point? Yet we are, by that account, made to reflect on a distinctive quality of James's art—a quality that makes it possible for an intelligent critic to slight the irony and see the book as Mr. Winters does. Isn't there, in fact, something evasive about James's inexplicitness; something equivocal about his indirectness and the subtlety of implication with which he pursues his aim of excluding all but the 'essential?' What, we ask, thinking by contrast of the fulness with which we have Gwendolen, is the *substance* of Isabel's interest for us? In spite of such things as the fine passage in Chapter XLII of *The Portrait of a Lady* that evokes her finding 'the infinite vista of a multiplied life to be a dark alley with a dead wall at the end,' we see that James's marvellous art is devoted to contenting us with very little in the way of inward realization of Isabel, and to keeping us interested, instead, in a kind of psychological detective work—keeping us intently wondering from the outside, and constructing, on a strict economy of evidence, what is going on inside. And, if we consider, we find that the constructions to which we are led are of such a kind as not to challenge, or to bear with comfort, any very searching test in terms of life. The difference between James and George Eliot is largely a matter of what he leaves out. The leaving out, of course, is a very positive art that offers the compensation. But it is not the less fair to say that what James does with

Gwendolen Harleth throws a strong light on the characteristic working of that peculiar moral sense which Mr. Winters discusses in relation to the New England background—a light in which its limiting tendency appears as drastic indeed. *The Portrait of a Lady* belongs to the sappiest phase of James's art, when the hypertrophy of technique hadn't yet set in; but, in the light of the patent relation to *Gwendolen Harleth,* we can see already a certain disproportion between an intensity of art that has at the same time an effect of moral intensity and the actual substance of human interest provided. That James should have done *this* with what he found in George Eliot, and done it with such strenuously refined art!—that registers our reaction.

Actually, we can see that the trouble is that he derives so much more from George Eliot than he suspects: he largely mistakes the nature of his inspiration, which is not so much from life as he supposes. He has been profoundly impressed by the irony of Gwendolen's married situation, and is really moved by a desire to produce a similar irony. But he fails to produce the fable that gives inevitability and moral significance. He can remain unaware of his failure because he is so largely occupied (a point that can be illustrated in detail) in transposing George Eliot, whose power is due to the profound psychological truth of her conception, and the consistency with which she develops it.

Isabel Archer, for all James's concern (if Mr. Winters is right) to isolate in her the problem of ethical choice, has neither a more intense nor a richer moral significance than Gwendolen Harleth; but very much the reverse. If this way of stating James's interest in her seems obtuse, and we are to appreciate a fully ironical intention in his presentment of the irony of her case, and are to say (as surely we are) that he intends an ironical 'placing' of her illusion, the adverse criticism of James still holds. For we can still see Mr. Winters' excuse for stating things in *his* way: beyond any question we are invited to share a valuation of Isabel that is incompatible with a really critical irony. We can't even say that James makes an implicit critical comment on the background of American idealism that fostered her romantic confidence in life and in her ability to choose: he admires her so much, and demands for her such admiration and homage, that he can't be credited with 'placing' the conditions that, as an admirable American girl, she represents. James's lack of specificity favours an evasiveness, and the evasiveness, if at all closely questioned, yields inconsistency of a kind that partly empties the theme of *The Portrait of a Lady* of moral substance.

He exempts Isabel from the conditions that engage our sympathy for Gwendolen—of whom we are nevertheless not expected to be uncritical: economic pressure, and the pressure (for, where Grandcourt's suit is in question, it is more than mere approval that Mr. Gascoigne enacts) brought quasi-paternally to bear on her by her uncle, the representative of the approving expectation of the society that constitutes her world. For the 'free' Isabel it can't even be urged that she is the victim of bad advice or a tacit general conspiracy that favours Madame Merle's designs; on the contrary, all those whose judgment Isabel has most reason to respect—Ralph Touchett, Mrs. Touchett, Lord Warburton—argue cogently against Osmond by their valuation of him. That she shouldn't be led by their unanimity to question her own valuation convicts her of a notable lack of sense, not to say extremely unintelligent obstinacy (which nothing we are shown mitigates)—at least, one would think so; but James doesn't let us suppose that he shares this view. After the marriage she is shown to us enjoying, in her proudly dissimulated desolation, the admiring pity due to a noble victim who is above criticism.

These inconsistencies, these moral incoherences, which become apparent when we ponder the story, pass undetected at first because of the brilliant art with which James, choosing his *scènes à faire*, works in terms of dramatic presentation. His dramatic triumphs often turn out to have been prompted (without, one judges, his recognizing the fact) by felicities of dramatic presentation in George Eliot; but his art is his own. All the same, when we make

the comparison, we find that her art is not less remarkable
than his for command of the dramatic—that she enjoys
here, in fact, a characteristic superiority. With her advantage in specificity, she is certainly not inferior in vividness
and immediate power; and when we reflect critically and
relate the scene to what goes before and what comes after
we discover more and more reason for admiring her
moral and psychological insight, and the completeness
with which she has grasped and realized her theme.

In what James does with *Gwendolen Harleth* there is
something premonitory. Again and again in his later work
we find ourselves asking: What is the moral substance?
what, definable in terms of human interest, is there to justify this sustained and strenuous suggestion that important
issues are involved, important choices are to be made? His
kind of preoccupation with eliminating the inessential
clearly tends to become the pursuit of an essential that
is illusory.

If any doubt should linger as to whether one is justified in talking about 'what James does with *Gwendolen
Harleth*,' it should be settled finally by a consideration of
Osmond in relation to Grandcourt: Osmond so plainly *is*
Grandcourt, hardly disguised, that the general derivative
relation of James's novel to George Eliot's becomes quite
unquestionable. It is true that Grandcourt is no aesthetic
connoisseur, but Osmond's interest in articles of *virtù*
amounts to nothing more than a notation of a kind of
cherished fastidiousness of conscious, but empty, superiority that is precisely Grandcourt's: 'From the first she
had noticed that he had nothing of the fool in his composition but that by some subtle means he communicated
to her the impression that all the folly lay with other
people, who did what he did not care to do.' That might
very well be on account of the effect of Osmond on Isabel,
but it comes from George Eliot. Grandcourt, as an English
aristocrat whose status licenses any amount of languid disdain, doesn't need a symbolic dilettantism:

'He himself knew what personal repulsion was—nobody better: his mind was much furnished with a sense of what brutes his fellow-creatures were, both masculine and feminine; what odious familiarities they had, what smirks, what modes of flourishing their handkerchiefs, what costumes, what lavender-water, what bulging eyes, and what foolish notions of making themselves agreeable by remarks which were not wanted. In this critical view of mankind there was affinity between him and Gwendolen before their marriage, and we know that she had been attractingly wrought upon by the refined negations he presented to her.' (Chapter LIV.)

This equally describes Osmond, of whom it might equally well be said that 'he is a man whose grace of bearing has long been moulded on an experience of boredom,' and that 'he has worn out all his healthy interest in things.' All either cares about is to be assured that he feels superior; and the contemptible paradox of a superiority that is nothing unless assured of itself by those whose judgment it affects to despise is neatly 'placed' by George Eliot here:

'It is true that Grandcourt went about with the sense that he did not care a languid curse for any one's admiration; but this state of not-caring, just as much as desire, required its related object—namely, a world of admiring or envying spectators: for if you are fond of looking stonily at smiling persons, the persons must be there and they must smile—a rudimentary truth which is surely forgotten by those who complain of mankind as generally contemptible, since any other aspect of the race must disappoint the voracity of their contempt.'

In Grandcourt, of course, we have as elsewhere her strength, her advantage, of specificity. Our sense of the numbing spell in which his languidly remorseless domination holds Gwendolen doesn't depend upon suggestive inexplicitnesses, sinister overtones and glimpses from a distance. 'Grandcourt had become a blank uncertainty to her in everything but this, that he would do just what he willed': we don't feel him as less sinister and formidable than Osmond because we see him deliberately working to produce this effect (of which we understand perfectly the conditions) in a number of dramatic scenes that have all George Eliot's explicitness and fulness of actuality. Such scenes are that in which he lets her know that he understands perfectly why she had made the surreptitious call on Miss Lapidoth from which he catches her returning; that in which he tells her that she is to learn about his will from the hated Lush; and that, very short, but with an extraordinary power to disturb, in which he surprises her with Deronda—the scene that ends, with reference to the announced yachting cruise which she sees as blessedly releasing her to her mother's company: 'No, you will go with me.' (All these are in Chapter XLVIII.)

In these scenes the sharpness of significant particularity with which the outward action is registered is very striking.

'She was frightened at her own agitation, and began to unbutton her gloves that she might button them again, and bite her lips over the pretended difficulty.'

The whole is *seen*, and the postures and movements are given with vivid precision. James's Constantius, contrasting George Eliot with Turgenev—he the 'poet,' she the 'philosopher'—says: 'One cares for the aspect of things and the other cares for the reason of things.' Nowhere is this characterization more patently wide of the mark than in those places where her supreme *intelligence* is most apparent. It is precisely because she cares for the 'reason' of things that she can render the aspect so vividly; her intelligence informs her perception and her visual imagination. The vividness of the rendering is significance.

As fine a sustained example of this power of hers is to be found in Chapter XXX, where Grandcourt visits Gadsmere in order to tell Mrs. Glasher of the coming marriage and to get from her the diamonds for Gwendolen. Not only is Mrs. Glasher afraid of him, he is afraid of her, for 'however he might assert his independence of Mrs. Glasher's past, he had made a past for himself which was a stronger yoke than any he could impose. He must ask for the diamonds which he had promised Gwendolen.' The inner drama in each as they act upon each other is so vividly present to us in outer movement that we seem to be watching a play; till 'Amid such caressing signs of mutual fear they parted.'

The diamonds, it may be noted at this point, exemplify George Eliot's characteristic subtle and inevitable use of symbolism. They are his mother's diamonds, 'long ago' given Lydia to wear. His demanding them back for Gwendolen is his means of announcing to Lydia that the relations they symbolize—marital, virtually—are to cease. But he can't force her to give them up when she refuses; her strength is that they were given to her as his wife, and she has been that, in all but legal form and social recognition. 'Her person suited diamonds, and made them look as if they were worth some of the money given for them'—the natural validity of the relation is suggested there. They come to Gwendolen on the night of her wedding-day with the enclosed message that turns them to poison (Chapter XXXI): 'I am the grave in which your chance of happiness is buried. . . .' Gwendolen has a hysterical fit: the diamonds are for her the consciousness of that past of Grandcourt's with Lydia which precludes any possibility of good married relations between him and herself.

'Shall you like to stand before your husband with these diamonds on you, and these words of mine in his thoughts and yours? Will he think you have any right to complain when he has made you miserable? You took him with your eyes open. The willing wrong you have done me will be your curse.'

The first glimpse we have of Gwendolen in public after her marriage, she is wearing the diamonds. We are told that her 'belief in her power of dominating had utterly gone.' And again and again, with inevitable naturalness, they play their pregnantly symbolic part. They come to represent Nemesis: they are what Gwendolen married

Grandcourt for, and her punishment is having to wear them.

James's use of symbols, famous as he is for it, looks weak in comparison with George Eliot's. They are thought out independently of the action and then introduced. We have an instance in the valuable coffee-cup, 'precious' to Madame Merle but 'attenuated,' that Osmond, in the showdown scene with Madame Merle (Chapter XLIX), picks up and observes, 'dryly,' to be cracked. It symbolizes very obviously, in its *ad hoc* way, the relations between the two, the crack being the resentment Osmond feels against Madame Merle for the 'service' she had done him in marrying him to Isabel. And here, it is worth noting, we have the first form of the celebrated Golden Bowl symbol, which, in the novel called after it, is used for so many purposes, but which, for all the modish esteem it enjoys, is always applied elaborately from the outside, with an effect of strain. The introduction of George Eliot's diamonds arises naturally from the social drama, and they play a natural part in the action. The turquoise necklace that represents Gwendolen's relations with Deronda is a symbol of the same order.

Lydia Glasher (to revert to her) is one of the admirably done subordinate characters in the book, which, when we have cut away the bad half, is not left thinly populated. Mrs. Davilow, the Gascoigne family, Gwendolen's *bête noire* Mr. Lush ('with no active compassion or good-will, he had just as little active malevolence, being chiefly occupied in liking his particular pleasure'), Mrs. Arrowpoint, Miss Arrowpoint (near kin to Mary Garth)—these are all *there* with a perfect rightness of presence, and with a quality of life that makes them George Eliot characters and no one else's.

And then there is Herr Klesmer, who, though a minor actor, has, for us, a major significance. Pointing to him, we can say: here we have something that gives George Eliot an advantage, not only over Jane Austen (against whom we feel no challenge to press the point), but also over Henry James in *The Portrait of a Lady*. The point is so important that a generous measure of illustration seems in place. Here, then, is Herr Klesmer's incongruous presence at the Archery Meeting:

'We English are a miscellaneous people, and any chance fifty of us will present many varieties of animal architecture or facial ornament; but it must be admitted that our prevailing expression is not that of a lively, impassioned race, preoccupied with the ideal and carrying the real as a mere make-weight. The strong point of the English gentleman pure is the easy style of his figure and clothing; he objects to marked ins and outs in his costume, and he also objects to looking inspired.

'Fancy an assemblage where the men had all that ordinary stamp of the well-bred Englishman, watching the entrance of Herr Klesmer—his mane of hair floating backward in massive inconsistency with the chimney-pot hat, which had the look of having been put on for a joke above his pronounced but well-modelled features and powerful clean-shaven mouth and chin; his tall, thin figure clad in a way which, not being strictly English, was all the worse for its apparent emphasis of intention. Draped in a loose garment with a Florentine *berretta* on his head, he would have been fit to stand by the side of Leonardo da Vinci; but how when he presented himself in trousers which were not what English feeling demanded about the knees?—and when the fire that showed itself in his glances and the movements of his head, as he looked round him with curiosity, was turned into comedy by a hat which ruled that mankind should have well-cropped hair and a staid demeanour, such, for example, as Mr. Arrowpoint's, whose nullity of face and perfect tailoring might pass everywhere without ridicule? One sees why it is often better for greatness to be dead, and to have got rid of the outward man.

'Many present knew Klesmer, or knew of him; but they had only seen him on candle-light occasions when he appeared simply as a musician, and he had not yet that supreme, world-wide celebrity which makes an artist great to the most ordinary people by their knowledge of his great expensiveness. It was literally a new light for them to see him in—presented unexpectedly on this July afternoon in an exclusive society: some were inclined to laugh, others felt a little disgust at the want of judgment shown by the Arrowpoints in this use of the introductory card.

' "What extreme guys those artistic fellows usually are!" said young Clintock to Gwendolen.'

The foreigner at English social and sporting functions, intrinsically ludicrous because of his ignorance of what's done—or, rather, what isn't done, what isn't said, and what isn't worn—has always been a familiar figure in *Punch*. George Eliot doesn't miss the comic element in Klesmer's appearance, but she uses him to 'place' the Philistinism[22] of English society, and the complacent unintelligence of its devotion to Good Form. James, in *The Portrait of a Lady*, can exhibit no such freely critical attitude towards the country-house and its civilization.

George Eliot's use of Herr Klesmer is the more effective because her attitude is so complete and balanced: she sees what is genuinely laughable in the Teutonic Intellectual and licensed and conscious Artist:

---

[22] We can guess where, in relation to Philistinism on the one hand and the 'social' values on the other, she would have placed the complacent confidence and radical provinciality of this: 'Moreover, like all Victorian rationalists, she is a Philistine. She pays lip-service to art, but like Dorothea Brooke confronted with the Statues of the Vatican, she does not really see why people set such a value on it.' (Lord David Cecil, *Early Victorian Novelists*, p. 322.) We have to confess that she doesn't know the kind of thing the best people to-day say about 'art.' But on the other hand, reading what is written about her (and other novelists) by the critic for whom this makes her a Philistine, we can't help asking why he should suppose he puts a high value on literature.

'. . . Gwendolen had accepted Klesmer as a partner; and that wide-glancing personage, who saw everything and nothing by turns, said to her when they were walking, "Mr. Grandcourt is a man of taste. He likes to see you dancing."

' "Perhaps he likes to look at what is against his taste," said Gwendolen, with a light laugh: she was quite courageous with Klesmer now. "He may be so tired of admiring that he liked disgust for a variety."

' "Those words are not suitable to your lips," said Klesmer, quickly, with one of his grand frowns, while he shook his hand as if to banish the discordant sounds.

' "Are you as critical of words as of music?"

' "Certainly I am. I should require your words to be what your face and form are—always among the meanings of a noble music."

' "That is a compliment as well as a correction. I am obliged for both. But do you know I am bold enough to wish to correct *you*, and require you to understand a joke?"

' "One may understand jokes without liking them," said the terrible Klesmer. "I have had opera books sent me full of jokes; it was just because I understood them that I did not like them. The comic people are ready to challenge a man because he looks grave. 'You don't see the witticism, sir?' 'No, sir, but I see what you meant.' Then I am what we call ticketed as a fellow without *esprit*. But, in fact," said Klesmer, suddenly dropping from his quick narrative to a reflective tone, with an impressive frown, "I am very sensible to wit and humour."

' "I am glad you tell me that," said Gwendolen, not without some wickedness of intention. But Klesmer's thoughts had flown off on the wings of his own statement, as their habit was, and she had the wickedness all to herself. "Pray, who is that standing near the card-room door?" she went on, seeing there the same stranger with whom Klesmer had been in animated talk on the archery-ground. "He is a friend of yours, I think."

' "No, no; an amateur I have seen in town: Lush, a Mr. Lush—too fond of Meyerbeer and Scribe—too fond of the mechanical-dramatic."

' "Thanks. I wanted to know whether you thought his face and form required that his words should be among the meanings of a noble music?" Klesmer was conquered, and flashed at her a delightful smile which made them quite friendly until she begged to be deposited by the side of her mamma.'

—The Teutonic trait is beautifully got in that 'But, in fact, I am very sensible to wit and humour.' Yet the balance of this exchange, which is managed with so flexible a sureness, hardly lies against Klesmer.

But perhaps, in the light of our present interest, the richest episode in which he figures is that with Mr. Bult (perfect name—how good George Eliot's names are):

'Meanwhile enters the expectant peer, Mr. Bult, an esteemed party man who, rather neutral in private life, had strong opinions concerning the districts of the Niger, was much at home also in the Brazils, spoke with decision of affairs in the South Seas, was studious of his parliamentary and itinerant speeches, and had the general solidity and suffusive pinkness of a healthy Briton on the central table-land of life. Catherine, aware of a tacit understanding that he was an undeniable husband for an heiress, had nothing to say against him but that he was thoroughly tiresome to her. Mr. Bult was amiably confident, and had no idea that his insensibility to counterpoint could ever be reckoned against him. Klesmer he hardly regarded in the light of a serious human being who ought to have a vote; and he did not mind Miss Arrowpoint's addiction to music any more than her probable expenses in antique lace. He was consequently a little amazed at an after-dinner outburst of Klesmer's on the lack of idealism in English politics, which left all mutuality between distant races to be determined simply by the need of a market: the crusades, to his mind, had at least this excuse, that they had a banner of sentiment round which generous feelings could rally: of course, the scoundrels rallied too, but what then? they rally in equal force round your advertisement van of "Buy cheap, sell dear." On this theme Klesmer's eloquence, gesticulatory and other, went on for a little while like stray fireworks accidentally ignited, and then sank into immovable silence. Mr. Bult was not surprised that Klesmer's opinions should be flighty, but was astonished at his command of English idiom and his ability to put a point in a way that would have told at a constituents' dinner—to be accounted for probably by his being a Pole, or a Czech, or something of that fermenting sort, in a state of political refugeeism which had obliged him to make a profession of his music; and that evening in the drawing-room he for the first time went up to Klesmer at the piano, Miss Arrowpoint being near, and said—

'"I had no idea before that you were a political man."

'Klesmer's only answer was to fold his arms, put out his nether lip, and stare at Mr. Bult.

'"You must have been used to public speaking. You speak uncommonly well, though I don't agree with you. From what you said about sentiment, I fancy you are a Panslavist."

'"No; my name is Elijah. I am the Wandering Jew," said Klesmer, flashing a smile at Miss Arrowpoint, and suddenly making a mysterious wind-like rush backwards and forwards on the piano. Mr. Bult felt this buffoonery rather offensive and Polish, but—Miss Arrowpoint being there—did not like to move away.

'"Herr Klesmer has cosmopolitan ideas," said Miss Arrowpoint, trying to make the best of the situation. "He looks forward to a fusion of races."

'"With all my heart," said Mr. Bult, willing to be gracious. "I was sure he had too much talent to be a mere musician."

'"Ah, sir, you are under some mistake there," said Klesmer, firing up. "No man has too much talent to be a musician. Most men have too little. A creative artist is no more a mere musician than a great statesman is a mere politician. We are not ingenious puppets, sir, who live in a box and look out on the world only when it is gaping for amusement. We help to rule the nations and make the age as much as any other public men. We count ourselves on level benches with legislators. And a man who speaks effectively through music is compelled to something more difficult than parliamentary eloquence."

'With the last word Klesmer wheeled from the piano and walked away.

'Miss Arrowpoint coloured, and Mr. Bult observed with his usual phlegmatic solidity, "Your pianist does not think small beer of himself."

'"Herr Klesmer is something more than a pianist," said Miss Arrowpoint, apologetically. "He is a great musician, in the fullest sense of the word. He will rank with Schubert and Mendelssohn."

'"Ah, you ladies understand these things," said Mr. Bult, none the less convinced that these things were frivolous because Klesmer had shown himself a coxcomb.' (Chapter XXII.)

What we see here is not a novelist harmed, or disabled, by the intellectual of *The Westminster Review*. The knowledge and interest shown, the awareness of the political world, is that of the associate of Spencer and Mill. But the attitude is not theirs. Bult is a far more effective 'placing' of a prevailing Victorian ethos than Podsnap: George Eliot really understands what she is dealing with—understands as well as the professional student of politics and the man of the public world; and more, understands as these cannot. In short, it is her greatness that she retains all the provincial strength and virtue while escaping, as no other Victorian novelist does, the limitations of provinciality.

As for the bad part of *Daniel Deronda*, there *is* nothing to do but cut it away—in spite of what James, as Constantius, finds to say for it:

'The universe forcing itself with a slow, inexorable
pressure into a narrow, complacent, and yet after all
extremely sensitive mind—that is Gwendolen's story.
And it becomes completely characteristic in that her supreme perception of the fact that the world is whirling
past her is in the disappointment not of a base but of
an exalted passion. The very chance to embrace what
the author is so fond of calling a "larger life" seems refused to her. She is punished for being "narrow," and
she is not allowed a chance to expand. Her finding Deronda pre-engaged to go to the East and stir up the race-
feeling of the Jews strikes me as wonderfully happy
invention. The irony of the situation, for poor Gwendolen, is almost grotesque, and it makes one wonder
whether the whole heavy structure of the Jewish question in the story was not built up by the author for the
express purpose of giving its proper force to this particular stroke.'

If it was (which we certainly can't accept as a complete
account of it) built up by the author for this purpose, then
it is too disastrously null to have any of the intended force
to give. If, having entertained such a purpose, George Eliot had justified it, *Daniel Deronda* would have been a
very great novel indeed. As things are, there is, lost under
that damning title, an actual great novel to be extricated.
And to extricate it for separate publication as *Gwendolen
Harleth* seems to me the most likely way of getting recognition for it. *Gwendolen Harleth* would have some rough
edges, but it would be a self-sufficient and very substantial
whole (it would by modern standards be a decidedly
long novel). Deronda would be confined to what was necessary for his rôle of lay-confessor to Gwendolen, and the
final cut would come after the death by drowning, leaving
us with a vision of Gwendolen as she painfully emerges
from her hallucinated worst conviction of guilt and confronts the daylight fact about Deronda's intentions.

It has seemed necessary to carry this examination so
much into detail in order to give due force to the conten-

tion that George Eliot's greatness is of a different kind
from that she has been generally credited with. And by
way of concluding on this emphasis I will adduce once
again her most intelligently appreciative critic, Henry
James:

> 'She does not strike me as naturally a critic, less still
> as naturally a sceptic; her spontaneous part is to observe
> life and to feel it, to feel it with admirable depth. Con-
> templation, sympathy and faith—something like that, I
> should say, would have been her natural scale. If she
> had fallen upon an age of enthusiastic assent to old
> articles of faith, it seems to me possible that she would
> have had a more perfect, a more consistent and graceful
> development than she actually had.'

There is, I think, a complete misconception here. George
Eliot's development may not have been 'perfect' or 'graceful,' and 'consistent' is not precisely the adjective one
would choose for it; yet she went on developing to the end,
as few writers do, and achieved the most remarkable expression of her distinctive genius in her last work: her art
in *Gwendolen Harleth* is at its maturest. And her profound insight into the moral nature of man is essentially
that of one whose critical intelligence has been turned
intensively on her faiths. A sceptic by nature or culture—
indeed no; but that is not because her intelligence, a very
powerful one, doesn't freely illuminate all her interests
and convictions. That she should be thought depressing
(as, for instance, Leslie Stephen thinks her) always surprises me. She exhibits a traditional moral sensibility expressing itself, not within a frame of 'old articles of faith'
(as James obviously intends the phrase), but nevertheless
with perfect sureness, in judgments that involve confident
positive standards, and yet affect us as simply the report
of luminous intelligence. She deals in the weakness and
ordinariness of human nature, but doesn't find it contemptible, or show either animus or self-deceiving indulgence towards it; and, distinguished and noble as she is, we
have in reading her the feeling that she is in and of the

humanity she presents with so clear and disinterested a vision. For us in these days, it seems to me, she is a peculiarly fortifying and wholesome author, and a suggestive one: she might well be pondered by those who tend to prescribe simple recourses—to suppose, say, that what Charlotte Yonge has to offer may be helpfully relevant—in face of the demoralizations and discouragements of an age that isn't one of 'enthusiastic assent to old articles of faith.'

As for her rank among novelists, I take the challenge from a representative purveyor of currency, Oliver Elton: what he says we may confidently assume that thousands of the cultivated think it reasonable to say, and thousands of students in 'Arts' courses are learning to say, either in direct study of him, or in the lecture-room. He says,[23] then, in discussing the 'check to George Eliot's reputation' given by the coming 'into fuller view' of 'two other masters of fiction'—Meredith and Hardy: 'Each of these novelists saw the world of men and women more freely than George Eliot had done; and they brought into relief one of her greatest deficiencies, namely, that while exhaustively describing life, she is apt to miss the spirit of life itself.' I can only say that this, for anyone whose critical education has begun, should be breath-taking in its absurdity, and affirm my conviction that, by the side of George Eliot—and the comparison shouldn't be necessary —Meredith appears as a shallow exhibitionist (his famous 'intelligence' a laboured and vulgar brilliance) and Hardy,

---

[23] *A Survey of English Literature*, 1830-1880, Vol. II, Chapter XXIII. This chapter, 'George Eliot and Anthony Trollope,' is very representative of Elton—who is very representative of the academically esteemed 'authority.' It contains a convenient and unintentionally amusing conspectus of the ideas about George Eliot I have been combating. He exemplifies the gentleman's attitude towards Gwendolen: 'The authoress drops on her a load of brickbats, and seems to wish to leave the impression that Gwendolen deserved them. She is young, and rather too hard, sprightly and rather domineering.' (He says of *Middlemarch*: 'This is almost one of the great novels of the language.')

decent as he is, as a provincial manufacturer of gauche and heavy fictions that sometimes have corresponding virtues. For a positive indication of her place and quality I think of a Russian; not Turgenev, but a far greater, Tolstoy—who, we all know, is pre-eminent in getting 'the spirit of life itself.' George Eliot, of course, is not as transcendently great as Tolstoy, but she *is* great, and great in the same way. The extraordinary reality of *Anna Karenina* (his supreme masterpiece, I think) comes of an intense moral interest in human nature that provides the light and courage for a profound psychological analysis. This analysis is rendered in art (and *Anna Karenina, pace* Matthew Arnold, is wonderfully closely worked) by means that are like those used by George Eliot in *Gwendolen Harleth* —a proposition that will bear a great deal of considering in the presence of the text. Of George Eliot it can in turn be said that her best work has a Tolstoyan depth and reality.

III. HENRY JAMES

(i) To 'The Portrait of a Lady'

I HAVE said enough about the part played in James's development by George Eliot, and what I have said has not, I'm afraid, tended to convey that *The Portrait of a Lady* is an original masterpiece. That, however, is what I take it to be; it is one of the great novels in the language. And what I propose to do in the earlier part of the space I devote to James is, in effect, to discuss the conditions that enabled him to make of a variation on *Gwendolen Harleth* —a description I think I have justified—something so different, positively, from that work, and so different from anything George Eliot could have done. By conditions I mean the inner conditions—largely determined as they are by outer. I mean the essential interests and attitudes that characterize his outlook on the world and his response to life.

This seems to me a good course to set in embarking on a brief treatment of James. It ensures that a major stress shall be laid on achievement. I am very conscious of the danger that, for various reasons, the stress shouldn't be laid sufficiently there. James was so incredibly productive over so long a period, and offers so many aspects for study, that nothing short of a book on him, and a book of formidable length, could pretend to adequacy. I have also in mind the way in which the cult of James of the last quarter of a century (a cult that, to judge by what has been written on them, doesn't seem to have involved intensive cultivation of the works admired) makes him pre-eminently the author of the later works. We are asked to admire *The Ambassadors* (1903); and *The Ambassadors* seems to me to be not only *not* one of his great books, but to be a bad one. If, as I was on the point of saying, it exhibits senility, then senility was more than setting in at the turn of the century in *The Sacred Fount*. It is as a matter of fact a more interesting disease than senility.

This is not to deny that there are achieved works in distinctively 'late' styles. Critical admirers of *The Awkward Age* (1899), that astonishing work of genius (about which they will have reserves on some points), and of *What Maisie Knew* (which is perfect), will know of many fine short stories and *nouvelles*. But they will also be largely occupied, where this later work is concerned, with sifting, rejecting, qualifying and deploring: that is, they are faced inescapably with James's 'case'—with the question of what went wrong in his later development; for something certainly did go wrong. The phase when his genius functioned with freest and fullest vitality is represented by *The Portrait of a Lady* (1881), together with *The Bostonians* (1885). That is my position, and that seems to me the right emphasis for a brief appreciation. And in discussing the interests that meet to condition supreme achievement in *The Portrait of a Lady*, I aim at finding my illustrations in other works that, for all the lack of recognition, are classical in quality. One can in this way hope to suggest the nature of James's achievement in general, while frankly avowing inadequacy of treatment and a drastic selectiveness of attention.

By 'interests' I mean the kinds of profound concern—having the urgency of personal problems, and felt as moral problems, more than personal in significance—that lie beneath Jane Austen's art, and enable her to assimilate varied influences and heterogeneous material and make great novels out of them. It is not for nothing that, like George Eliot, he admired her immensely, and that from him too passages can be found that show her clear influence. For he goes back to her, not only through George Eliot, but directly. Having two novelists of that kind of moral preoccupation in his own language to study, he quickly discovered how much, and how little, the French masters had to teach him, and to what tradition he belonged. Hence the early and decisive determination—a surprising one (if they knew of it) for the modish Gallophils of our time—against Paris.

His interests, of course, are very different from Jane Austen's, being determined by a contrasting situation. His problem was not to balance the claims of an exceptional and very sensitive individual against the claims of a mature and stable society, strong in its unquestioned standards, sanctions and forms. The elements of his situation are well known. He was born a New Yorker at a time when New York society preserved a mature and refined European tradition, and when at the same time any New Yorker of literary and intellectual bent must, in the formative years, have been very much aware of the distinctive and very different culture of New England. Here already we have an interplay likely to promote a critical attitude, and an emancipation from any complete adherence to one code or ethos. Then there was the early experience of Europe and the final settling in England. It is not surprising that, in the mind of a genius, the outcome should be a bent for comparison, and a constant profound pondering of the nature of civilized society and of the possibility of imagining a finer civilization than any he knew.

It was the profundity of the pondering that I had in mind when I referred to him as a 'poet-novelist': his 'interests' were not of the kind that are merely written *about*. Here is an apt passage from the Preface to *The Golden Bowl*:

'. . . the whole growth of one's "taste": a blessed comprehensive name for many of the things deepest in us. The "taste" of the poet is, at bottom and so far as the poet in him prevails over everything else, his active sense of life: in accordance with which truth to keep one's hand on it is to hold the silver clue to the whole labyrinth of his consciousness.' [1]

---

[1] The passage (which I had marked years before) is quoted by Mr. Quentin Anderson in an essay in *The Kenyon Review* for Autumn, 1946, which arrived as I was correcting

James's use of the word 'poet' to cover the novelist, and his associating it in this explanatory way with the term 'taste,' indicates the answer to the not uncommon suggestion that his work exhibits taste trying to usurp the function of a moral sense. In calling him 'poet-novelist' I myself was intending to convey that the determining and controlling interests in his art engage what is 'deepest in him' (he being a man of exceptional capacity for experience), and appeal to what is deepest in us.

This characteristic of his art manifests itself in his remarkable use of symbolism—see, for instance, *The Jolly Corner, The Figure in the Carpet* and *The Great Good Place* (I specify these as obvious instances and obviously successful). But to stress the symbolism too much would tend to misunderstanding: the qualities of his art that derive from the profound seriousness of his interest in life—it is these in general that one stresses in calling him a poet, and they are to be found widely in forms and places that the reference to his use of symbolism doesn't immediately bring up for attention. When these qualities are duly recognized it becomes ridiculous to save the word 'poet' for the author of *The Waves* and *The Years*—works that offer something like the equivalent of Georgian poetizing. (Even *To the Lighthouse,* which may be distinguished among her books as substantially justifying her so obviously 'poetical' method, is a decidedly minor affair—it is *minor* art.) 'Hawthorne,' says James in the early study he wrote for the *English Men of Letters* series, 'is perpetually looking for images which shall place themselves in pictur-

---

my typescript. In this essay, 'Henry James and the New Jerusalem,' Mr. Anderson argues, very persuasively, that James was deeply influenced by his father's system and symbolism (the nature of which may be indicated by saying that Swedenborg counts for something in it). What Mr. Anderson doesn't appear to recognize sufficiently is that a preoccupation with such interests wouldn't necessarily be identifiable with the novelist's true creative preoccupation. But I look forward to Mr. Anderson's promised book. (Essays also in *Scrutiny,* XIV, 4, and XV, 1.)

esque correspondence with the spiritual facts with which he is concerned, and of course the search is of the very essence of poetry.' James's own constant and profound concern with spiritual facts expresses itself not only in what obviously demands to be called symbolism, but in the handling of character, episode and dialogue, and in the totality of the plot, so that when he seems to offer a novel of manners he gives us more than that, and the 'poetry' is major.

And here, prompted by James, we have to recognize a great debt to Hawthorne, that original genius (for, whatever the limitations of his achievement, he is that) whom it is difficult to relate to any earlier novelist—unless we are to count Bunyan one. With James and Melville he constitutes a distinctively American tradition. The more we consider James's early work (and his early work in relation to the later), the more important does Hawthorne's influence appear. With none of James's sophistication or social experience, and no interest in manners, Hawthorne devotes himself to exploring profoundly moral and psychological interests in a poetic art of fiction. It is an art at the other extreme from Jane Austen's, for whom moral interests are intimately bound up with manners. Hawthorne's approach to morals is psychological, and his psychology, a striking achievement of intuition, anticipates (compare Tolstoy and Lawrence) what are supposed to be modern findings. His influence on James can be seen to have countered hers, and must have had much to do with James's emancipation from the English tradition we may represent by Thackeray. It clearly counts with George Eliot's in his renunciation of France (see pp. 23 and 25 above).

I think it well to start with this emphasis on James's greatness because of the almost inevitable way in which any brief survey of his work that is focussed on what is most significant in it tends to be, in effect, unjust. As I have said, the very bulk of the *œuvre* (he had in a very remarkable degree the productivity of genius) leads to a centring of attention upon development, rather than upon the achieved thing as such. Let me insist, then, at once, on the striking measure of achievement that marks even the opening phase of his career as a novelist.

In fact, his 'first attempt at a novel,' *Roderick Hudson* (1874), in spite of its reputation, is a very distinguished book that deserves permanent currency—much more so than many novels passing as classics. It is the work of a writer with mature interests, who shows himself capable of handling them in fiction. The interests are those of a very intelligent and serious student of contemporary civilization. Suppose, James asks himself, there were an American genius born in a small town of pristine New England: what would be the effect of Europe on him—Europe, the culture of the ages, tradition, Rome? There is a weakness in the book that James, retrospectively, puts a finger on: the artist's decay—the break-up in dissipation at Baden-Baden and the end in suicide—is accomplished too rapidly. But *Roderick Hudson* is essentially a dramatic study, evaluative and exploratory, in the interplay of contrasted cultural traditions (a glimpsed ideal being at the centre of James's preoccupation), and the sustained maturity of theme and treatment qualifies the book as a whole to be read at the adult level of demand in a way that no novel of Thackeray's will bear.

As might have been guessed from what I said above about the use of symbolism and from James's relevant remark about Hawthorne—though the instances I gave were from a much later period—the influence of Hawthorne is very apparent in some of James's earliest stories. But the influence we note in *Roderick Hudson* is not that of Hawthorne. Here is a passage from Chapter X:

'Mr. Leavenworth was a tall, expansive, bland gentleman, with a carefully-brushed whisker and a spacious, fair, well-favoured face, which seemed somehow to have more room in it than was occupied by a smile of superior benevolence, so that (with his smooth white forehead) it bore a certain resemblance to a large parlour with a very florid carpet, but without mural decoration. He held his head high, talked impressively, and told Roderick within five minutes that he was a widower travelling to distract his mind, and that he had lately retired from the proprietorship of large mines of borax in the Middle West. Roderick supposed at first that under the influence of his bereavement he had come to order a tombstone; but observing the extreme benevolence of his address to Miss Blanchard he credited him with a judicious prevision that on the day the tombstone should be completed a monument of his inconsolability might appear mistimed. Mr. Leavenworth, however, was disposed to give an Order—to give it with a capital letter.

'"You'll find me eager to patronize our indigenous talent," he said. "You may be sure that I've employed a native architect for the large residential structure that I'm erecting on the banks of the Ohio. I've sustained a considerable loss; but are we not told that the office of art is second only to that of religion? That's why I have come to you, sir. In the retreat that I'm preparing, surrounded by the memorials of my wanderings, I hope to recover a certain degree of tone. They're doing what they can in Paris for the fine effect of some of its features; but the effect I have myself most at heart will be that of my library, filled with well-selected and beautifully-bound authors in groups, relieved from point to point by high-class statuary. I should like to entrust you, can we arrange it, with the execution of one of these appropriate subjects. What do you say to a representation, in pure white marble, of the idea of Intellectual Refinement?"

'. . . the young master good-naturedly promised to do his best to rise to his client's conception. "His conception be hanged!" Roderick exclaimed none the less after Mr. Leavenworth had departed. "His conception is sitting on an india-rubber cushion with a pen in her ear and the lists of the stock exchange in her hand. It's a case for doing, of course, exactly as one likes—yet how *can* one like, by any possibility, anything that such a blatant humbug as that possibly can? It's as much as one can do to like his awful money. I don't think," our young man added, "that I ever swallowed anything that wanted so little to go down, and I'm doubtless on my way now to any grovelling you please." '

The influence of Dickens is plain here. It is the Dickens, not, as in *The Princess Casamassima*, of *Little Dorrit*, but of *Martin Chuzzlewit*. This passage of *Roderick Hudson*, of course, couldn't possibly have been written by Dickens: something has been done to give the Dickensian manner a much more formidable intellectual edge. We feel a finer and fuller consciousness behind the ironic humour, which engages mature standards and interest such as Dickens was innocent of. It is quite personal, a remarkably achieved manner for a first novel. *Roderick Hudson*, in fact, is a much more distinguished, lively and interesting work than, at the prompting of the retrospective James, is generally supposed.

What I offer this passage as illustrating is not merely James, in the way I have suggested earlier in this book, seeing life through literature—and English literature. More importantly, what we have here is a good instance of the way in which a great original artist learns from another. Incomparably more mature in respect of standards as James was than Dickens, his debt to Dickens involves more than a mere manner; he was helped by him to see from the outside, and critically place, the life around him.

To bring out the full force of this point I will jump forward a dozen years and quote, for comparison, a passage from one of James's acknowledged masterpieces, *The Bostonians*:

'Towards nine o'clock the light of her hissing burners smote the majestic person of Mrs. Farrinder, who might have contributed to answer that question[2] of Miss

---

[2] '. . . in a career in which she was constantly exposing herself to laceration her most poignant suffering came from the injury of her taste. She had tried to kill that nerve, to persuade herself that taste was only frivolity in the guise of knowledge;

Chancellor's in the negative. She was a copious, handsome woman, in whom angularity had been corrected by the air of success; she had a rustling dress (it was evident what *she* thought about taste), abundant hair of a glossy blackness, a pair of folded arms, the expression of which seemed to say that rest, in such a career as hers, was as sweet as it was brief, and a terrible regularity of feature. I apply that adjective to her fine placid mask because she seemed to face you with a question of which the answer was preordained, to ask you how a countenance could fail to be noble of which the measurements were so correct. You could contest neither the measurements nor the nobleness, and had to feel that Mrs. Farrinder imposed herself. There was a lithographic smoothness about her, and a mixture of the American matron and the public character. There was something public in her eye, which was large, cold, and quiet; it had acquired a sort of exposed reticence from the habit of looking down from a lecture-desk, over a sea of heads, while its distinguished owner was eulogized by a leading citizen. Mrs. Farrinder, at almost any time, had the air of being introduced by a few remarks. She talked with great slowness and distinctness, and evidently a high sense of responsibility; she pronounced every syllable of every word and insisted on being explicit. If, in conversation with her, you attempted to take anything for granted, or to jump two or three steps at a time, she paused, looking at you with a cold patience as if she knew that trick, and then went on at her own measured pace. She lectured on temperance and the rights of women; the ends she laboured for were to give the ballot to every woman in the country and to take the flowing bowl from every man. She was held to have a very fine manner, and to embody the domestic virtues and the graces of the drawing-

---

but her susceptibility was constantly blooming afresh and making her wonder whether an absence of nice arrangements were a necessary part of the enthusiasm of humanity.'

room; to be a shining proof, in short, that the forum, for ladies, is not necessarily hostile to the fireside. She had a husband, and his name was Amariah.'

This, in itself, would perhaps not have suggested a relation to Dickens, but when it is approached by way of the passage from *Roderick Hudson* the relation is plain. What we have now, though, is pure James. And, as we find it in the description of Miss Birdseye, the un-Dickensian subtlety—the penetrating analysis and the implicit reference to mature standards and interests—is pretty effectually disassociating:

'She was a little old lady, with an enormous head; that was the first thing Ransom noticed—the vast, fair, protuberant, candid, ungarnished brow, surmounting a pair of weak, kind, tired-looking eyes, and ineffectually balanced in the rear by a cap which had the air of falling backward, and which Miss Birdseye suddenly felt for while she talked, with unsuccessful irrelevant movements. She had a sad, soft, pale face, which (and it was the effect of her whole head) looked as if it had been soaked, blurred, and made vague by exposure to some slow dissolvent. The long practice of philanthropy had not given accent to her features; it had rubbed out their transitions, their meanings. The waves of sympathy, of enthusiasm, had wrought upon them in the same way in which the waves of time finally modify the surface of old marble busts, gradually washing away their sharpness, their details. In her large countenance her dim little smile scarcely showed. It was a mere sketch of a smile, a kind of instalment, of payment on account; it seemed to say that she would smile more if she had time, but that you could see, without this, that she was gentle and easy to beguile.'

We are a long way from Dickens here. And the subtlety is never absent. Nevertheless, it remains obviously right in suggestion to say that, in his rendering of the portentous efflorescences of American civilization, as represented by the publicists, the charlatans, the cranks, the new-religionists, the femininists, and the newspapermen, he gives us *Martin Chuzzlewit* redone by an enormously more intelligent and better educated mind. The comedy is rich and robust as well as subtle.

But when we come to Olive Chancellor, New England spinster and representative of the earnest refinement of Boston culture, we have something that bears no relation to anything Dickens could have done, though it bears an essential relation to this comedy. James understands the finer civilization of New England, and is the more effective as an ironic critic of it because he is not merely an ironic critic. He understands it because he both knows it from inside and sees it from outside with the eye of a professional student of civilization who has had much experience of non-Puritan cultures. Here, in the opening of the book, are the reflections of Basil Ransom:

> 'What her sister had imparted to him about her mania for "reform" had left in his mouth a kind of unpleasant after-taste; he felt, at any rate, that if she had the religion of humanity—Basil Ransom had read Comte, he had read everything—she would never understand him. He, too, had a private vision of reform, but the first principle of it was to reform the reformers.'

The easy reference to Comte is significant; James, we are sure, has a right to the ease. Not that we suppose him to have made a close study of Comte—or to have needed to. But he brings to the business of the novelist a wide intellectual culture, as well as, in an exceptionally high degree, the kind of knowledge of individual humans and concrete societies that we expect of a great novelist— knowledge that doesn't favour enthusiasm for such constructions as the religion of humanity. We are not to identify him with Ransom, but we don't suspect him of enthusiasm for that religion, and it is made very plain that he shares Ransom's ironical vision of the 'reformers.'

In fact, *The Bostonians* has a distinct political interest. James deals with the feminist movement with such dispas-

sionate lightness and sureness, with an insight so utterly
unaccompanied by animus, if not by irony, that Miss
Rebecca West couldn't forgive him (in her book on James
she can find nothing to say in favour of *The Bostonians*).
The political interest, it is true, is incidental; but to that
it owes its provocative strength: James's preoccupation is
centred in the presentment of Miss Chancellor and of
her relations with the red-haired and very Americanly vital
and charming girl, Verena Tarrant, whom she is intent
on saving from the common fate of woman—love and marriage—and dedicating to the Cause. And James's genius
comes out in a very remarkable piece of psychological
analysis, done in the concrete (and done, it is worth noting, decades before the impact of Freud had initiated a
general knowingness about the unconscious and the sub-
conscious).

The relation of Miss Chancellor to Verena is at bottom,
and essentially, a very painful matter, but it provides
some very fine psychological comedy. Here, for instance, is
Miss Chancellor dealing with one of her most difficult
problems:

'A day or two after this, Mr. Henry Burrage left a card
at Miss Chancellor's door, with a note in which he expressed the hope that she would take tea with him on
a certain day on which he expected the company of his
mother. Olive responded to this invitation, in conjunction with Verena; but in doing so she was in the position, singular for her, of not quite understanding what
she was about. It seemed to her strange that Verena
should urge her to take such a step when she was free
to go without her, and it proved two things: first, that
she was much interested in Mr. Henry Burrage, and
second, that her nature was extraordinarily beautiful.
Could anything, in effect, be less underhand than such
an indifference to what she supposed to be the best opportunities for carrying on a flirtation? Verena wanted
to know the truth, and it was clear that by this time
she believed Olive Chancellor to have it, for the most

part, in her keeping. Her insistence, therefore, proved, above all, that she cared more for her friend's opinion of Henry Burrage than for her own—a reminder, certainly, of the responsibility that Olive had incurred in undertaking to form this generous young mind, and of the exalted place that she now occupied in it. Such revelations ought to have been satisfactory; if they failed to be completely so, it was only on account of the elder girl's regret that the subject as to which her judgment was wanted should be a young man destitute of the worst vices. Henry Burrage had contributed to throw Miss Chancellor into a "state," as these young ladies called it, the night she met him at Mrs. Tarrant's; but it had none the less been conveyed to Olive by the voices of the air that he was a gentleman and a good fellow.

'This was painfully obvious when the visit to his rooms took place; he was so good-humoured, so amusing, so friendly and considerate, so attentive to Miss Chancellor, he did the honours of his bachelor-nest with so easy a grace, that Olive, part of the time, sat dumbly shaking her conscience, like a watch that wouldn't go, to make it tell her some better reason why she shouldn't like him. She saw that there would be no difficulty in disliking his mother; but that, unfortunately, would not serve her purpose nearly so well.'

And after the charming tea-party:

' "It would be very nice to do that always—just to take men as they are, and not to have to think about their badness . . . so that one could sit there . . . and listen to Schubert and Mendelssohn. *They* didn't care anything about female suffrage! And I didn't feel the want of a vote to-day at all, did you?" Verena inquired, ending, as she always ended in these speculations, with an appeal to Olive.

'This young lady thought it necessary to give her a very firm answer. "I always feel it—everywhere—night and day. I feel it *here*"; and Olive laid her hand solemnly on her heart. "I feel it as a deep, unforgettable wrong; I feel it as one feels a stain that is on one's honour."

'Verena gave a clear laugh, and after that a soft sigh, and then said, "Do you know, Olive, I sometimes wonder whether, if it wasn't for you, I should feel it so very much!"

'"My own friend," Olive replied, "you have never yet said anything to me which expressed so clearly the closeness and sanctity of our union."

'"You do keep me up," Verena went on. "You are my conscience."'

On the relation of the feminism to the conscience James is very good—the New England conscience, of course, is for him a central theme. In Olive Chancellor he relates the conscience, the feminism, the culture and the refinement. 'Olive almost panted' when she proposed to herself as the ideal happiness 'winter evenings under the lamp with falling snow outside, and tea on a little table, and successful renderings, with a chosen companion, of Goethe' (*Entsagen sollst du, sollst entsagen!* being the text immediately in question), 'almost the only foreign author she cared about; for she hated the writings of the French in spite of the importance they have given to women.' As for vulgarity: 'Olive Chancellor despised vulgarity and had a scent for it which she followed up in her own family. . . . There were times, indeed, when every one seemed to have it; every one but Miss Birdseye (who had nothing to do with it—she was an antique) and the poorest, humblest people' . . . 'Miss Chancellor would have been much happier if the movements she was interested in could have been carried on only by the people she liked, and if revolutions, somehow, didn't always have to begin with one's self—with internal convulsions, sacrifices, executions.'

It is her representative plight, of course, that she has to take the impact of vulgarity in its most fantastically gross forms. She has, for instance, to receive a visit, being unable to keep him out, from Mr. Matthias Pardon (Chapter XVII), whom Verena's parents favour as a *parti*. 'For this ingenuous son of his age all distinction between the person and the artist had ceased to exist; the writer was personal, the person food for newsboys, and everything and every one were every one's business.' The unsnubbable, invulnerable, and hardly conscious impudence of the American newspaperman, servant of a 'vigilant public opinion,' is rendered with a force so much surpassing Dickens's (we remember the theme in *Martin Chuzzlewit*) because of the so much greater subtlety of James's art and the significance drawn from the whole context. The cold, forbidding distinction of the well-born Boston spinster goes for nothing here. 'She thought Mr. Pardon's visit a liberty; but if she expected to convey this idea to him by withholding any suggestion that he should sit down, she was greatly mistaken, inasmuch as he cut the ground from under her feet by himself offering her a chair. His manner represented hospitality enough for both of them. . . .'

I specify this scene (as I might equally well have specified a number of others) for its typical value. This play of contrasts—thin refinement against confident vulgarity, fastidiousness against expansive publicity, restrictive scruple against charlatanism in tropical luxuriance—runs all through James's rendering of the New England aspect of American civilization.[3] *The Bostonians* is a wonderfully rich, intelligent and brilliant book. I said that it is an acknowledged masterpiece, but I don't in fact think that it has anything like the reputation it deserves. It could have been written only by James, and it has an overt richness of life such as is not commonly associated with him. It is incomparably witty and completely serious, and it makes

---

[3] The clash represented by the impact of the American newspaperman, invulnerable in his nationally sanctioned office of unrestricted and unscrupulous publicity, is a recurrent theme in James. We find it notably in *The Reverberator*, a *nouvelle* of 1888.

the imputed classical status of all but a few of the admired
works of Victorian fiction look silly. It is one of James's
achieved major classics, and among the works that he devoted to American life it is supreme.

He wrote, of course, other 'American' classics. Not to
speak of short-stories and things of less than novel-length,
there is *Washington Square* (1880). It is on a smaller
scale than *The Bostonians,* and very different in kind. It
is not in the same sense a 'study' of American civilization,
but the New York setting gives James an opportunity for
such a record of the *mœurs* of a past age as he alone could
have done. *Washington Square* is a 'tale of silent suffering'
that very obviously recalls *Eugénie Grandet*—to say which
doesn't mean that it isn't a very original and very characteristic creation, fine in a way that is beyond Balzac. Its
unlikeness in excellence to *The Bostonians* evinces strikingly the flexibility and range as well as the maturity that
James commanded in the early eighteen-eighties.

This summary dismissal of so fine a work as *Washington Square* illustrates the impossibility of being fair to
James in any directed and limited survey. I have, as anyone must have in dealing with an author so voluminous,
so complex and of so interesting a development, a given
exploratory line in view. I must accordingly hark back at
once from *The Bostonians* to an earlier book that comes
between it and *Roderick Hudson: The Europeans* (1878).
In this book, as the title suggests, the 'international situation' appears. But the Europeans, the visiting cousins, are
there mainly to provide a foil for the American family, a
study of the New England ethos being James's essential
purpose.

"The sudden irruption into the well-ordered consciousness of the Wentworths of an element not allowed
for in its scheme of usual obligations, required a re-
adjustment of that sense of responsibility which constituted its principal furniture. To consider an event,
crudely and baldly, in the light of the pleasure it might
bring them, was an intellectual exercise with which

Felix Young's American cousins were almost wholly unacquainted, and which they scarcely supposed to be largely pursued in any section of human society. The arrival of Felix and his sister was a satisfaction, but it was an extension of duty, of the exercise of the more recondite virtues. . . .'

Of Felix we are told:

'It is beside the matter to say he had a good conscience; for the best conscience is a sort of self-reproach, and this young man's brilliantly healthy nature spent itself in objective good intentions which were ignorant of any test save exactness in hitting their mark.'

The 'irruption' is beneficent. Felix confirms Gertrude, the younger daugher, in her dawning realization that she is no Puritan, and doesn't belong *here* (he carries her off), and helps in various ways, by his warm and electric presence, to vindicate the claims of life against the constrictions of the braced conscience. Nevertheless James's irony is far from being unkind; he sees too much he admires in the ethos he criticizes to condemn it. The reaction he attributes here (not, of course, as a permanent one) to the worldly Baroness is made more than plausible:

'There were tears in her eyes. The luminous interior, the gentle, tranquil people, the simple, serious life— the sense of these things pressed upon her with an overmastering force, and she felt herself yielding to one of the most genuine emotions she had ever known. "I should like to stay here," she said. "Pray take me in."'

And the advantage isn't wholly on the side of the Europeans here:

'Mr. Wentworth also observed his young daughter.
'"I don't know what her manner of life may have been," he said; "but she certainly never can have enjoyed a more refined and salubrious home."
'Gertrude stood there looking at them all. "She is the wife of a Prince," she said.

' "We are all princes here," said Mr. Wentworth; "and
I don't know of any palace in this neighbourhood that
is to let." '

This compares interestingly with the passages quoted
above—from *Roderick Hudson* and from *The Bostonians*
—as illustrating the relation to Dickens. We remark the
distinctively American note both of Mr. Wentworth's observation and of his retort; but we notice also that the
attitude *towards* him, which might appear to be simply
Dickensian, shifts as we pass from the one to the other,
and in shifting makes one of James's essential discriminations. When a wooden house, 'eighty years old,' is thus
exalted we can't doubt the intention; we know that we are
to feel an ironical amusement at a characteristic American complacency characteristically expressed, and that
the nicely chosen adjectives, 'refined' and 'salubrious,'
register, on James's part, a critical irony induced by certain
elements of the New England ethos. But if we have been
giving the attention demanded (and deserved), we perceive, when we come to the retort, that Mr. Wentworth
at this point has his creator's backing, and, opposed as he
is here to the Baroness, stands for an American democracy
that James offers, with conviction, as an American superiority.

The Baroness and her brother, we shall have noted, are
themselves opposed in value to one another; as representative Europeans, they are complementary, and establish,
in their difference, another essential discrimination for
James. In fact, all the figures in the book play their parts
in this business of discriminating attitudes and values,
which is performed with remarkable precision and economy; the total effect being an affirmation, made with the
force of inspired art. James is not condemning or endors-
ing either New England or Europe; separating in both
what he prizes from what he dislikes, he is defining an
imagined satisfying positive. *The Europeans* (as the very
names of the characters suggest) is a moral fable. It has
suffered the same fate as *Hard Times*—for, we have to

conclude, the same reasons; the critical tradition regarding 'the English novel'—if 'critical' is the word—deals in the 'creation of real characters,' measures vitality by external abundance, and expects a loosely generous provision of incident and scene, but is innocent of any adult criterion of point and relevance in art. (It can give us Thackeray as a major novelist.) So when it is offered concentrated significance—close and insistent relevance to a serious and truly rich theme, it sees merely insignificance: *Hard Times* passes unnoticed, and *The Europeans* is dismissed as 'slight.' Yet this small book, written so early in James's career, is a masterpiece of major quality.[4]

He had already, in respect of the 'international situation' (for it is to this that we must now turn), taken a positively American line. *The American* (1875) is the novel that follows on *Roderick Hudson*, and it inaugurates the long series of works in which James may be said to offer his native country its revenge for *Martin Chuzzlewit*. Unfortunately he chooses, in this book, as the representative of American decency and genuineness, a type of which he knows virtually nothing—the business-man—and offers us a quite incredible idealization. Christopher Newman, having started from nothing, emerges from making his pile in the post-Civil-War decade crude (in the sense of being socially innocent) but unworldly, and finely sensitive to moral values; and because of this is at a disadvantage in dealing with the corrupt and subtle French aristocrats who victimize him. It is romantic, unreal and ridiculous.

To say, however, that Newman is a romantic concep-

---

[4] It may be suggested that a comparison with *The Europeans* helps us to define the unsatisfactoriness of *The Spoils of Poynton* (1896), a novel that contains so much that is strikingly good. In this later book James has not been closely enough controlled by his scheme of essential significance, but has allowed himself to over-develop partial interests, and to go in for some free—that is, loose—'representation.' (*Hard Times* is analysed, pp. 273 ff. below).

tion is not enough. As his name suggests, he represents a
very positive and significant intention on James's part.
His christian name recalls Christopher Columbus, and
'Newman' explains itself: James, that is, intends him to
have a peculiar symbolic value. He is the answer to the
question: What, separating off and putting aside that
which comes from Europe—the heritage brought across—
can we offer as the distinctively American contribution?
That James should so transfigure the type he first presented, in *Roderick Hudson,* as Mr. Leavenworth shows
both the urgency with which he felt the question, and
the difficulty of finding a satisfactory answer. The 'new
man,' being without the refinements of European culture,
is to be also without its corruptions; he is to represent
energy, uncompromising moral vitality and straightfor-
ward will. We meet him again as Caspar Goodwood in
The Portrait of a Lady; we find him in the extremely sophisticated later art, and he culminates in Adam Verver
of *The Golden Bowl.* In *The Ivory Tower* we have him
in the significantly named Frank Betterman.

   The American is in many ways an interesting book, but
it is not one of James's successes. He deals more impressively with the international theme in a story—a *nouvelle,*
not a novel—dated a year earlier, *Madame de Mauves*
(1874). The heroine, an American heiress, having idealized into real human distinction the 'high' descent of a
fortune-hunting French aristocrat, and married him,
shows in the resulting disillusionment her own invincible
superiority of spirit. Madame de Mauves' situation clearly
foreshadows Isabel Archer's, and there is a further likeness
represented by the young American whom, worthily devoted as he is, her own self-idealization forbids her to accept as a lover. The story deserves to be read for its fine
qualities, though it has obvious weaknesses and the reader
may feel in the close a possible ambiguity in James's total
attitude; for Madame de Mauves remains unyielding, not
only towards the young American, but, when her husband repents and is 'converted' (incredibly—this, we feel,

is romantic), towards him too, the consequence being
that he blows his brains out.

There is no ambiguity about *Daisy Miller* (1878). It
offers a variant of a favourite theme of James's: the superiority of the American girl to all the world. The story is a
master's work, and we can see why it enjoyed an immediate
success. But it has to be classed with *The American* as
giving us a James who takes an American stand on insufficient ground. Daisy Miller's freedom in the face of
European social conventions is of a kind that would make
her insufferable in any civilized society. She belongs with
the characteristics of the American scene that are ironically presented by James in *The Bostonians*. She is utterly uneducated, and no intelligent man could stand her
for long since there could be no possible exchange of
speech with her: she has nothing to recommend her but
looks, money, confidence and clothes (James must have
been told that only the American girl knows how to dress).
And, whatever there may be in my suggestion about Isabel
Archer (a very different case), it is plain that the sympathetic vision of Daisy Miller presented by James depends
on her being seen through the eyes of an American gentleman—at not so close a range that he is committed to
personal or social relations with her.

Daisy Miller, in significance, is closely related to Christopher Newman. Her incomparably greater reality only
serves to emphasize the poverty of the answer she represents—answer to the same question that produced
Newman. James offers us something more interesting in
the Pandora Day of *Pandora* (1884), which, though not
among the best known, is one of his finer *nouvelles*. Pandora, from the Middle-Western Utica, hasn't even beauty;
she has nothing but her American vitality, initiative, 'freedom' and confidence, and in her person American democracy is very effectively vindicated (for she preserves
an unashamed loyalty to her early connexions) as against
what is represented by the German diplomatist Count Vo-
gelstein. But the attempt to isolate and exalt the distinctively and uniquely American is—on the showing of the

consequences in James's art—misconceived. He had, for creative impulse driving at something over and above mere representation, a more valid ideal positive before him. The 'Americanism' results ultimately (to consider now James's women) in a feebleness and in a perversity of valuation we may figure by Milly Theale of *The Wings of the Dove*. An American heiress, merely because she is an American heiress, is a Princess, and such a Princess as, just for being one, is to be conceived as a supreme moral value: that is what it amounts to. And, in bearing this significance, Milly Theale has, in the Jamesian *œuvre*, a sufficient company of other examples.

Madame de Mauves has a real moral superiority, combined with a distinction of manners. And what, with an eye on James's development, we find interesting is his evident glimpse of a possible 'civilization' in which the manners belonging to a ripe art of social intercourse shall be the index of a moral refinement of the best American kind and a seriousness that shall entail a maturity of humane culture. The preoccupation defines itself further in an admirable story that is to be found in the *Daisy Miller* volume—*An International Episode*. This story shows us Bessy Alden, the 'Boston sister' of a New York 'society hostess,' finding herself attracted by the visiting Lord Lambeth. She is intelligent, sophisticated socially, and serious as well ('at concerts Bessy always listened'):

'She was perfectly conscious, moreover, that she liked to think of his more adventitious merits—that her imagination was excited and gratified by the sight of a handsome young man endowed with such large opportunities—opportunities she hardly knew for what, but, as she supposed, for doing great things—for setting an example, for exerting an influence, for conferring happiness, for encouraging the arts. She had a kind of ideal of conduct for a young man who should find himself in this magnificent position, and she tried to adapt it to Lord Lambeth's deportment, as you might attempt to fit a silhouette in cut paper upon a shadow projected upon a wall. But Bessy Alden's silhouette refused to coincide with his Lordship's image; and this want of harmony sometimes vexed her more than she thought reasonable.'

This is when, with her sister, she had come to England and met him again. Lord Lambeth is nice, and not stupid, but he is utterly without intellectual interests:

'If Lord Lambeth should appear anywhere, it was a symbol that there would be no poets and philosophers; and in consequence—for it was almost a strict consequence—she used to enumerate to the young man these objects of her admiration.

'"You seem to be awfully fond of that sort of people," said Lord Lambeth one day, as if the idea had just occurred to him.

'"They are the people in England I am most curious to see," Bessy Alden replied.

'"I suppose that's because you have read so much," said Lord Lambeth, gallantly.

'"I have not read so much. It is because we think so much of them at home."

'"Oh, I see!" observed the young nobleman. "In Boston."

'"Not only in Boston; everywhere," said Bessy. "We hold them in great honour; they go to the best dinner-parties."

'"I daresay you are right. I can't say I know many of them."'

As Bessy Alden takes in the fact, settling down to it as undeniably a fact, that the curious and offensive preoccupation with precedence distinguishing Lord Lambeth's world goes with a complete and complacent Philistinism, we have James's criticism of English society—a criticism that he was to go on making throughout his life, often with a bitterly contemptuous accent. When Lord Lambeth's mother and sister call to exhibit their patrician insolence and warn her off, she has already decided against him. She rejects him and leaves England at once, without regret.[5]

We observe, then, a marked complexity in James's attitude towards the international theme—not to speak of inconstancy and inconsistency. He exhibits a variety of tendencies. In *Roderick Hudson*, aided by Dickens, he has already achieved a maturely poised 'placing' irony in the treatment of certain characteristics of American life. He can, all the same, offer us in the immediately following novel, *The American*, his Christopher Newman, a masterful, self-made business-man, as the representative of American superiority over a corrupt, materialistic, and therefore victoriously self-seeking Europe. He is capable, too, of exalting the American girl in the guise of Daisy Miller. Yet he can criticize the moral and intellectual culture of New England by bringing to bear his knowledge of a maturer civilization, and further, in *The Bostonians*, do again—more devastatingly—the work of *Martin Chuzzle-*

---

[5] In *Lady Barbarina* (1888), which is in many ways the most interesting of the anti-English stories of cultural comparison (as they may be called), we have a kind of inversion of the theme of *An International Episode*. Jackson Lemon, an American doctor of keen scientific interests, whose father's suddenly acquired wealth makes the young man a desirable *parti*, marries Lady Barb (named with a kind of suggestiveness often found in James, but not always noticed—'Barbarina' suggests Arnold's 'Barbarian' and 'Barb' the equine thoroughbred) because he sees in her 'the beautiful mother of beautiful children in whom the appearance of "race" should be conspicuous.' He insists on taking her back to New York and settling there. She, for whom life has no meaning except in terms of hunting and the English social code, can, in New York society, find nothing to keep interest alive, for though her 'social traditions were rich and ancient' she is incapable of conversation—the poor Doctor had hoped to initiate an American *salon*. She succeeds in getting him back to England for a visit, their indefinite stay settles into permanence, and his life, which is bound up with his profession and his feeling for his native land, lapses into futility. At the end of the story he is seen scanning his infant daughter's face for 'the look of race'—but apprehensively.

wit. And he can, on the other hand, show us, as characteristically American, conscience and seriousness joined with a superiority of true intellectual culture and a fineness of manners. We have further an intimation that, in the depths of his mind, in the interplay between the diverse actualities of his experience, there is forming an imagined ideal positive that is not to be identified with any one of them. And this brings us to *The Portrait of a Lady*.

But, before going on to consider that book, I will, briefly and by the way, guard against appearing to slight his remarkable achievement in the rendering of actualities. Pound says[6] that James 'has put America on the map . . . giving to her a reality such as is attained only by scenes recorded in the arts and the writing of masters.' 'No one but an American,' he says, 'can ever know, really know, how good he is at bottom, how good his America is.' But an English reader can know how well James renders essential characteristics of English civilization and representative English types (though these, we sometimes find, are seen—as, for instance, Lord Warburton is—distinctly through the eyes of an outsider). And any reader, English or American, can see that he is, more generally, an incomparable master at differentiating national tones and qualities—the indices of radical differences of temper, tradition and moral outlook. After the Americans and the English, of course, he pays most attention to the French, and there are some French types finely observed and done as early as *The American*. He gives us Italians too. Germans are not frequent presences in his books, but they are to be found, and, in their 'doing,' exhibit his usual penetration. Within a decade after 1870 he gives us the new Herrenvolk German—see *A Bundle of Letters* (and there is another German type, 'a Junker of Junkers,' in the not much later *Pandora*).

It was to *The Portrait of a Lady* that the argument had brought me. The greatness of that book, it seems to me, is essentially conditioned by the inclusive harmony (or

6 In *Make it New*.

something approaching it) that it represents—the vital poise between the diverse tendencies and impulses I have noted. In Isabel Archer we have again the supremacy of the American girl; but in her we can recognize a real superiority, even if, pondering it critically, we judge it to depend on a large measure of idealization. Her freedom in the face of English conventions appears—and she is a firmly realized presence for us—as a true emancipation of spirit. Unlike Daisy Miller she has her own superior code, in her scruple, her self-respect and her sensitiveness; she is educated and highly intelligent. She is more idealized, it is true, than Bessy Alden. Nevertheless, however idealized, and whatever I may have said in comparing her with Gwendolen Harleth, she is convincing and impressive: the idealization stands for a true fineness, worthily imagined by James.

Lord Warburton, on the other hand, is very much superior to Lord Lambeth of *An International Episode*. He is far from stupid or impermeable to ideas ('he had a lively grey eye'), and he sees the order to which he belongs as standing for something more than precedence and privilege. In fact, that order is still in some ways idealized in *The Portrait of a Lady*, and the presentation of it has a mellow fulness that has much to do with the effect of rich beauty characterizing the book. The opening scene, on the lawn, giving us, with a ripe and subtle art that at once proclaims a great master, the old American banker and his company against the background of country-house, sets the tone. He admires and respects Lord Warburton and Lord Warburton's world, while, at the same time, the quite different standards he himself represents (he remains an American after thirty successful years in England), and the free play of mind and spirit that, with his son, he introduces into that world, constitutes, as I suggested earlier, an implicit criticism of it. We have here a sufficient hint at the way in which, in the total effect of the book, the idealization and the criticism are reconciled.

The admirableness of Lord Warburton and the impressiveness of his world, as we are made to feel them, are essential to the significance of Isabel's negative choice. That her rejection of them doesn't strike us as the least capricious, but as an act of radically ethical judgment, is a tribute to the reality with which James has invested her (she is *not*, we must concede, Gwendolen Harleth):

'At the risk of adding to the evidence of her self-sufficiency it must be said that there had been moments when this possibility of admiration by a personage represented to her an aggression almost to the degree of an affront, quite to the degree of an inconvenience. She had never yet known a personage; there had been no personages, in this sense, in her life; there were probably none such at all in her native land. When she had thought of individual eminence she had thought of it on the basis of character and wit—of what one might like in a gentleman's mind and in his talk. She herself was a character—she couldn't help being aware of that; and hitherto her visions of a completed consciousness had concerned themselves largely with moral images—things as to which the question would be whether they pleased her sublime soul. Lord Warburton loomed up before her, largely and brightly, as a collection of attributes and powers, which were not to be measured by this simple rule, but which demanded a different sort of appreciation—an appreciation that the girl, with her habit of judging quickly and freely, felt she lacked the patience to bestow. He appeared to demand of her something that no one else, as it were, had presumed to do. What she felt was that a territorial, a political, a social magnate had conceived the design of drawing her into the system in which he rather invidiously lived and moved. A certain instinct, not imperious, but persuasive, told her to resist—murmured to her that, virtually, she had a system and an orbit of her own.'

James goes on immediately to tell us that there was 'a young man lately come from America who had no system at all.' This, in the guise of Caspar Goodwood from New England, is the American business-man. He represents what America has to offer Isabel—stark unpliant integrity and self-reliant practical will, as opposed to 'system' and the civilized graces. 'His jaw was too square and set and his figure too straight and stiff: these things suggested a want of consonance with the deeper rhythms of life.'[7] But in spite of this promising description he is sentimentalized —in so far as he is 'there' at all—and he is one of the weaknesses of the book. However, the ineffectualness of the intention he stands for leaves Isabel's rejection of Lord Warburton all its significance.

This significance is beautifully intimated in such touches as the lapse (it is not unique) that Lord Warburton is guilty of on the occasion of Mrs. Touchett's forbidding Isabel to stay up alone with the gentlemen (Chapter VII):

'"Need I go, dear aunt? I'll come up in half an hour."

'"It is impossible I should wait for you," Mrs. Touchett answered.

'"Ah, you needn't wait! Ralph will light my candle," Isabel gaily engaged.

'"I'll light your candle; do let me light your candle, Miss Archer!" Lord Warburton exclaimed. "Only I beg it shall not be before midnight."

'Mrs. Touchett fixed her bright little eyes upon him a moment and transferred them to her niece.'

Warburton would not have used this tone to an English girl. Perceiving that she has the American freedom where the English *convenances* are concerned, he immediately classifies her as 'an American girl,' and slips into a manner that would have been in place with Henrietta Stackpole, the bright young journalist who habitually 'walks in without knocking at the door.' It shocks us, such is the power

[7] This description represents a kind of subtlety, expressive of a profundity of interest in life such as is not suggested by the phrase 'novelist of manners,' that is highly characteristic of James's notation. It is a character of 'style' that derives from the same radical bent as his stronger uses of symbolism.

of James's art. It shocks us more than it shocks Isabel, and
it serves none the less for that to bring to a concrete point
for us the rightness of her decision against him. For it
reveals to us an obtuse complacency, in assuming which
for a moment Lord Warburton seems to reveal the spirit of
the 'system' he belongs to.

This passage has its retroactive parallel in the later exchange (Chapter X) between Ralph Touchett and Henrietta, in which he pretends, to her confusion, to think that
she is making love to him. Ralph's 'lapse' doesn't matter.
It merely leads us to say that he knows how to treat Henrietta, just as he knows how to treat everyone. For Ralph
Touchett is the centre, the key-figure, of James's 'system'
—the poise of harmony I have spoken of as characterizing
The Portrait of a Lady. He is neither American nor English—or he is both: that is, he combines the advantages,
while being free from the limitations. He can place everyone, and represents the ideal civilization that James
found in no country.[8]

He understands why Isabella likes Henrietta, but, when
told that Henrietta carries in her garments 'the strong,
sweet, fresh odour' of her great country, he replies: she
'does smell of the Future—it almost knocks one down!' For
her he is just another expatriate, like Osmond. And when
Isabel asks the Parisian Americans, whom, in their obvious-
ness, she *can* place, 'You all live this way, but what does it
lead to?', Mrs. Touchett, placing herself, 'thought the question worthy of Henrietta Stackpole.' The discriminations,
in fact, are established with beautiful precision all along

---

[8] We have here, in fact, the positive ideal that we can see to be
implied in this passage from a letter of 1888 to his brother:
'. . . I aspire to write in such a way that it would be impossible to an outsider to say whether I am at a given moment
an American writing about England or an Englishman writing
about America (dealing as I do with both countries), and so
far from being ashamed of such an ambiguity I should be
exceedingly proud of it, for it would be highly civilized.' *Letters*, Vol. I, p. 143.

the scale. Isabel herself notices that Ralph seems to re-
semble Osmond in having a fastidious taste—and that yet
there is a difference. Ralph himself, in placing Osmond for
her (she, of course, doesn't take it in, and that is the tragic
irony), explains what it is: 'He has a great dread of vulgarity; that's his special line; he hasn't any other that I
know of.' He places Madame Merle too—again without
effect:

> '"Ah, with Madame Merle you may go anywhere
> *de confiance*," said Ralph. "She knows none but the best
> people."'

This will suffice to indicate the kind of essential organization that makes *The Portrait of a Lady*, for all the
critical points I made about it in discussing George
Eliot, a great book. Its greatness derives from his peculiar
genius and experience, and it embodies an organization of
his vital interests. These interests inform everything in it:
the wit, the dialogue, the plot, the characterization.

The creative wealth of the book is all distinctively
Jamesian. Madame Merle, for instance, couldn't have been
done by George Eliot. The vision here is Isabel's, who
hasn't yet seen through her:

> 'She had become too flexible, too useful, was too ripe
> and too final. She was in a word too perfectly the
> social animal that man and woman are supposed to have
> been intended to be; and she had rid herself of every
> remnant of that tonic wildness which we may assume
> to have belonged even to the most amiable persons in
> the ages before country-house life was the fashion. Isa-
> bel found it difficult to think of her in any detachment
> or privacy, she existed only in her relations, direct or
> indirect, with her fellow-mortals. One might wonder
> what commerce she could possibly hold with her own
> spirit. One always ended, however, by feeling that a
> charming surface doesn't necessarily prove one super-
> ficial; this was an illusion in which, in one's youth, one

had but just escaped being nourished. Madame Merle was not superficial—not she. She was deep. . . .'

She represents, that is, a social 'civilization' ('the great round world itself') That is not of the kind James himself is after (just as she is, with Osmond, the complete expatriate who has none of the American virtues). The contrasting Mrs. Touchett reminds us of an American type we meet in some of Lawrence's best work (*St. Mawr*, for instance). James presents her with his characteristic wit—which, as I have said, is no mere surface-habit of expression: 'The edges of her conduct were so very clear-cut that for susceptible persons it sometimes had a knife-like effect.' Henrietta Stackpole is another American type, perfectly done—marvellously escaping the effect of caricature, and remaining for all her portentous representativeness, sufficiently sympathetic. Then there is Osmond's sister, the Countess Gemini, 'a lady who had so mismanaged her improprieties that they had ceased to hang together at all . . . and had become the mere floating fragments of a wrecked renown, incommoding social circulation,' and who would plunge into a lucid conversation 'as a poodle plunges after a thrown stick.'

The Countess Gemini, though so well done, is a weakness in the book, in the sense that she is too simply there to serve as a piece of machinery. She alone can reveal to Isabel the clandestine relations of Osmond and Madame Merle, and the fact that Pansy is their daughter, and she is given no sufficient motives for performing the service. Pansy herself raises the question of James's attitude toward the pure protected *jeune fille* (the 'blank page'), a type to which he seems curiously drawn. In *The Awkward Age* he shows the good little Aggie, the foil to Nanda, developing after marriage into something approaching, at the level of Edwardian smart society, a vulgar trollop: and we readily accept the implication that, in such a *milieu*, the development follows naturally out of such 'innocence.' In *The Ambassadors* he seems to confirm this implication by giving the decidedly not innocent Madame Vionnet another carefully guarded 'blank page' for daughter.

Though Pansy serves obvious functions as machinery in the relations between Isabel and Osmond, her presence in the book has, in addition, some point. As a representative figure, 'the white flower of cultivated sweetness,' she pairs in contrast with Henrietta Stackpole, the embodiment of a quite different innocence—a robust American innocence that thrives on free exposure to the world. She brings us, in fact, to the general observation that almost all the characters can be seen to have, in the same way, their values and significances in a total scheme. For though *The Portrait of a Lady* is on so much larger a scale than *The Europeans*, and because of its complexity doesn't invite the description of 'moral fable,' it is similarly organized: it is all intensely significant.[9] It offers no largesse of irrelevant 'life'; its vitality is wholly that of art.

This is clearly why it has had nothing like due recognition—in an age when Trollope, Mrs. Gaskell, and the rest are being revived. And the same explanation covers the neglect of the masterpieces that keep it company. *The Portrait of a Lady*, *The Bostonians*, *The Europeans*, *Washington Square*, not to speak of the shorter things—how can this magnificent group of classics have missed being acclaimed as placing the novelist in established preeminence with Jane Austen and George Eliot? They are not difficult of approach, and they present no appearance of esotericism, while they have overt attractions that might seem to qualify them for popularity. The answer is that the real pre-eminence neither of Jane Austen nor of George Eliot, for all the general acceptance they have enjoyed, has in fact succeeded in getting itself really and

[9] What he says about Maisie in the Preface to *What Maisie Knew* he might have said about Pansy; the kind of 'economy' he so characteristically and significantly describes here is his constant preoccupation: 'so that we get, for our profit, and get by an economy of process interesting in itself, the thoroughly pictured creature, the striking figured symbol.'

generally recognized. The tradition of 'the English novel' is such that even critics who are too sophisticated to subscribe to the view that *The Cloister and the Hearth* is a great novel have expectations that prevent them from distinguishing, in fiction, the signs of serious art. It is a disastrous tradition.

It undoubtedly accounts for the misdirection and waste of much talent. It probably accounts for the fact that Gissing, who showed his powers in his one memorable novel, *New Grub Street,* in which the pressure of personal experience served him well, produced no other, though he produced many negligible ones. To pass from talent to genius, it accounts for the neglect—ultimately disastrous for his art—suffered by James himself. It accounts for the neglect that embittered Conrad's life as a writer. It meant that Lawrence, after *Women in Love,* had to give up wrestling with his creative problems, as had been his habit, in an intensive and prolonged process of writing and rewriting a slowly shaped major work, and, instead, dashed off and published novel after novel in quick succession, turned his genius to journalism, and confined his finished art to short stories.

However, the point to emphasize is that, for all the discouragement he suffered even in his early phase, James produced in it a cluster of achieved masterpieces. *The Portrait of a Lady* is a great novel, and we can't ask for a finer exhibition of James's peculiar gifts than we get there and in *The Bostonians* (they seem to me the two most brilliant novels in the language). The later development brings extraordinary subtleties of art—and poetic triumphs such as the method by which in *The Lesson of the Master* James dramatizes the complexities of his own attitude towards his career (about which he was clearly given to radical self-questioning)—but, for all the interest of the development, with its rich product of masterly tales, we can hardly follow it unregretting.

(ii) The Later James

The cue for the low current estimation of *Roderick Hudson* seems, I have remarked, to have been given, in his Preface to it, by James himself. But the James of the Prefaces—the famous prefaces that he wrote for the 'New York' edition of his works—is so much *not* the James of the early books that he certainly shouldn't be taken as a critical authority upon them, at any rate where valuation is concerned. The interest of the Prefaces is that they come from the mind that conceived the late work—which is to say that, if they are not in any sense critically satisfying, they have distinct critical bearings.

In bringing them together in *The Art of the Novel* Mr. R. P. Blackmur did something worth doing: James is so decidedly one of the very great, and such documents ought to be conveniently accessible. (It is very good news that the notebooks are at last going to be edited by Mr. F. O. Matthiessen.) Yet, if we find Mr. Blackmur's Introduction disappointing, we have, after reading the book through, to recognize that the disappointment goes back to the Prefaces themselves.

'Criticism has never been more ambitious, nor more useful. There has never been a body of work so eminently suited to criticism as the fiction of Henry James, and there has never been an author who so saw the need and had the ability to criticize specifically and at length his own work. He was avid of his opportunity and both proud and modest as to what he did with it. "These notes," he wrote in the Preface to *Roderick Hudson*, "represent, over a considerable course, the continuity of an artist's endeavour, the growth of his whole operative consciousness. . . ."'

—If this is high promise, it is a promise answering to our expectation, to our general sense of Henry James.

Mr. Blackmur, in the succeeding thirty pages of his Introduction, disappoints because, though besides classifying the Prefaces and enumerating James's themes he also summarizes and comments, he conveys no effect of vigorous and lucid argument, of issues clearly perceived and decisively set forth: the Introduction, in fact, seems laboured and unenlightening. If we at first think this due to excessive modesty or lack of ambition in Mr. Blackmur —to his having confined himself too much to listing and grouping, we afterwards discover that to have done anything more satisfying he would have to have been very much the reverse of modest and unambitious: he would have to have done what Henry James has not. And if we have finally a criticism to pass against him it is that he encourages us to expect what we are not, in fact, given.

For such a failure (as I judge it) to come to the necessary recognition there is a great deal of excuse: the Prefaces make not merely difficult but unrepaying reading. The extraordinary distinction of the mind they come from is apparent in them, and this distinction asserts itself in the very difficulty; the impressed, modest and tired reader comes away crediting James with achievement that is not really there. If Mr. Blackmur, as we must grant, is an unusually well-qualified reader, he is also a specialist, and a formal introducer preoccupied with establishing his author's claims to attention.

Mr. Blackmur has certainly read the Prefaces and knows them through and through. It is characteristic of the contemporary cult of Henry James (if it can be called that), and evidence of a real need for re-stating his claims in general to attention, that several of the contributors to the Henry James number of the *Hound and Horn* (April-June 1934) in which Mr. Blackmur's Introduction first appeared expose themselves as not having read, or having not been able to read, the works they write about. *The Portrait of a Lady* is not of the late, difficult period (to which the Prefaces very much belong), but one critic (H. R. Hays, writing on *Henry James the Satirist*) tells us that the situation it presents 'is resolved into a conventional

190 HENRY JAMES

happy ending with a divorce and a rescue by the American business man.' It is difficult to believe that anyone who had actually read, however carelessly or incompetently, to the end could have made that of it. But then it is difficult to believe that anyone capable of making anything at all of Henry James could pronounce as another contributor, Mr. Stephen Spender, does: 'A third of this book is taken up with brush work which has nothing to do with the story, but much to do with James's determination that he would really present Isabel Archer to us.' After that we are hardly surprised when Mr. Spender tells us that 'there is something particularly obscene about *What Maisie Knew*, in which a small girl is, in a rather admiring way, exhibited as prying into the sexual lives of her very promiscuous elders'—hardly surprised, though the consummately 'done' theme of *What Maisie Knew* is the incorruptible innocence of Maisie; innocence that not merely preserves itself in what might have seemed to be irresistibly corrupting circumstances, but can even generate decency out of the egotistic squalors of adult personal relations. The intention described by James in the Preface is, in the story, realized:

'No themes are so human as those that reflect for us, out of the confusion of life, the close connexion of bliss and bale, of the things that help with the things that hurt, so dangling before us for ever that bright hard metal, of so strange an alloy, one face of which is somebody's right and ease and the other somebody's pain and wrong. To live with all intensity and perplexity and felicity in its terribly mixed little world would thus be the part of my interesting small mortal; bringing people together who would be at least more correctly separate; keeping people separate who would be at least more correctly together; flourishing, to a degree, at the cost of many conventions and proprieties, even decencies, really keeping the torch of virtue alive in an air tending infinitely to smother it; really in short making confusion worse confounded by drawing some stray fragrance of

an ideal across the scent of selfishness, by sowing on
barren strands, through the mere fact of presence, the
seed of the moral life.'

It would, one would have thought, be possible to read
The Portrait of a Lady quite lazily, 'for the story,' without
missing the whole point as completely as Mr. Spender
misses it. *What Maisie Knew,* on the other hand, does certainly demand of the reader a close and unrelaxed
attention, an actively intelligent collaboration; it never per-
mits us to find it 'as easy to read as a novel.' Nevertheless,
that the general nature of the theme could, on any perusal,
escape recognition still seems remarkable. Yet it is not very
especially remarkable in the criticism and appreciation of
James's later work. For instance, as respectable a critic as
Mr. Van Wyck Brooks can write[10]: 'A young man who is
represented as "a gentleman, generally sound and generally
pleasant," straightway appears without any adequate explanation as engaged in the most atrocious of conspiracies
(Merton Densher in *The Wings of the Dove*).' That
would appear to amount to nothing better than the reading given us by H. R. Hays in the *Hound and Horn*: 'The
villain, Merton Densher, or Kate, in *The Wings of the
Dove*, Madame Merle in the *Portrait*. . . .'

Now, wherever *The Wings of the Dove* may fail, it is
not in the presentment of Kate Croy and Merton Densher. All the subtleties, obliquities and indirections of
Henry James's art are devoted, triumphantly, to showing
us Densher being drawn, resisting and never acquiescing,
into a position in which he cannot but, in spite of himself,
be a party to a conspiracy—a conspiracy which he has
never connived at or countenanced. He is in love with
Kate—they are 'in love' in the full common sense of the
phrase, and the direct strength with which the attraction
between the lovers is conveyed (a strength not common,
it must be confessed, in James, whose lack of freedom with
the physical Mr. Spender finds 'vulgar') makes the pre-

---

[10] *The Pilgrimage of Henry James*, p. 133.

sentment of Densher's unwilling complicity the more convincing. And even Kate Croy, whose resolute intention
constitutes the conspiracy, is not presented as a villain—
if 'villain' denotes a character whose 'wicked' behaviour we
simply, without any motions of sympathy, condemn. Her
resoluteness, as a matter of fact, appears to us as partly
admirable: the pressures driving her—her hateful outlawed
father, the threatening fate represented by her married
sister's overwhelming domestic squalors, the inflexible ambition of her magnificently vulgar aunt, Mrs. Lowder—are
conveyed with such force as to make them seem, for a
person of such proud and admirable vitality, irresistible.
Henry James's art, that is, has a moral fineness so far beyond the perception of his critics that they can accuse him
of the opposite. This fineness, this clairvoyant moral
intelligence, is the informing spirit of that technique by
the indirections and inexplicitnesses of which these critics
are baffled.

This fineness it is that, at James's best, the technique
serves and expresses. But *The Wings of the Dove* is nevertheless not a successful work; it does not as a whole show
James at his best. The great, the disabling failure is in the
presentment of the Dove, Milly Theale. As he says in the
Preface,

> 'the case prescribed for its central figure a sick young
> woman, at the whole course of whose disintegration
> and the whole ordeal of whose consciousness one would
> have quite honestly to assist.'

But later in the Preface he notes (finding it on re-perusal
of the book 'striking, charming and curious')

> 'the author's instinct everywhere for the *indirect* pres-
> entation of his main image. I note how, again and
> again, I go but a little way with the direct—that is, with
> the straight exhibition of Milly; it resorts for relief, this
> process, whenever it can, to some kinder, more merciful
> indirection: all as if to approach her circuitously, deal
> with her at second hand, as an unspotted princess is

ever dealt with; the pressure all round her kept easy for her, the sounds, the movements, regulated, the forms and ambiguities made charming.'

James was deceived. A vivid, particularly realized Milly might for him stand in the midst of his indirections, but what for his reader these skirt round is too much like emptiness; she isn't there, and the fuss the other characters make about her as the 'Dove' has the effect of an irritating sentimentality.[11]

This inveterate indirectness of the later James, this aim of presenting, of leaving presented, the essential thing by working round and behind so that it shapes itself in the space left amidst a context of hints and apprehensions, is undoubtedly a vice in the Prefaces; it accounts for their unsatisfactoriness. It appears there, in criticism, as an inability to state—an inability to tackle his theme, or to get anything out clearly and finally. Not that the Prefaces don't contain a good deal that arrests the reader and that is particularly impressive in quotation; but the developed and done is exasperatingly disproportionate to the laboured doing and the labour of reading.

Still, the novels are another matter. Criticism is not the art of fiction, and James's technical preoccupations, the development of his style and method, are obviously bound up with his essential genius; they are expressions of his magnificent intelligence, of his intense and delicate interest in human nature. No direct and peremptory grasp could handle the facts, the data, the material that concerned him most; and the moral situations that seemed to him most worth exploring were not such as invited blunt and confident judgments of simple 'good' and 'bad.' Mr. Edmund Wilson, writing for the memorial number of the *Hound and Horn* what is by far the most distinguished contribution, calls his theme *The Ambiguity of Henry*

---

[11] She was associated for him with his beloved and idealized cousin, Minny Temple, who died young; but that doesn't give her any more substance for us.

James. After giving an original and extremely persuasive account of *The Turn of the Screw,* he goes on to argue that, as the later manner developed, the subtleties of James's technique, the inexplicitnesses and indirections of his methods of presentment, tended to subserve a fundamental ambiguity; one, that is, about which he was not himself clear. For instance, of the central figure in *The Sacred Fount* we are left asking: 'Is the obnoxious week-end guest one of what used to be called the élite, a fastidious highly civilized sensibility, or is he merely morbid and a bore?' And Mr. Wilson suggests that James himself doesn't really know. The explanation?—

> 'In Henry James's mind, there disputed all his life the European and the American points of view; and their debate, I believe, is closely connected with his inability sometimes to be clear as to what he thinks of a certain sort of person.'

Now it is certainly true that James's development was towards over-subtlety, and that with this development we must associate a loss of sureness in his moral touch, an unsatisfactoriness that in some of the more ambitious late works leads us to question his implicit valuations. But this unsatisfactoriness at its worst—at any rate at its most important—seems to be something more decided than the ambiguity that Mr. Wilson illustrates from *The Sacred Fount.* It is what we have in *The Golden Bowl,* for example, which is one of the late 'great' novels, and, beyond any question, representatively on the line of his development. There James clearly counts on our taking towards his main persons attitudes that we cannot take without forgetting our finer moral sense—our finer discriminative feeling for life and personality. Adam Verver, the American plutocrat, and his daughter Maggie 'collect' the Prince in much the same spirit as that in which they collect their other 'pieces.' James is explicit about it:

> 'Nothing perhaps might strike us queerer than this application of the same measure of value to such differ-

ent pieces of property as old Persian carpets, say, and new human acquisitions; all the more, indeed, that the amiable man was not without an inkling that he was, as a taster of life, economically constructed. He put into his own little glass everything he raised to his lips. . . .' (Vol. I, p. 175.)

He acquires later Charlotte Stant, another fine 'piece'—acquires her as a wife in order to settle the uneasiness that Maggie feels about the difference made in his life by her own marriage (though actually father and daughter seem to be as constantly and completely together as before). This is how he sees them in the concluding scene of the novel:

'The two noble persons seated in conversation and at tea fell then into the splendid effect and the general harmony: Mrs. Verver and the Prince fairly "placed" themselves, however unwittingly, as high expressions of the kind of human furniture required esthetically by such a scene. The fusion of their presence with the decorative elements, their contribution to the triumph of selection, was complete and admirable; though to a lingering view, a view more penetrating than the occasion really demanded, they might have figured as concrete attestations of a rare power of purchase.' (Vol. II, p. 317.)

And yet, though James can on occasion come to this point of explicitness, our attitude towards the Ververs isn't meant to be ironical. We are to feel for and with them. We are to watch with intense sympathy Maggie's victorious struggle to break the clandestine relation between her husband and Charlotte, establish the pretence that nothing has occurred, and get Charlotte safely packed off under a life-sentence to America, the penal settlement. Actually, if our sympathies are anywhere they are with Charlotte and (a little) the Prince, who represent what, against the general moral background of the book, can only strike us as decent passion; in a stale, sickly and oppressive atmosphere they represent life. That in our feelings about the Ververs there would be any element of distaste Henry James, in spite of the passages quoted, seems to have had no inkling.

Mr. Wilson, of course, might find here another illustration for his theme of ambiguity. But actually what we have in this aspect of *The Golden Bowl* would seem to be, rather than any radical ambiguity in James, a partial inattention—an inadvertence. It is as if his interest in his material had been too specialized, too much concentrated on certain limited kinds of possible development, and as if in the technical elaboration expressing this specialized interest he had lost his full sense of life and let his moral taste slip into abeyance.[12] *The Ambassadors* too, which he seems to have thought his greatest success, produces an effect of disproportionate 'doing'—of a technique the subtleties and elaborations of which are not sufficiently controlled by a feeling for value and significance in living. What, we ask, is this, symbolized by Paris, that Strether feels himself to have missed in his own life? Has James himself sufficiently inquired? Is it anything adequately realized? If we are to take the elaboration of the theme in the spirit in which we are meant to take it, haven't we to take the symbol too much at the glamorous face-value it has for Strether? Isn't, that is, the energy of the 'doing' (and the energy demanded for the reading) disproportionate to the issues—to any issues that are concretely held and presented?

It is characteristic of Henry James's fate that, while it should be generally agreed that something went wrong with his development, it should at the same time be almost as generally agreed that the books we ought to know —the books he ought to be known by—are the last three long novels, *The Wings of the Dove* (1902), *The Ambassadors* (1903), and *The Golden Bowl* (1905). *The Ambassadors* in particular has probably, since Mr. Percy Lub-

---

[12] The kind of interest in symbolism discussed by Mr. Quentin Anderson would have the same tendency.

bock picked on it in *The Craft of Fiction* (Mr. E. M. Forster confirmed him in *Aspects of the Novel*), been the book most commonly attempted by those wishing to qualify in Henry James. This is to be deplored, since not only is *The Portrait of a Lady* much more likely, once started, to be read through and read with unfeigned enjoyment; it is much more worth reading. At any rate, as I have said, it seems to me to be James's finest achievement, and one of the great novels of the English language.

The Portrait of a Lady (1881) belongs to his early maturity. Just before and after come *Washington Square* and *The Bostonians*. The two last named are wholly American in theme and setting, and all three have the abundant, full-blooded life of well-nourished organisms. It is, of course, in terms of his deracination that Henry James's unsatisfactory development is commonly explained. The theory is what we find, in its most respectable statement, advanced by Mr. Van Wyck Brooks in *The Pilgrimage of Henry James*. The less delicate expositions more or less bluntly censure James for not having stayed in America and become a thoroughly American novelist. He should have devoted his genius to his own country and inaugurated modern American—the first truly American—literature.

What, we ask, when the theory becomes explicit to this point, does it mean? That Henry James ought to have forestalled the work of Dreiser and Sinclair Lewis? That he ought to have devoted himself to preparing the way for a much earlier Dos Passos? It means that he ought at any rate to have been a totally different kind of writer from what he actually, either by endowment or through early life and environment, was.

For his essential interests were inseparable from an interest in highly civilized manners, in the refinements of civilized intercourse. The social civilization that in America might have yielded him (or seemed to yield) what he needed was, as Mrs. Wharton, in her autobiographical book, *A Backward Glance*, points out, vanishing with his youth. England had certainly more to offer him than America had. But, says Mr. Van Wyck Brooks, 'England was impenetrable.'

> 'Granting that he had lost the immediate sense of life and character, that America had faded from his mind and that he knew that he could never write of English manners with the intimacy and freedom which his conception of the novelist's task necessitated . . .'

—But how, remembering (for instance) *The Awkward Age* (1899) and *What Maisie Knew* (1897), can we grant this last proposition? The author of these two masterpieces, which were written after that notorious dividing phase, the sustained and frustrate attempt upon the theatre (during which, as a matter of fact, he turned out a steady succession of stories), hardly suffered from any sense that he was not qualified to write of English manners with freedom and intimacy. Rather he knew English manners too well; he had penetrated too thoroughly.

The obvious constatation to start from, when the diagnosis of his queer development is in question, is that he suffered from being too much a professional novelist: being a novelist came to be too large a part of his living; that is, he did not live enough. His failure in this respect suggests, no doubt, some initial deficiency in him. Nevertheless, the peculiarities in terms of which it demands to be discussed are far from appearing as simple weakness. It is no doubt at first appearances odd that his interest in manners should have gone with such moral-intellectual intensity. But the manners he was interested in were to be the outward notation of spiritual and intellectual fineness, or at least to lend themselves to treatment as such. Essentially he was in quest of an ideal society, an ideal civilization. And English society, he had to recognize as he lived into it, could not after all offer him any sustaining approximation to his ideal. Still less, he knew, could America. So we find him developing into something like a paradoxical kind of recluse, a recluse living socially in the midst of society.

But a real recluse, living in unmetaphorical retreat,

is just what we cannot imagine him. In saying this we are, no doubt, touching on certain limiting characteristics of his genius. It was not the explorer's or the pioneer's, and it had nothing prophetic about it. It was not of a kind to manifest itself in lonely plumbings of the psyche or passionate questionings of the familiar modes of human experience. It was not, in short, D. H. Lawrence's or anything like it. James had no such immediate sense of human solidarity, no such nourishing intuition of the unity of life, as could make up to him for the deficiencies of civilized intercourse: life for him must be humane or it was nothing. There was nowhere in his work that preoccupation with ultimate sanctions which we may call religious.[13] (There comes to my mind here the significant badness of *The Altar of the Dead*, that morbidly sentimental and extremely unpleasant tale which—it is, of course, late—also illustrates poor James's weary, civilized loneliness of spirit.) It was to the artist as such that the discrepancy between the desiderated civilization and English society was peculiarly brought home:

'The artist may, of course, in wanton moods, dream of some Paradise (for art) where the direct appeal to the intelligence might be legalized; for to such extravagances as these his yearning mind can scarce hope ever completely to close itself. The most he can do is to remember they *are* extravagances.'

James has already remarked in this Preface (it is that to *The Portrait of a Lady*) that the novelist

'is entitled to nothing, he is bound to admit, that can come to him, from the reader, as a result on the latter's part of any act of reflexion or discrimination.'

---

[13] This statement will have to be reconsidered in the light of Mr. Quentin Anderson's argument, when this is fully accessible (see footnote, p. 157, above). But I suspect that what will turn out to be required will be not so much withdrawal as a less simple formulation.

These bitter ironies abound in the Prefaces, which, he wrote to W. D. Howells,

> 'are, in general, a sort of plea for Criticism, for Discrimination, for Appreciation on other than infantile lines—as against the so almost universal Anglo-Saxon absence of these things; which tends, in our general trade, it seems to me, to break the heart. . . .'

The comments in the Preface to *The Lesson of the Master* on the story called *The Figure in the Carpet* are especially significant. Speaking of his great unappreciated author James says:

> 'I came to Hugh Vereker, in fine, by this travelled road of a generalization; the habit of having noted for many years how strongly and helplessly, among us all, what we call criticism—its curiosity never emerging from the limp state—is apt to stand off from the intended sense of things, from such finely attested matters, on the artist's part, as a spirit and a form, a bias and a logic, of his own.'

He has already referred with less detachment to

> 'the poor man's attributive dependence, for the sense of being understood, on some responsive reach of critical perception that he is destined never to waylay with success. . . .'

And the force of that attribution comes out unmistakably in the eloquent reticence of this:

> 'As for the ingenious *Figure in the Carpet*, let me perhaps a little pusillanimously conclude, nothing would induce me to come to close quarters with you on the correspondences of this anecdote. . . . All I can at this point say is that if ever I was aware of ground and matter for a significant fable, I was aware of them in that connexion.'

He was indeed; and if he could have foreseen the criticism

and appreciation, starting with Miss Rebecca West's characteristic tribute, his work would receive in the two decades following his death, he would hardly have been consoled.

The same conditions, then, that drove him back on his art made him profoundly aware that his art wasn't likely to be appreciated by many besides himself.[14] So he came to live in it—and not the less so for living strenuously—the life of a spiritual recluse; a recluse in a sense in which not only no novelist but no good artist of any kind can afford to become one. His technique came to exhibit an unhealthy vitality of undernourishment and etiolation. His technical preoccupation, to put it another way, lost its balance, and, instead of being the sharp register of his finest perceptions, as informed and related by his fullest sense of life, became something that took his intelligence out of its true focus and blunted his sensitiveness. That is the mischief of what he discusses in the Prefaces as a possible tendency in himself towards 'overtreatment.' Correlated with this tendency is that manifested in the extraordinarily specialized living of his characters:

> 'The immensity didn't include *them*; but if he had an idea at the back of his head she had also one in a recess as deep, and for a time, while they sat together, there was an extraordinary mute passage between her vision of this vision of his, his vision of her vision, and her vision of his vision of her vision.'[15]

---

[14] *Cf.* what the author says to his young visitor in *The Author of Beltraffio*: 'If you're going into this kind of thing there's a fact you should know beforehand; it may save you some disappointment. There's a hatred of art, there's a hatred of literature—I mean of the genuine kinds. Oh the shams—*those* they'll swallow by the bucket!'

[15] *What Maisie Knew*, p. 163 (Pocket Edition). *Cf.* 'There were other marble terraces, sweeping more purple prospects, on which he would have known what to think, and would have enjoyed thereby at least the small intellectual fillip of a discerned relation between a given appearance and a taken meaning.' *The Golden Bowl*, I, 318.

This last aspect of his development is the more significant—significant in the sense suggested—in that he was, it seems, quite unaware of it. Mrs. Wharton records (*A Backward Glance*, p. 191):

> 'Preoccupied by this, I one day said to him: "What was your idea in suspending the four principal characters in *The Golden Bowl* in the void? What sort of life did they lead when they were not watching each other, and fencing with each other? Why have you stripped them of all the *human fringes* we necessarily trail after us through life?"
>
> 'He looked at me in surprise, and I saw at once that the surprise was painful, and wished I had not spoken. I had assumed that his system was a deliberate one, carefully thought out, and had been genuinely anxious to hear his reasons. But after a pause of reflection he answered in a disturbed voice: "My dear—I didn't know I had!" and I saw that my question, instead of starting one of our absorbing literary discussions, had only turned his startled attention on a peculiarity of which he had been completely unconscious.' [16]

Of the peculiarities of his later style, with its complexities and exhausting delicacies and its incapacity for directness ('her vision of his vision of her vision' and 'the small intellectual fillip of a discerned relation between a given appearance and a taken meaning'—James himself is the complete Jamesian character), he cannot have been wholly unconscious. That there really was incapacity, essential loss of a power, that something had gone wrong in his life, Mrs. Wharton brings amusingly home to us. She relates an episode showing him unable to ask the way

---

[16] Mrs. Wharton goes on: 'This sensitiveness to criticism or comment of any sort had nothing to do with vanity; it was caused by the great artist's deep consciousness of his powers, combined with a bitter, a life-long disappointment at his lack of popular recognition.'

THE LATER JAMES 203

so as to be understood.[17] The author of *The Portrait of a Lady* most certainly was not like that.

The nature of the change comes out notably in James's imagery—his metaphors, analogies and so on. There is an extraordinary wealth of these in the earlier style, where they strike us with their poetic immediacy and their rightness to feeling as well as their wit. They are to be found at any opening of *The Portrait of a Lady*, and it would be easy to illustrate; but illustration, by taking each natural unobtrusive effect out of the easy flow in which it comes, would convey a false impression (unless one quoted the

---

[17] ' "My good man, if you'll be good enough to come here, please; a little nearer—so," and as the old man came up: "My friend, to put it to you in two words, this lady and I have just arrived here from *Slough;* that is to say, to be more strictly accurate, we have recently *passed through* Slough on our way here, having actually motored to Windsor from Rye, which was our point of departure; and the darkness having overtaken us, we should be much obliged if you would tell us where we are now in relation, say, to the High Street, which, as you of course know, leads to the Castle, after leaving on the left hand the turn down to the railway station."

'I was not surprised to have this extraordinary appeal met by silence, and a dazed expression on the old wrinkled face at the window; nor to have James go on: "In short" (his invariable prelude to a fresh series of explanatory ramifications), "in short, my good man, what I want to put to you in a word is this: supposing we have already (as I have reason to think we have) driven past the turn down to the railway station (which, in that case, by the way, would probably not have been on our left hand, but on our right), where are we now in relation to . . ."

' "Oh, please," I interrupted, feeling myself utterly unable to sit through another parenthesis, "do ask him where the King's Road is."

' "Ah—? The King's Road? Just so! Quite right! Can you, as a matter of fact, my good man, tell us where in relation to our present position the King's Road exactly *is?*"

' "Ye're in it," said the aged face at the window.'

sustained passage in Book II,[18] in which we are for the
first time shown Isabel realizing the 'dark, narrow alley
with a drab wall at the end' into which her marriage has
trapped her). Things of the same kind may be found in
the later books, but what goes characteristically with the
developed Jamesian style is a more deliberate and elaborated kind of figure, the kind exemplified at its most elaborate by the famous pagoda that opens Book II of *The
Golden Bowl* or by the caravan later on in the same volume
(p. 209). We are conscious in these figures more of analysis, demonstration and comment than of the realizing imagination and the play of poetic perception. Between any
original perception or feeling there may have been and
what we are given there has come a process of judicial
stock-taking; the imagery is not immediate and inevitable
but synthetic. It is diagrammatic rather than poetic. And
that is so even when it makes a show of sensuous vividness,
as here:

> 'Just three things in themselves, however, with all the
> rest, with his fixed purpose now, his committed deed,
> the fine pink glow, projected forward, of his ships, be-
> hind him, definitely blazing and crackling—this quan-
> tity was to push him harder than any word of his own
> could warn him. All that she was herself, moreover,
> was so lighted, to its advantage, by the pink glow.'

This hasn't the concrete immediacy of metaphor[19]; it is,
rather, coloured diagram.

---

[18] See p. 166 *et seq.*, the Pocket Edition.
[19] As the following, also from *The Golden Bowl*, has: 'Ah
then it was that the cup of her conviction, full to the brim,
overflowed at a touch! *There* was his idea, the clearness of
which for an instant almost dazzled her. It was a blur of light
in the midst of which she saw Charlotte like some object
marked by contrast in blackness, saw her waver in the field of
vision, saw her removed, transported, doomed. And he had
named Charlotte, named her again, and she had *made* him—
which was all she had needed more: it was as she had held a
blank letter to the fire and the writing had come out still

The trouble with the late style is that it exacts so intensely and inveterately analytic an attention that no sufficient bodied response builds up: nothing sufficiently approaching the deferred concrete immediacy that has been earned is attainable. Of Henry James himself we feel that the style involves for him, registers as prevailing *in* him, a kind of attention that doesn't favour his realizing his theme, in the whole or locally, as full-bodied life. The relation between deficiency of this order (a deficiency—in spite of the tremendous output of intellectual energy represented by each work—in vitality) and the kind of moral unsatisfactoriness that we have observed in *The Golden Bowl* should be fairly plain. James himself suggests it well enough in the Preface to *The Portrait of a Lady*:

> 'There is, I think, no more nutritive or suggestive truth in this connexion than that of the perfect dependence of the "moral" sense of a work of art on the amount of felt life concerned in producing it. The question comes back thus, obviously, to the kind and degree of the artist's prime sensibility, which is the soil out of which his subject springs.'

—We do not feel in the late style a rich and lively sensibility freely functioning.

But qualifications impose themselves at once. It will not do to suggest that there are not, in the late period, admirable successes, works in which distinctively late and difficult characteristics appear merely or mainly as achieved subtlety and fineness. Of these the most notable are *The Awkward Age* and *What Maisie Knew*. Of the latter something has already been said. Though it occupies only part of a volume, it might, with its packed and intensively organized three hundred pages, stand as a

---

larger than she had hoped.'—The analogy in the last sentence brings out by contrast the metaphorical immediacy of what goes before.

novel. *The Awkward Age* occupies a whole volume and may (though it doesn't occupy two) fairly be considered one of James's major achievements. It seems unlikely, however, to gain general acceptance as such: it was received at its first appearance, James tells us, with 'complete disrespect,' and the critics who have written about it seem to have found it not worth the extremely close and alert reading it demands. So qualified a critic as Mr. Edmund Wilson, for instance, opines that 'James could never have known how we should feel about the gibbering disembowelled crew who hover around one another with sordid shadowy designs in *The Awkward Age*.' Actually, the various ways in which we are to feel about the various characters are delicately but surely defined; and the whole point of the book depends upon our feeling a strong distaste for some of the characters and sharing with James a critical attitude towards most of them. Yet for the general complete misreading James possibly bears some responsibility—responsibility other than that of having merely been difficult and subtle. When, for example, Mr. Percy Lubbock in *The Craft of Fiction* sees the 'highly sophisticated circle of men and women, who seem so well practised in the art of living that they could never be taken by surprise' (p. 191) as an admirable coterie to which one would be proud to belong ('Their intelligence counts for everything . . .' 'It is a charmed world . . .') he might reasonably point to the Preface for his warrant. And he might reasonably invoke the same authority for his account of James's theme:

> 'The girl Nanda, supposedly a helpless spectator, takes control of the situation and works it out for her elders. She is the intelligent and expert and self-possessed one of them all; they have only to leave everything to her light manipulations, and the awkwardness—which is theirs, not hers—is surmounted. By the time she has displayed all her art the story is at an end; her action has answered the question and provided the issue.'

That is the notion of the theme one gets from the Preface. It is an ironical commentary on the significance and drift of James's later technical preoccupation that, discussing ten years after having written *The Awkward Age* the triumphant *tour de force* that it was for him (a novel completely dramatized, 'triumphantly scientific,' 'the *quantity* of finish it stows away'), he should have forgotten to say anything about his essential theme—about the intense moral and tragic interest that here justifies his technique and is justified by it. For *The Awkward Age*, though it exhibits James's genius for social comedy at its most brilliant, is a tragedy; a tragedy conceived in an imagination that was robustly, delicately and clairvoyantly moral.

The dialogue (and *The Awkward Age* is nearly all dialogue) is marvellously good, an amazing exhibition of genius. It is in this life of the dialogue that *The Awkward Age* differs most obviously from the late 'great,' conventionally admired novels, where, while granting the author's right to stylize, we have to complain that his characters speak in a stylization that is too often intolerably like the author's own late style. And this life of the dialogue, fascinating in itself, also means a subtle, vivid and varied life of character. Nevertheless, perhaps even *The Awkward Age*, brilliant success as it is, represents a disproportionate amount of 'doing,' a disproportionate interest in technique. Certainly Nanda, the tragic heroine, is a more rarefied presence than Isabel Archer. To say which, of course, is to invite the reply that James didn't intend either to give us Isabel again or to give us with the same relative fulness anyone. Yet it still seems a fair comment that a James who had as much fulness of life to impart as informs *The Portrait of a Lady* couldn't have chosen to restrict himself by so 'triumphantly scientific' and so *excluding* a method of presentment as that of *The Awkward Age*. Interest in technique is usurping here upon the interest that, in the greatest art, technique subserves.

'Ah, aren't we very much the same—simple lovers of

life? That is of the finer essence of it which appeals to
the consciousness—!'

This is said by one of the characters in *The Awkward
Age*. The phrase, 'the finer essence . . . which appeals to
the consciousness,' suggests very well the nature of James's
own preoccupation. In *The Portrait of a Lady*, we may say,
he seeks the essence of a very much richer life than in
The Awkward Age. In connexion with the latter book
'consciousness' takes on a limiting suggestion: it suggests
something too close to what is represented by the witty
and sophisticated conversation into which the theme is
distilled. And the reading that *The Awkward Age* exacts
is, strongly sympathetic as are the feelings generated towards Nanda, Mr. Longdon and Mitchy, too intensively
and predominantly a matter of the 'wits,' in a limiting
sense, to permit of the profoundest and most massive imaginative effect.

Isabel Archer, who in *The Portrait of a Lady*, loving
life, seeks 'the finer essence of it that appeals to the consciousness,' may be said to symbolize for James that essence
at his richest apprehension of it. It is not for nothing that
a whole volume is required to present, place and duly
charge Isabel before the 'story,' in Mr. Stephen Spender's
sense, begins; or that the process involves the evocation of
a rich and varied environment and background. And convincingly 'there' as scene and persons are, and though the
imagination that makes them so present to us is ironically
perspicacious and supremely intelligent, there is something of James's ideal civilization about the England he
evokes. Manners, the arts of social intercourse, do, in that
mellow and spacious world—the world of Lord Warburton
and his sisters, Ralph Touchett, and the old American
banker his father—seem to express something truly and
maturely humane, a spiritual fineness. That element of
warm faith, or illusion, disappears from James's work along
with the generous fulness of actuality as the 'scientific'
elaborateness of 'doing' comes in. It is significant too that
we cannot believe that the later James—the James of *The*

Golden Bowl—would have dealt so mercilessly, would not have dealt at least a little complaisantly, with Gilbert Osmond, the aesthetic dilettante to whom Isabel falls a prey.

This development might suggest critical reflections regarding the essential nature and conditions of James's concern for 'the finer essence.' So peculiar an intensity of concern for consciousness might perhaps be seen as in itself an index of some correlated deficiency—an index of something, from the beginning, not quite sound, whole and thriving within and below. True, *The Bostonians*, with the poised wisdom of its comedy, and its richness of substance, derived from the experience and observation of childhood and youth, doesn't encourage such reflections. But even of *The Portrait of a Lady* it might perhaps be suggested that its effect of rich vitality isn't quite simply an expression of rich and free first-hand living.[20] The young American in *The Author of Beltraffio* says of the Author's house:

> 'there was imagination in the carpets and curtains, in the pictures and books, in the garden behind it, where certain old brown walls were muffled in creepers that appeared to me to have been copied from a masterpiece of one of the pre-Raphaelites. That was the way many things struck me at that time in England as reproduc-

---

[20] It is relevant here (and see pp. 197-99 above) to note that, for such an upbringing as that of the young Jameses, there was a price. Never allowed to become rooted in any *milieu*, one would be remarkable indeed to develop a strong sense of society as a system of functions and responsibilities. H. J.'s interest in 'civilization' betrays, tested by his actual selectiveness in the concrete field before him, a grave deficiency. 'He didn't know the right people,' 'Q' once said to me, discussing James's criticism of the country-house. A fair point: after all, the admirable types, the public spirit and the fine and serious culture we come on when we study, *e.g.*, the *milieu* of Henry Sidgwick (intense and intelligent admirer of George Eliot) were characteristic products of the England of the 'best families' in James's time. Why does he seem to know nothing about this real and most impressive best?

tions of something that had existed primarily in art or
literature. It was not the picture, the poem, the fictive
page, that seemed to me a copy; these things were the
originals, and the life of happy and distinguished people was fashioned in their image.'

—Something of the effect of *The Portrait of a Lady* is suggested there. And when, as in *The Princess Casamassima*
(which brings so little comfort to those who would like to
justify James by his interest in the class-war), he offers,
uncharacteristically, something like an earthy and sappy
vitality, it derives, significantly, from Dickens.

But this is not the note to end on. It is a measure of our
sense of the greatness of Henry James's genius that discussion should tend to stress mainly what he failed to do
with it. But what achievement in the art of fiction—fiction
as a completely serious art addressed to the adult mind—
can we point to in English as surpassing his? Besides *The
Europeans, The Portrait of a Lady, The Bostonians, Washington Square, The Awkward Age* and *What Maisie
Knew,* there is an impressive array of things—novels, *nouvelles,* short stories—that will stand permanently as classics.

IV. JOSEPH CONRAD

(i) *Minor Works and 'Nostromo'*

An announcement once appeared in a quarterly, against
the name of the present writer, of an article to be entitled
Conrad, the Soul and the Universe. The exasperation registered in this formula explains, perhaps, why the article
was never written. For that Conrad has done classical
work is as certain as that his classical status will not rest
evenly upon his whole *œuvre*, and the necessary discriminations and delimitations, not being altogether simple,
clearly oughtn't to be attempted in any but a securely
critical frame of mind. He has, of course, long been generally held to be among the English masters; the exasperation records a sense that the greatness attributed to him
intended to be identified with an imputed profundity,
and that this 'profundity' was not what it was taken to be,
but quite other, and the reverse of a strength. The final
abandonment of the article may have been partly determined by Mr. E. M. Forster's note on Conrad that appeared in *Abinger Harvest*:

> 'What is so elusive about him is that he is always
> promising to make some general philosophic statement
> about the universe, and then refraining with a gruff
> disclaimer. . . . Is there not also a central obscurity,
> something noble, heroic, beautiful, inspiring half-a-
> dozen great books, but obscure, obscure? . . . These
> essays do suggest that he is misty in the middle as well
> as at the edges, that the secret casket of his genius con-
> tains a vapour rather than a jewel; and that we needn't
> try to write him down philosophically, because there is,
> in this direction, nothing to write. No creed, in fact.
> Only opinions, and the right to throw them overboard
> when facts make them look absurd. Opinions held un-

der the semblance of eternity, girt with the sea, crowned with stars, and therefore easily mistaken for a creed.'

—This might well have gratified the exasperation, and made its expression seem unnecessary.

Mr. Forster, however, doesn't attempt discriminations or precisions (his note is a reprinted review of *Notes on Life and Letters*). And he doesn't suggest those manifestations of the characteristic he describes in which we have something simply and obviously deplorable—something that presents itself, not as an elusively noble *timbre*, prompting us to analysis and consequent limiting judgments, but as, bluntly, a disconcerting weakness or vice. Consider, for instance, how *Heart of Darkness* is marred.

Heart of Darkness is, by common consent, one of Conrad's best things—an appropriate source for the epigraph of *The Hollow Men*: 'Mistah Kurtz, he dead.' That utterance, recalling the particularity of its immediate context, represents the strength of *Heart of Darkness*:

'He cried in a whisper at some image, at some vision —he cried out twice, a cry that was no more than a breath—

'"The horror! The horror!"

'I blew the candle out and left the cabin. The pilgrims were dining in the mess-room, and I took my place opposite the manager, who lifted his eyes to give me a questioning glance, which I successfully ignored. He leaned back, serene, with that peculiar smile of his sealing the unexpressed depth of his meanness. A continuous shower of small flies streamed upon the lamp, upon the cloth, upon our hands and faces. Suddenly the manager's boy put his insolent face in the doorway, and said in a tone of scathing contempt—

'"Mistah Kurtz—he dead."

'All the pilgrims rushed out to see. I remained, and went on with my dinner. I believe I was considered brutally callous. However, I did not eat much. There was a lamp in there—light, don't you know—and outside it was so beastly, beastly dark.'

This passage, it will be recognized, owes its force to a whole wide context of particularities that gives the elements here—the pilgrims, the manager, the manager's boy, the situation—their specific values. Borrowing a phrase from Mr. Eliot's critical writings, one might say that *Heart of Darkness* achieves its overpowering evocation of atmosphere by means of 'objective correlatives.' The details and circumstances of the voyage to and up the Congo are present to us as if we were making the journey ourselves and (chosen for record as they are by a controlling imaginative purpose) they carry specificities of emotion and suggestion with them. There is the gunboat dropping shells into Africa:

'There wasn't even a shed there, and she was shelling the bush. It appears the French had one of their wars going on thereabouts. Her ensign dropped limp like a rag; the muzzles of the long six-inch guns stuck out all over the low hull; the greasy, slimy swell swung her up lazily and let her down, swaying her thin masts. In the empty immensity of earth, sky and water, there she was, incomprehensible, firing into a continent. Pop, would go one of the six-inch guns; a small flame would dart and vanish, a tiny projectile would give a feeble screech —and nothing happened. Nothing could happen. There was a touch of insanity in the proceeding, a sense of lugubrious drollery in the sight; and it was not dissipated by somebody on board assuring me earnestly there was a camp of natives—he called them enemies! —hidden out of sight somewhere.

'We gave her her letters (I heard the men in that lonely ship were dying of fever at the rate of three a day) and went on. We called at some more places with farcical names, where the merry dance of death and trade goes on in a still and earthy atmosphere as of an overheated catacomb. . . .'

There is the arrival at the Company's station:

'I came upon a boiler wallowing in the grass, then

found a path leading up the hill. It turned aside for the boulders, and also for an undersized railway-truck lying there on its back with its wheels in the air. One was off. The thing looked as dead as the carcass of some animal. I came upon more pieces of decaying machinery, a stack of rusty nails. To the left a clump of trees made a shady spot, where dark things seemed to stir feebly. I blinked, the path was steep. A horn tooted to the right, and I saw black people run. A heavy, dull detonation shook the ground, a puff of smoke came out of the cliff, and that was all. No change appeared on the face of the rock. They were building a railway. The cliff was not in the way of anything; but this objectless blasting was all the work going on.

'A slight clanking behind me made me turn my head. Six black men advanced in a file, toiling up the path. They walked erect and slow, balancing small baskets full of earth on their heads, and the clink kept time with their footsteps. Black rags were wound round their loins, and the short ends behind waggled to and fro like tails. I could see every rib, the joints of their limbs were like knots in a rope; each had an iron collar on his neck, and all were connected together with a chain whose bights swung between them, rhythmically clinking. Another report from the cliff made me think suddenly of that ship of war I had seen firing into a continent. It was the same kind of ominous voice; but these men could by no stretch of imagination be called enemies. They were called criminals. . . .'

There is the grove of death:

'At last I got under the trees. My purpose was to stroll into the shade for a moment; but no sooner within it than it seemed to me that I had stepped into the gloomy circle of some Inferno. The rapids were near, and an uninterrupted, uniform, headlong, rushing noise filled the mournful stillness of the grove, where not a breath stirred, not a leaf moved, with a mysterious sound—as though the tearing pace of the launched earth had suddenly become audible.

'Black shapes crouched, lay, sat beneath the trees, leaning against the trunks, clinging to the earth, half coming out, half effaced within the dim light, in all the attitudes of pain, abandonment, and despair. Another mine of the cliff went off, followed by a slight shudder of the soil under my feet. The work was going on. The work! And this was the place where some of the helpers had withdrawn to die.

'They were dying slowly—it was very clear. They were not enemies, they were not criminals, they were nothing earthly now,—nothing but black shadows of disease and starvation, lying confusedly in the greenish gloom. . . . These moribund shapes were free as air and nearly as thin. I began to distinguish the gleam of the eyes under the trees. There, glancing down, I saw a face near my hand. The black bones reclined at full length with one shoulder against the tree, and slowly the eyelids rose and the sunken eyes looked up at me, enormous and vacant, a kind of blind, white flicker in the depths of the orbs, which died out slowly.'

By means of this art of vivid essential record, in terms of things seen and incidents experienced by a main agent in the narrative, and particular contacts and exchanges with other human agents, the overwhelming sinister and fantastic 'atmosphere' is engendered. Ordinary greed, stupidity and moral squalor are made to look like behaviour in a lunatic asylum against the vast and oppressive mystery of the surroundings, rendered potently in terms of sensation. This mean lunacy, which we are made to feel as at the same time normal and insane, is brought out by contrast with the fantastically secure innocence of the young harlequin-costumed Russian ('son of an arch-priest . . . Government of Tambov'), the introduction to whom is by the way of that copy of Tower's (or Towson's) *Inquiry into Some Points of Seamanship*, symbol of tradition, sanity and the moral idea, found lying, an incongruous mystery, in the dark heart of Africa.

Of course, as the above quotations illustrate, the author's comment cannot be said to be wholly implicit. Nevertheless, it is not separable from the thing rendered, but seems to emerge from the vibration of this as part of the tone. At least, this is Conrad's art at its best. There are, however, places in *Heart of Darkness* where we become aware of comment as an interposition, and worse, as an intrusion, at times an exasperating one. Hadn't he, we find ourselves asking, overworked 'inscrutable,' 'inconceivable,' 'unspeakable' and that kind of word already?—yet still they recur. Is anything added to the oppressive mysteriousness of the Congo by such sentences as:

'It was the stillness of an implacable force brooding over an inscrutable intention?'

The same vocabulary, the same adjectival insistence upon inexpressible and incomprehensible mystery, is applied to the evocation of human profundities and spiritual horrors; to magnifying a thrilled sense of the unspeakable potentialities of the human soul. The actual effect is not to magnify but rather to muffle. The essential vibration emanates from the interaction of the particular incidents, actions and perceptions that are evoked with such charged concreteness. The legitimate kind of comment, that which seems the inevitable immediate resonance of the recorded event, is represented here:

'And then I made a brusque movement, and one of the remaining posts of that vanished fence leaped into the field of my glass. You remember I told you I had been struck at the distance by certain attempts at ornamentation, rather remarkable in the ruinous aspect of the place. Now I had suddenly a nearer view, and its first result was to make me throw my head back as if before a blow. Then I went carefully from post to post with my glass, and I saw my mistake. Those round knobs were not ornamental but symbolic; they were expressive and puzzling, striking and disturbing—food for thought and also for the vultures if there had been any looking down from the sky; but at all events for such ants as were industrious enough to ascend the pole. They would have been even more impressive, those heads on the stakes, if their faces had not been turned to the house. Only one, the first I had made out, was facing my way. I was not so shocked as you may think. The start back I had given was really nothing but a movement of surprise. I had expected to see a knob of wood there, you know. I returned deliberately to the first I had seen—and there it was, black, dried, sunken, with closed eyelids,—a head that seemed to sleep at the top of that pole, and, with the shrunken dry lips showing a narrow white line of the teeth, was smiling too, smiling continuously at some endless and jocose dream of that eternal slumber.

'I am not disclosing any trade secrets. In fact, the manager said afterwards that Mr. Kurtz's methods had ruined the district. I have no opinion on that point, but I want you clearly to understand that there was nothing exactly profitable in those heads being there. They only showed that Mr. Kurtz lacked restraint in the gratification of his various lusts, that there was something wanting in him—some small matter which, when the pressing need arose, could not be found under his magnificent eloquence. Whether he knew of this deficiency himself I can't say. I think the knowledge came to him at last—only at the very last, but the wilderness had found him out early, and had taken on him a terrible vengeance for the fantastic invasion. I think it had whispered to him things about himself which he did not know, things of which he had no conception till he took counsel with this great solitude—and the whisper had proved irresistibly fascinating. It echoed loudly within him because he was hollow at the core. . . . I put down the glass, and the head that had appeared near enough to be spoken to seemed at once to have leaped away from me into inaccessible distance.'

—That the 'admirer of Mr. Kurtz,' the companion of the narrator here, should be the fantastically sane and innocent young Russian is part of the force of the passage.

By such means as it illustrates we are given a charged sense of the monstrous hothouse efflorescences fostered in Kurtz by solitude and the wilderness. It is a matter of such things as the heads on posts—a direct significant glimpse, the innocent Russian's explanations, the incidents of the progress up the river and the moral and physical incongruities registered; in short, of the charge generated in a variety of highly specific evocations. The stalking of the moribund Kurtz, a skeleton crawling through the long grass on all fours as he makes his bolt towards the fires and the tom-toms, is a triumphant climax in the suggestion of strange and horrible perversions. But Conrad isn't satisfied with these means; he feels that there is, or ought to be, some horror, some significance he has yet to bring out. So we have an adjectival and worse than supererogatory insistence on 'unspeakable rites,' 'unspeakable secrets,' 'monstrous passions,' 'inconceivable mystery,' and so on. If it were only, as it largely is in *Heart of Darkness*, a matter of an occasional phrase it would still be regrettable as tending to cheapen the tone. But the actual cheapening is little short of disastrous. Here, for instance, we have Marlow at the crisis of the episode just referred to:

'I tried to break the spell—the heavy, mute spell of the wilderness—that seemed to draw him to its pitiless breast by the awakening of forgotten and brutal instincts, by the memory of gratified and monstrous passions. This alone, I was convinced, had driven him out to the edge of the forest, towards the gleam of the fires, the throb of drums, the drone of weird incantations; this alone had beguiled his unlawful soul beyond the bounds of permitted aspirations. And, don't you see, the terror of the position was not in being knocked on the head—though I had a very lively sense of that danger too —but in this, that I had to deal with a being to whom I could not appeal in the name of anything high or low

. . . I've been telling you what we said—repeating the phrases we pronounced—but what's the good? They were common everyday words—the familiar vague sounds exchanged on every waking day of life. But what of that? They had behind them, to my mind, the terrific suggestiveness of words heard in dreams, of phrases spoken in nightmares. Soul! If anybody had ever struggled with a soul, I am the man. And I wasn't arguing with a lunatic either. . . . But his soul was mad. Being alone in the wilderness, it had looked within itself, and, by heavens! I tell you, it had gone mad. I had—for my sins, I suppose—to go through the ordeal of looking into it myself. No eloquence could have been so withering to one's belief in mankind as his final burst of sincerity. He struggled with himself too, I saw it—I heard it. I saw the inconceivable mystery of a soul that knew no restraint, no faith, and no fear, yet struggling blindly with itself.'

—Conrad must here stand convicted of borrowing the arts of the magazine-writer (who has borrowed his, shall we say, from Kipling and Poe) in order to impose on his readers and on himself, for thrilled response, a 'significance' that is merely an emotional insistence on the presence of what he can't produce. The insistence betrays the absence, the willed 'intensity' the nullity. He is intent on making a virtue out of not knowing what he means. The vague and unrealizable, he asserts with a strained impressiveness, is the profoundly and tremendously significant:

'I've been telling you what we said—repeating the phrases we pronounced—but what's the good? They were common everyday words—the familiar vague sounds exchanged on every waking day of life. But what of that? They had behind them, to my mind, the terrific suggestiveness of words heard in dreams, of phrases spoken in nightmares.'

What's the good, indeed? If he cannot through the concrete presentment of incident, setting and image invest the words with the terrific something that, by themselves, they fail to convey, then no amount of adjectival and ejaculatory emphasis will do it.

> 'I saw the inconceivable mystery of a soul,' etc.

—That, of course, is an ambiguous statement. I see that there is a mystery, and it remains a mystery for me; I can't conceive what it is; and if I offer this inability to your wonder as a thrilling affair of 'seeing an inconceivable mystery,' I exemplify a common trait of human nature. Actually, Conrad had no need to try and inject 'significance' into his narrative in this way. What he shows himself to have successfully and significantly seen is enough to make *Heart of Darkness* a disturbing presentment of the kind he aimed at. By the attempt at injection he weakens, in his account of Kurtz's death, the effect of that culminating cry:

> 'He cried in a whisper at some image, at some vision —he cried out twice, a cry that was no more than a breath—"The horror! The horror!"'

—The 'horror' there has very much less force than it might have had if Conrad had strained less.

This final account of Kurtz is associated with a sardonic tone, an insistent irony that leads us on to another bad patch, the closing interview in Brussels with Kurtz's 'Intended':

> 'The room seemed to have grown darker, as if all the sad light of the cloudy evening had taken refuge on her forehead. This fair hair, this pale visage, this pure brow, seemed surrounded by an ashy halo from which the dark eyes looked out at me. Their glance was guileless, profound, confident, and trustful. She carried her sorrowful head as though she were proud of that sorrow, as though she would say, I—I alone know how to mourn for him as he deserves.'

It is not part of Conrad's irony that there should be anything ironical in this presentment of the woman. The irony lies in the association of her innocent nobility, her purity of idealizing faith, with the unspeakable corruption of Kurtz; and it is developed (if that is the word) with a thrilled insistence that recalls the melodramatic intensities of Edgar Allan Poe:

'I felt like a chill grip on my chest. "Don't," I said in a muffled voice.

'"Forgive me. I—I—have mourned so long in silence —in silence. . . . You were with him—to the last? I think of his loneliness. Nobody near to understand him as I would have understood. Perhaps no one to hear. . . ."

'"To the very end," I said shakily. "I heard his very last words. . . ." I stopped in a fright.

'"Repeat them," she murmured in a heart-broken tone.

'"I want—I want—something—something to live with."

'I was on the point of crying at her "Don't you hear them?" The dark was repeating them in a persistent whisper all around us, in a whisper that seemed to swell menacingly, like the first whisper of a rising wind. "The horror! the horror!"

'"His last words—to live with," she insisted. "Don't you understand I loved him—I loved him—I loved him!"

'I pulled myself together and spoke slowly.

'"The last word he pronounced was—your name."

'I heard a light sigh and then my heart stood still, stopped dead short by an exulting and terrible cry, by the cry of inconceivable triumph and of an unspeakable pain.

'"I knew it—I was sure!" . . . She knew. She was sure.'

Conrad's 'inscrutable,' it is clear, associates with Woman as it does with the wilderness, and the thrilling mystery of the Intended's innocence is of the same order as the thrilling mystery of Kurtz's corruption: the profundities are complementary. It would appear that the cosmopolitan Pole, student of the French masters, who became a British master-mariner, was in some respects a simple soul. If anyone should be moved to question the propriety of this way of putting it, perhaps the following will be found something of a justification:

> 'Woman and the sea revealed themselves to me together, as it were: two mistresses of life's values. The illimitable greatness of the one, the unfathomable seduction of the other, working their immemorial spells from generation to generation fell upon my heart at last: a common fortune, an unforgettable memory of the sea's formless might and of the sovereign charm in that woman's form wherein there seemed to beat the pulse of divinity rather than blood.'

This comes from a bad novel, one of Conrad's worst things, *The Arrow of Gold*. It is a sophisticated piece of work, with a sophistication that elaborates and aggravates the deplorable kind of naïvety illustrated in the quotation. Not that the author's talent doesn't appear, but the central theme—and the pervasive atmosphere—is the 'unfathomable seduction' of the 'enigmatic' Rita; a glamorous mystery, the evocation of which (though more prolonged and elaborated) is of the same order as the evocation of sinister significance, the 'inconceivable' mystery of Kurtz, at the close of *Heart of Darkness*. If any reader of that tale had felt that the irony permitted a doubt regarding Conrad's attitude towards the Intended, the presentment of Rita should settle it.

'Woman' figures in *The Rescue*, the book that in publication preceded *The Arrow of Gold* (both came out just after the 1914 war, though *The Rescue* belongs essentially to Conrad's early period). The glamour here is a simpler affair—less sophisticated and more innocent. But if *The Rescue* lacks the positive badness of *The Arrow of Gold*, it is, on a grand scale, boring in its innocence. The seduction of Woman as represented by Mrs. Travers is less insistently and melodramatically 'unfathomable' than in the

later book, but cannot sustain the interest Conrad demands
for it; so to say that it is, in the formal design, adequate to
balancing Heroic Action as represented by Lingard—King
Tom, idealized seaman-adventurer—is not to say anything
very favourable about the whole. *The Rescue,* in short,
is an Academy piece—'sombre, colourful, undeniably a
classic' the reviewers may have said, and its Grand Style
staging of the conflict between Love and Honour (a king-
dom at stake) against a sumptuously rendered *décor* of
tropical sea, sunset, and jungle is, in its slow and conscientious magnificence, calculated to engender more deference than thrill, and so can't even be recommended as
good boy's reading—though it offers little to adults. The
book, in fact, is not altogether a surprising kind of thing
to have come from a sailor of pertinacious literary talent
and French literary education. The reason for bringing it
in just here is to enforce the point that Conrad, for all his
sophistication, exhibits a certain simplicity of outlook and
attitude. About his attitude towards women there is perceptible, all the way through his literary career, something
of the gallant simple sailor.

The sailor in him, of course, is rightly held to be a main
part of his strength. It is not for nothing that *Heart of
Darkness,* a predominantly successful tale, is told by the
captain of the steamboat—told from that specific and concretely realized point of view: appraisal of the success of
the tale is bound up with this consideration. But the stress
up till now has fallen upon Conrad's weaknesses. It is
time to ask where the strength may be found in its purest
form. There will, I think, be general approval of the choice
of *Typhoon* as a good example. But I am not sure that
there is as general a recognition of just where the strength
of *Typhoon* lies. The point may be made by saying that it
lies not so much in the famous description of the elemental
frenzy as in the presentment of Captain MacWhirr, the
chief mate Jukes and the chief engineer Solomon Rout
at the opening of the tale. Of course, it is a commonplace
that Conrad's distinctive genius comprises a gift for rendering the British seaman. But is it a commonplace that

the gift is the specific gift of a novelist, and (though the
subtler artist doesn't run to caricature and the fantastic)
relates Conrad to Dickens? Consider, for instance, this:

'He was rather below the medium height, a bit round-
shouldered, and so sturdy of limb that his clothes always
looked a shade too tight for his arms and legs. As if unable to grasp what is due to the difference of latitudes,
he wore a brown bowler hat, a complete suit of a brown-
ish hue, and clumsy black boots. These harbour togs
gave to his thick figure an air of stiff and uncouth
smartness. A thin silver watch-chain looped his waistcoat, and he never left his ship for the shore without
clutching in his powerful, hairy fist an elegant umbrella of the very best quality, but generally unrolled.
Young Jukes, the chief mate, attending his commander
to the gangway, would sometimes venture to say, with
the greatest gentleness, "Allow me, sir,"—and, possessing
himself of the umbrella deferentially, would elevated
the ferrule, shake the folds, twirl a neat furl in a jiffy,
and hand it back: going through the performance with a
face of such portentous gravity, that Mr. Solomon Rout,
the chief engineer, smoking his morning cigar over the
skylight, would turn away his head in order to hide a
smile. "Oh! aye! The blessed gamp. . . . Thank 'ee,
Jukes, thank 'ee," would mutter Captain MacWhirr
heartily, without looking up.'

Consider the exchanges between Captain MacWhirr
and Jukes over the Siamese flag, deplorably, poor Jukes
feels ('Fancy having a ridiculous Noah's ark elephant in
the ensign of one's ship'), substituted for the Red Ensign.
Consider the accounts of the home backgrounds of Mac-
Whirr and the chief engineer.

It is to be noted further that these backgrounds in their
contrast with the main theme of the tale afford a far more
satisfactory irony (it is, in fact, supremely effective) than
that, in *Heart of Darkness,* of the scenes at Brussels. At
the same time it is to be noted that there is in *Typhoon* no
sardonic Marlow, commenting on an action that he is

made to project; whereas, though *Heart of Darkness* is given from the point of view of the captain of the steamboat, that captain *is* Marlow—Marlow, for whom Conrad has more than one kind of use, and who is both more and less than a character and always something other than just a master-mariner. For comment in *Typhoon* we have the letters home of Solomon Rout, the chief engineer, and the letter of Jukes to his chum. In short, nothing in the story is forced or injected; the significance is not adjectival, but resides in the presented particulars—the actors, the incidents and the total action: we are given the ship, her cargo and her crew of ordinary British seamen, and the impact on them of the storm.

The ordinariness is, with a novelist's art, kept present to us the whole time; the particular effect of heroic sublimity depends on that.

> 'And again he heard that voice, forced and ringing feeble, but with a penetrating effect of quietness in the enormous discord of noises, as if sent out from some remote spot of peace beyond the black wastes of the gale; again he heard a man's voice—the frail and indomitable sound that can be made to carry an infinity of thought, resolution and purpose, that shall be pronouncing confident words on the last day, when heavens fall, and justice is done—again he heard it, and it was crying to him, as if from very, very far—"All right."'

—Conrad can permit himself this, because the voice is that of the unheroically matter-of-fact Captain MacWhirr, whose solid specific presence, along with that of particularized ordinary sailors and engineers, we are never allowed to forget:

> 'A lull had come, a menacing lull of the wind, the holding of a stormy breath—and he felt himself pawed all over. It was the boatswain. Jukes recognized these hands, so thick and enormous that they seemed to belong to some new species of man.
>
> 'The boatswain had arrived on the bridge, crawling

on all fours against the wind, and had found the chief
mate's legs with the top of his head. Immediately he
crouched and began to explore Jukes' person upwards,
with prudent, apologetic touches, as became an inferior.'

Or take this:

'The boatswain by his side kept on yelling. "What?
What is it?" Jukes cried distressfully; and the other repeated, "What would my old woman say if she saw me
now?"

'In the alleyway, where a lot of water had got in and
splashed in the dark, the men were still as death, till
Jukes stumbled against one of them and cursed him sav-
agely for being in the way. Two or three voices then
asked, eager and weak, "Any chance for us, sir?"

' "What's the matter with you fools?" he said brutally.
He felt as though he could throw himself down amongst
them and never move any more. But they seemed
cheered; and in the midst of obsequious warning. "Look
out! Mind that manhole lid, sir," they lowered him into
the bunker. The boatswain tumbled down after him,
and as soon as he had picked himself up he remarked
"She would say, 'Serve you right, you old fool, for going
to sea.' "

'The boatswain had some means, and made a point of
alluding to them frequently. His wife—a fat woman—
and two grown-up daughters kept a greengrocer's shop
in the East-end of London.'

The seamen are their ordinary selves, the routine goes
forward in the engine-room, and the heroic triumphs of
the *Nan-Shan* emerge as matters-of-fact out of the ordinariness:

' "Can't have . . . fighting . . . board ship," '

says Captain MacWhirr through the typhoon, and down
into the 'tween-deck, into the human hurricane of fighting

coolies, go Jukes and his men as a routine matter-of-fact course, to restore order and decency:

> '"We have done it, sir," he gasped.
> '"Thought you would," said Captain MacWhirr.
> '"Did you?" murmured Jukes to himself.
> '"Wind fell all at once," went on the Captain.
> 'Jukes burst out: "If you think it was an easy job—"
> 'But his captain, clinging to the rail, paid no attention.
> '"According to the books the worse is not over yet."'

And the qualities which, in a triumph of discipline—a triumph of the spirit—have enabled a handful of ordinary men to impose sanity on a frantic mob are seen unquestionably to be those which took Captain MacWhirr, in contempt of 'Storm-strategy,' into the centre of the typhoon. Without any symbolic portentousness the Captain stands there the embodiment of a tradition. The crowning triumph of the spirit, in the guise of a matter-of-fact and practical sense of decency, is the redistribution—ship devastated, men dropping with fatigue—of the gathered-up and counted dollars among the assembled Chinese.

In *The Shadow-Line*, also in common recognition one of Conrad's masterpieces (it is, I think, superior to *Heart of Darkness* and even to *Typhoon*), we have the same art. It has been acclaimed as a kind of prose *Ancient Mariner*, and it is certainly a supremely sinister and beautiful evocation of enchantment in tropic seas. But the art of the evocation is of the kind that has been described; it is not a matter of engendering 'atmosphere' adjectivally, by explicitly 'significant' vaguenesses, insistent unutterablenesses, or the thrilled tone of an expository commentator, but of presenting concretely a succession of particulars from the point of view of the master of the ship, who, though notably sensitive, is not a Marlow, but just a ship's master; an actor among the other actors, though burdened with responsibilities towards the crew, owners and ship. The distinctive art of a novelist, and the art upon which the success of the prose *Ancient Mariner* essentially depends, is apparent in the rendering of personality, its re-actions and vibrations; the pervasive presence of the crew, delicately particularized, will turn out on analysis to account for the major part of the atmosphere. The young captain, entering the saloon for the first time and sitting in the captain's chair, finds he is looking into a mirror:

'Deep within the tarnished ormolu frame, in the hot half-light sifted through the awning, I saw my own face propped between my hands. And I stared back at myself with the perfect detachment of distance, rather with curiosity than with any other feeling, except of some sympathy for this latest representative of what for all intents and purposes was a dynasty; continuous not in blood, indeed, but in its experience, in its training, in its conception of duty, and in the blessed simplicity of its traditional point of view on life. . . .

'Suddenly I perceived that there was another man in the saloon, standing a little on one side and looking intently at me. The chief mate. His long, red moustache determined the character of his physiognomy, which struck me as pugnacious in (strange to say) a ghastly sort of way.'

The disobliging and disturbing oddity of the mate turns out to be due to the sinister vagaries and unseemly end of the late captain:

'That man had been in all essentials but his age just such another man as myself. Yet the end of his life was a complete act of treason, the betrayal of a tradition which seemed to me as imperative as any guide on earth could be. It appeared that even at sea a man could become the victim of evil spirits. I felt on my face the breath of unknown powers that shape our destinies.'

The sinister spell that holds the ship is characteristically felt in terms of contrast with the tradition and its spiritual values, these being embodied in the crew, a good one, who carry on staunchly against bad luck and disease. The visiting doctor himself is 'good' in the same way. The story ends, it will be noted, on the unexpected parting with the faithful Ransome, the exquisitely rendered seaman with a voice that is 'extremely pleasant to hear' and a weak heart:

> ' "But, Ransome," I said, "I hate the idea of parting with you."
> ' "I must go," he broke in. "I have a right!" He gasped and a look of almost savage determination passed over his face. For an instant he was another being. And I saw under the worth and the comeliness of the man the humble reality of things. Life was a boon to him—this precarious, hard life—and he was thoroughly alarmed about himself.
> ' "Of course I shall pay you off if you wish it."

> *   *   *   *   *   *

> 'I approached him with extended hand. His eyes, not looking at me, had a strained expression. He was like a man listening for a warning call.
> ' "Won't you shake hands, Ransome?" I said gently. He exclaimed, flushed up dusky red, gave my hand a hard wrench—and next moment, left alone in the cabin, I listened to him going up the companion stairs cautiously, step by step, in mortal fear of starting into sudden anger our common enemy it was his hard fate to carry consciously within his faithful breast.'

These things are worth many times those descriptions of sunsets, exotic seas and the last plunge of flaming wrecks which offer themselves to the compilers of prose anthologies.

This is at any rate to confirm the accepted notion of Conrad to this extent: that his genius was a unique and happy union of seaman and writer. If he hadn't actually been himself a British seaman by vocation he couldn't have done the Merchant Service from the inside. The cosmopolitan of French culture and French literary initiation is there in the capacity for detachment that makes the intimate knowledge uniquely conscious and articulate. We are aware of the artist by vocation, the intellectual who doubles the seaman, only when we stop to take stock of the perfection of the rendering and the subtle finish of the art.

But this fine balance, this identity, isn't always sustained. In Marlow, who (as remarked above) has a variety of uses, the detachment is separated off. As a main participant in events though, by his specific rôle as such, a detached one, he gives his technical function a dramatic status in the action, and the author a freedom of presence that, as we have seen, constitutes a temptation. Elsewhere Marlow is frankly a method of projection or presentation —one that we learn to associate with Conrad's characteristic vices and weaknesses. In *Youth,* for instance, one of the best-known of the tales, though not one of the best, he goes with the cheap insistence on the glamour, and with that tone which, here and in other places, makes one recall the formula of the early reviewer and reflect that the prose laureate of the British seaman does sometimes degenerate into a 'Kipling of the South Seas.' (And this is the point at which to note that Conrad can write shockingly bad magazine stuff—see the solemnly dedicated collection called *Within the Tides.*)

In *Lord Jim* Marlow is the means of presenting Jim with the appropriate externality, seen always through the question, the doubt, that is the central theme of the book. Means and effect are unobjectionable; it is a different matter from the use of Marlow elsewhere to pass off a vaguely excited incomprehension as tremendous significance. But *Lord Jim* doesn't deserve the position of pre-eminence among Conrad's works often assigned it: it is hardly one of the most considerable. There is, in fact, much to be said in support of those reviewers who (Conrad tells us) 'maintained that the work starting as a short story had got beyond the writer's control,' so that what we have is neither a very considerable novel, in spite of its 420 pages, nor one of Conrad's best short stories. The presentment of Lord Jim in the first part of the book, the account of

the inquiry and of the desertion of the *Patna,* the talk
with the French lieutenant—these are good Conrad. But
the romance that follows, though plausibly offered as a
continued exhibition of Jim's case, has no inevitability as
that; nor does it develop or enrich the central interest,
which consequently, eked out to provide the substance of
a novel, comes to seem decidedly thin.

The eking out is done mainly from the world of *Almay-
er's Folly, An Outcast of the Islands,* and *Tales of Unrest,*
those excessively adjectival studies in the Malayan exotic
of Conrad's earliest vein. Those things, it had better be
said here, though they are innocuous, and no doubt deserved for their originality of setting some respectful
notice when they came out, will not be urged by judicious
admirers of Conrad among his claims to classical rank. In
their stylistic eloquence, which suggests a descent from
Chateaubriand, their wearying exoticism, and their 'picturesque' human interest, they aren't easy to re-read.

No, *Lord Jim* is neither the best of Conrad's novels, nor
among the best of his short stories. If, on the other hand,
his most considerable work had had due recognition, it
would be known as one of the great novels of the language. For *Nostromo* is most certainly that. And it complicates the account of Conrad's genius in that it doesn't
answer to the formula arrived at above. He is not here the
laureate of the Merchant Service, the British seaman happily doubled with the artist—an artist whose 'outsideness'
with regard to the Merchant Service is to be constated
only in the essential degree of detachment involved in an
adequately recording art. In *Nostromo* Conrad is openly
and triumphantly the artist by *métier,* conscious of French
initiation and of fellowship in craft with Flaubert. The
French element so oddly apparent in his diction and idiom
throughout his career (he learnt French before English)
here reveals its full significance, being associated with so
serious and severe a conception of the art of fiction.

The controlling conception of the novelist's art is severe,
but the novel is luxuriant in its magnificence: it is Conrad's supreme triumph in the evocation of exotic life and

colour. Sulaco, standing beneath snow-clad Higuerota, with its population of Indians, mixed-bloods, Hidalgos, Italians and English engineers, is brought before us in irresistible reality, along with the picturesque and murderous public drama of a South American State. This aspect of Conrad's genius in *Nostromo* has had full recognition; indeed it could hardly be missed. What doesn't seem to be a commonplace is the way in which the whole book forms a rich and subtle but highly organized pattern. Every detail, character and incident has its significant bearing on the themes and motives of this. The magnificence referred to above addresses the senses, or the sensuous imagination; the pattern is one of moral significances.

Nostromo has a main political, or public, theme, the relation between moral idealism and 'material interests.' We see the Gould Concession become the rallying centre for all in Costaguana who desire peace and order—the constitutionalists, the patriotic idealists, the Robin Hood of the oppressed, the representatives of the financial power of Europe and North America. The ironical end of the book shows us a Sulaco in which order and ideals have triumphed, Progress forges ahead, and the all-powerful Concession has become the focus of hate for workers and the oppressed and a symbol of crushing materialism for idealists and defenders of the spirit. This public theme is presented in terms of a number of personal histories or, it might be said, private themes, each having a specific representative moral significance.

The Gould Concession is in the first place the personal history of its inheritor, Charles Gould—and the tragedy of his wife. He, like the other main characters, enacts a particular answer to the question that we feel working in the matter of the novel as a kind of informing and organizing principle: what do men find to live *for*—what kinds of motive force or radical attitude can give life meaning, direction, coherence? Charles Gould finds his answer in the ideal purpose he identifies with the success of the Gould Concession:

'What is wanted here is law, good faith, order, security. Anyone can declaim about these things, but I pin my faith to material interests. Only let the material interests once get a firm footing, and they are bound to impose the conditions on which alone they can continue to exist. That's how your money-making is justified here in the face of lawlessness and disorder. It is justified because the security which it demands must be shared with an oppressed people. A better justice will come afterwards. That's your ray of hope.'

Charles Gould's faith is parodied by his backer, the American financier Holroyd, whose interest in furthering a 'pure form of Christianity' and whose rhetorical faith in the manifest destiny of the United States cannot without irony be said to give ideal significance to his love of power. Charles himself is absorbed by the Concession that killed his father, and Emilia Gould, standing for personal relations and disinterested human sympathy, looks on in starved loneliness at the redeeming triumph that is an ironical defeat of the spirit.

Nostromo, picturesque indispensable to his patrons and popular hero, has no ideal purpose. He lives for reputation, 'to be well spoken of'—for his reflection in the eyes of others, and when, tempted by the silver, he condemns himself to clandestine courses the mainspring of his life goes slack. His return to find the new lighthouse standing on the lonely rock hard by his secret, and his consequent betrayal into devious paths in love, are magnificent and characteristic triumphs of symbolism. His appropriately melodramatic death is caused by the silver and occurs during a stealthy visit to it.

Martin Decoud, intellectual and 'dilettante in life,' Nostromo's companion in that marvellously rendered night of the Gulf (it is one of the most vivid pieces of sensuous evocation in literature), also has no ideal purpose. The voice of sceptical intelligence, with 'no faith in anything except the truth of his own sensations,' he enjoys conscious advantages, and has no difficulty in summing up Nostromo:

> 'Decoud, incorrigible in his scepticism, reflected, not cynically but with general satisfaction, that this man was made incorruptible by his enormous vanity, that finest form of egoism which can take on the aspect of every virtue.'

He can also place Charles Gould, that 'sentimental Englishman' who

> 'cannot exist without idealizing every simple desire or achievement. He could not believe his own motives if he did not make them first a part of some fairy tale.'

Decoud himself, contemptuously free from the 'sentimentalism of the people that will never do anything for the sake of their passionate desire, unless it comes to them clothed in the fair robes of an ideal,' is frankly moved by his passion for Antonio Avellanos, and that alone, when he initiates the step through which the mine is saved and the aims of the patriots and idealists achieved. In this respect he provides a criticism of Charles Gould's subtle infidelity to his wife. Yet, even apart from his passion, he is not quite self-sufficient. At a moment when we might have expected him to be wholly engrossed in practical considerations we find him, significantly, illustrating an essential human trait:

> 'all the objectless and necessary sincerity of one's innermost life trying to react upon the profound sympathies of another's existence.'

For

> 'In the most sceptical heart there lurks at such moments, when the chances of existence are involved, a desire to leave a correct impression of the feelings, like a light by which the action may be seen when personality is gone, gone where no light of investigation can ever reach the truth which every death takes out of the

world. Therefore, instead of looking for something to eat, or trying to snatch an hour or two of sleep, Decoud was filling the pages of a large pocket book with a letter to his sister.'

Marooned on the Great Isabel (site of the subsequent lighthouse) he discovers that his self-sufficiency is indeed radically qualified:

'Solitude from mere outward condition of existence becomes very swiftly a state of soul in which the affectations of irony and scepticism have no place. It takes possession of the mind, and drives forth the thought into the exile of utter unbelief. After three days of waiting for the sight of some human face, Decoud caught himself entertaining a doubt of his own individuality. It had merged into the world of cloud and water, of natural forces and forms of nature. . . .

'. . . He had recognized no other virtue than intelligence and had erected passions into duties. Both his intelligence and his passion were swallowed up easily in the great unbroken solitude of waiting without faith.'

He shoots himself. The whole episode is given in painful immediacy.

Of all the characters the one nearest to self-sufficiency is Dr. Monygham, the disliked and distrusted, and he, for all his sardonic scepticism about human nature, does hold to an ideal. His scepticism is based on self-contempt, for his ideal (he is, in fact, a stronger and quite unequivocal Lord Jim) is one he has offended against; it is an exacting ideal of conduct. He offers a major contrast with Nostromo too, since his success in the desperate venture that saves the situation and rehabilitates him (in his own eyes—he expects death) depends upon his having no reputation except for 'unsoundness' and a shady past, and his being ready to be ill-spoken of and ill-thought of. His ideal, of course, isn't merely personal—it is of the same order as the moral idea of the Merchant Service (he is 'an officer and a gentleman'): it owes its strength to a traditional and social sanction; and he has an outer stay in his devotion to Mrs. Gould.

Perhaps the completest antithesis to Decoud is Giorgio Viola, the serene old Garibaldino, also self-sufficient, or very near it—he by reason of his libertarian idealism, the disinterestedness of which is above all question. He represents with monumental massiveness the heroic age of the liberal faith—of *Songs before Sunrise* and the religion of humanity, and so provides a contrasting background for the representatives of Progress in Costaguana politics (by the end of *Nostromo* the Marxists are on the scene). He is commandingly real; but it is part of the irony of the book that the achievements he stands for should have produced the South America we are shown.

Captain Mitchell represents the Merchant Service. He is sane and stable to the point of stupidity. His inability to realize that he, Joe Mitchell ('I am a public character, sir'), has anything to fear from a ridiculously menacing Dago whose ruffians have stolen his presentation pocket-chronometer actually cows the all-powerful Dago into restoring both chronometer and freedom:

> 'The old sailor, with all his small weaknesses and absurdities, was constitutionally incapable of entertaining for any length of time a fear of his personal safety. It was not so much firmness of soul as the lack of a certain kind of imagination—the kind whose undue development caused intense suffering to Señor Hirsch; that sort of imagination which adds the blind terror of bodily suffering and of death, envisaged as an accident to the body alone, strictly—to all the other apprehensions on which the sense of one's existence is based. Unfortunately, Captain Mitchell had not much penetration of any kind; characteristic, illuminating trifles of expression, action, or movement, escaped him completely. He was too pompously and innocently aware of his own existence to observe that of others. For instance, he could not believe that Sotillo had been really afraid of him, and this simply because it would never have en-

tered into his head to shoot anyone except in the most pressing case of self-defence. Anybody could see he was not a murdering kind of man, he reflected quite gravely.'

These traits, it will be seen, qualify him for an essential function in the presentment of the action, to which he is related in a way symbolized by his triumphant sense—a sense uninformed by any comprehension of what is going forward—of being at the centre of things, whence history is directed, as he sits, an *habitué*, in Mrs. Gould's drawing-room.

On the significance of the other characters there is no need to enlarge: Señor Avellanos, the liberal idealist, who dies of disappointment, and the sheets of whose *Fifty Years of Misrule* are 'fired out as wads for trabucos loaded with handfuls of type' during the 'democratic' *émeute*; the fanatical Father Corbelàn; Hirsch, the embodiment of fear, and so on. Instead, a negative point had better be made by way of stressing the distinctive nature of the impressiveness of *Nostromo*. The impressiveness is not a matter of any profundity of search into human experience, or any explorative subtlety in the analysis of human behaviour. It is a matter rather of the firm and vivid concreteness with which the representative attitudes and motives are realized, and the rich economy of the pattern that plays them off against one another. To suggest, as Edward Garnett does in his introduction to *Conrad's Prefaces*, that perhaps this or that character wouldn't really have behaved just as he does in the book is misdirected criticism. The life-like convincingness of Conrad's persons (which is complete as we read, and undisturbed by properly critical reflection) doesn't entitle us to psychologize them as lives existing outside the book. I am reminded of certain remarks of T. S. Eliot's:

'A "living" character is not necessarily "true to life." It is a person whom we can see and hear, whether he be true or false to human nature as we know it. What the creator of character needs is not so much knowledge of motives as keen sensibility; the dramatist need not

JOSEPH CONRAD

understand people, but he must be exceptionally aware of them.'

It is an Elizabethan dramatist Eliot has in front of him; and it strikes me that there is something that recalls the strength of Elizabethan drama about the art of *Nostromo* —something Shakespearean, in fact. The keen sensibility and the exceptional awareness are apparent in the vividness with which we see and hear Conrad's persons, and there is nothing about them that, on reflection, we find untrue to human nature as we know it. But the seeing and hearing is adequate understanding: they are present to us and are plainly what they are; and to try, by way of appreciation or criticism, to go behind that is to misunderstand what the book offers us. There is plainly no room in *Nostromo* for the kind of illustrated psychology that many critics think they have a right to demand of a novelist (and of Shakespeare). Consider the number of personal centres of moral interest, and the variety of themes. Consider the number of vivid dramatic scenes and episodes. Consider the different strands that go to the totality of the action. There is the private tragedy of the Goulds; there is Nostromo's history, involving that of the Viola family; there is the story of Decoud and Antonia; there is that of Dr. Monygham and his self-rehabilitation; and all these and so much else are subsumed in the public historical drama—the study, concretely rendered, of the play of moral and material forces, political and personal motives, in the founding of the Occidental Republic.

Clearly, Conrad's study of motives, and of the relation between the material and the spiritual, doesn't depend for its impressiveness on any sustained analytic exhibition of the inner complexities of the individual psyche. The impressiveness lies in the vivid reality of the things we are made to see and hear, and the significance they get from their relations in a highly organized and vividly realized whole. It lies in such effects as that of the presence of Decoud and Nostromo in the lighter as it drifts with its load of silver and of Fear (personified by the stowaway

Hirsch) through the black night of the Gulf; and that of the unexpected nocturnal encounter between Nostromo and Dr. Monygham, two sharply contrasted consciousnesses, in the vast deserted Custom House, and their discovery that the 'shapeless high-shouldered shadow of somebody standing still, with lowered head' seen on the wall through a doorway, is thrown by the hanging body of the tortured Hirsch. We have it characteristically when Charles Gould, going out from his interview (consummate satiric comedy) with Pedrito Montero, would-be Duc de Morny to the new Napoleon, runs into the 'constitutionalist' deputation he has refused to support ('The acceptance of accomplished facts may save yet the precious vestiges of parliamentary institutions'):

'Charles Gould on going out passed his hand over his forehead as if to disperse the mists of an oppressive dream, whose grotesque extravagance leaves behind a subtle sense of bodily danger and intellectual decay. In the passages and on the staircases of the old palace Montero's troopers lounged about insolently, smoking and making way for no one; the clanking of sabres and spurs resounded all over the building. Three silent groups of civilians in severe black waited in the main gallery, formal and helpless; a little huddled up, each keeping apart from the others, as if in the exercise of a public duty they had been overcome by a desire to shun the notice of every eye. These were the deputations waiting for their audience. The one from the Provincial Assembly, more restless and uneasy in its corporate expression, was overtopped by the big face of Don Juste Lopez, soft and white, with prominent eyelids and wreathed in impenetrable solemnity as if in a dense cloud. The President of the Provincial Assembly, coming bravely to save the last shred of parliamentary institutions (on the English model), averted his eyes from the Administrador of the San Tomé mine as a dignified rebuke of his little faith in that only saving principle.'

Charles Gould's quiet unyieldingness in the face of Pe-

drito's threats and blandishments has already invested him
for the moment with a larger measure of our sympathy
than he in general commands. The brush with the deputation confirms this effect, while at the same time reinforcing
dramatically that pattern of political significance which
has a major part in *Nostromo*—a book that was written, we
remind ourselves in some wonder, noting the topicality of
its themes, analysis and illustrations, in the reign of Edward VII.

Again, we have the symbolic pregnancy of Conrad's
dramatic method in such a representative touch as this
(the context is the flight of aristocrats and adherents of
'law and order' to the protection of the 'master of the
Campo'):

> 'The emissary of Hernandez spurred his horse close
> up.
> ' "Has not the master of the mine any message to send
> the master of the Campo?"
> 'The truth of the comparison struck Charles Gould
> heavily. In his determined purpose he held the mine
> and the indomitable bandit held the Campo by the same
> precarious tenure. They were equals before the lawless-
> ness of the land. It was impossible to disentangle one's
> activities from its debasing contacts.'

There is—the adjective proposes itself at this point—
something rhetorical, in a wholly laudatory sense, about
Conrad's art in *Nostromo*. One might add, by way of insisting further on the Elizabethan in it, that it has a certain
robust vigour of melodrama. The melodrama, of course, is
completely controlled to the pattern of moral significance.
Consider, for instance, how the climax of the public
drama is given us: it is a thrilling nick-of-time *peripeteia*,
but it is given in retrospect through the pompous show-
manship and uncomprehending importance of Captain
Mitchell ('Fussy Joe'). The triumphs of the Progress he
hymns are already assured and commonplace, and already
(a few pages on) Dr. Monygham is asking:

'"Do you think that now the mine would march upon the town to save their Señor Administrador? Do you think that?"'

He has just pronounced:

'"There is no peace and no rest in the development of material interests. They have their law, and their justice. But it is founded on expediency, and it is inhuman; it is without rectitude, without the continuity and the force that can be found only in a moral principle."'

This is only one instance of that subtle play of the order of presentment against the time-order which the reader finds himself admiring in the book as a whole—subtle, yet, once taken stock of, appreciated as inevitable. It is characteristic of Conrad's method, to take another instance, that we should have seen, in a prospective glimpse given us at the very opening of the book, the pitiable *débâcle* of the Ribierist dictatorship of 'reform' before we are invited to contemplate the hopes and enthusiasms of its supporters at the inauguration.

It will probably be expected, after so much insistence on the moral pattern of *Nostromo,* that something will be said about the total significance. What, as the upshot of this exhibition of human motive and attitude, do we feel Conrad himself to endorse? What are his positives? It is easier to say what he rejects or criticizes. About the judgment on Decoud's scepticism we can have no doubt. And even Decoud concedes that the illusions 'those Englishmen' live on 'somehow or other help them to get a firm hold of the substance.' To this concession we can relate the observations of the engineer-in-chief:

'"Upon my word, doctor, things seem to be worth nothing by what they are in themselves. I begin to believe that the only solid thing about them is the spiritual value which everyone discovers in his own form of activity—"
'"Bah!" interrupted the doctor.'

The engineer has in mind Holroyd the millionaire and his preoccupation with a 'pure form of Christianity.' But although Dr. Monygham, himself devoted to a moral idea, is as such clearly not disapproved by the author, he is made to seem Quixotic, and it is difficult to feel that the ironic light in which the 'spiritual values' discovered by the other main characters in their forms of activity are shown is less essentially dissociating than the irony focussed upon Holroyd. In fact, though Decoud is so decisively dealt with in the action, he remains at the centre of the book, in the sense that his consciousness seems to permeate it, even to dominate it. That consciousness is clearly very closely related to the author's own personal *timbre*, that which becomes representable in quotation in such characteristic sardonic touches as:

> 'They had stopped near the cage. The parrot, catching the sound of a word belonging to his vocabulary, was moved to interfere. Parrots are very human.
> ' "Viva Costaguana!" he shrieked. . . .'

It is not a question of a 'philosophy'; Conrad cannot be said to have one. He is not one of those writers who clear up their fundamental attitudes for themselves in such a way that we may reasonably, in talking of them, use that portentous term. He does believe intensely, as a matter of concrete experience, in the kind of human achievement represented by the Merchant Service—tradition, discipline and moral ideal; but he has also a strong sense, not only of the frailty, but of the absurdity or unreality, in relation to the surrounding and underlying gulfs, of such achievement, a sense so strong that it often seems very close to Decoud's radical scepticism, which is, in the account of those last days, rendered with such significant power. In fact, Decoud may be said to have had a considerable part in the writing of *Nostromo*; or one might say that *Nostromo* was written by a Decoud who wasn't a complacent dilettante, but was positively drawn towards those capable of 'investing their activities with spiritual value'—Monygham, Giorgio Viola, Señor Avellanos, Charles Gould.

At any rate, for all the rich variety of the interest and the tightness of the pattern, the reverberation of *Nostromo* has something hollow about it; with the colour and life there is a suggestion of a certain emptiness. And for explanation it is perhaps enough to point to this reflection of Mrs. Gould's:

> 'It had come into her mind that for life to be large and full, it must contain the care of the past and of the future in every passing moment of the present.'

That kind of self-sufficient day-to-dayness of living Conrad can convey, when writing from within the Merchant Service, where clearly he has known it. We are made aware of hostile natural forces threatening his seamen with extinction, but not of metaphysical gulfs opening under life and consciousness: reality on board ship is domestic, assured and substantial. 'That feeling of life-emptiness which had made me so restless for the last few months,' says the young captain of *The Shadow-Line*, entering on his new command, 'lost its bitter plausibility, its evil influence.' For life in the Merchant Service there is no equivalent in *Nostromo*—no intimate sense conveyed of the day-by-day continuities of social living. And though we are given a confidential account of what lies behind Dr. Monygham's sardonic face, yet on the whole we see the characters from the outside, and only as they belong to the ironic pattern—figures in the futilities of a public drama, against a dwarfing background of mountain and gulf.

This kind of vision, this sense of life, corresponds, there can be no doubt, to something radical in Conrad. All his readers must have noticed how recurrent and important the theme of isolation is in his work. And they must have noticed too the close relation between the Decoud consciousness and the sympathetic hero of *Victory*, the English-speaking Swede, Axel Heyst.

JOSEPH CONRAD

(ii) *'Victory,' 'The Secret Agent,' 'Under Western Eyes,' and 'Chance'*

Heyst, 'uprooted' (his own word) and unattached, formed by a philosophically disillusioned father,

> 'in solitude and silence had been used to think clearly and sometimes even profoundly, seeing life outside the flattering delusion of everlasting hope, of conventional self-deception, of an ever-expected happiness.'

Having, in spite of himself, contracted a tie (the novel deals with his unwilling involvements and their consequences), he finds that 'that human being, so near and still so strange, gave him a greater sense of his own reality than he had ever known in all his life.' *Victory* is a study of Heyst's case; he is indisputably at the centre of the book. While he is wholly sympathetic in his scepticism, as Decoud is not, that scepticism presents itself as specifically conditioned, and, in the upshot of the action, it is renounced. A certain ambiguity does all the same attend it: Heyst's irony is dramatically rendered, yet it merges into the author's own—an intimate relation becomes at times unmistakable:

> 'The young man learned to reflect, which is a destructive process, a reckoning of the cost. It is not the clear-sighted who rule the world. Great achievements are accomplished in a blessed, warm mental fog, which the pitiless cold blast of the father's analysis had blown away from the son.'

—That is the author's own voice, and the tone is characteristic. Of Schomberg's infatuation we are told, a page later, by a Conrad whose relation to Heyst's father is plain:

> 'Forty-five is the age of recklessness for many men, as

if in defiance of the decay and death waiting with open arms in the sinister valley at the bottom of the inevitable hill. For every age is fed on illusions, lest men should renounce life early and the human race come to an end.'

Schomberg is in every way unadmirable: what we recognize in this tone is the Heyst-MacWhirr or Decoud-Mitchell antithesis—an antithesis that is implicit in the characteristic Conradian irony.

However, Conrad in *Victory* doesn't rest at that antithesis. Intelligence and fine consciousness in Heyst are represented as very specially conditioned; perverted, in fact, by the influence of a father who is a kind of genius of disillusion, and the 'victory' is a victory over scepticism, a victory of life. The tragic irony that makes it come too late and identifies it with death doesn't make it less a victory; it is unequivocal:

'"Ah, Davidson, woe to the man whose heart has not learned while young to hope, to love—and to put its trust in life."'

The process, a progressive self-discovery through relations with others, by which Heyst arrives here is rendered with poignant insight and convincing subtlety. To avoid the indignities, follies and illusions of involvement in life he has prescribed for himself an aloof self-sufficiency:

'Heyst was not conscious of either friends or of enemies. It was the essence of his life to be a solitary achievement, accomplished not by hermit-like withdrawal with its silence and immobility, but by a system of restless wandering, by the detachment of an impermanent dweller amongst changing scenes. In this scheme he had perceived the means of passing through life without suffering and almost without a single care in the world—invulnerable because elusive!'

But the wisdom of this scheme turns out to be inadequate, and life convicts Heyst of lack of self-knowledge. With his intelligence and moral fastidiousness goes a sensitive quickness of sympathy:

> 'No decent feeling was ever scorned by Heyst.'

That is the author's way of putting it. But Heyst is precluded from realizing the significance of this part of his make-up by habit, the persisting influence of his father, which may be represented by this:

> ' "You still believe in something, then," he said, in a clear voice, which had been growing feebler of late. "You believe in flesh and blood, perhaps? A full and equable contempt would soon do away with that too. But since you have not attained to it, I advise you to cultivate that form of contempt which is called pity." '

Moved by an irresistible sympathetic impulse that is of the essence of the self-respect that qualifies him for 'contempt,' Heyst comes to the rescue of the cornered Morrison, and the history—it is at first a comedy—of his unwilling involvement begins. Morrison, himself a quixotically sensitive and generous man (an admirable piece of Conradian characterization, realized in a physical presence with Conrad's Dickensian vividness—'He was tall and lantern-jawed and clean-shaven, and looked like a barrister who had thrown his wig to the dogs'), is overcome with the thought of his inability to repay Heyst:

> 'Poor Morrison actually laid his head on the cabin table, and remained in that crushed attitude while Heyst talked to him soothingly with the utmost courtesy. The Swede was as much distressed as Morrison, for he understood the other's feelings perfectly. No decent feeling was ever scorned by Heyst. But he was incapable of outward cordiality of manner, and he felt acutely his defeat. Consummate politeness is not the right tonic for an emotional collapse. They must have had, both of them, a fairly painful time of it in the cabin of the brig.'

The tragi-comedy of their relations is given us foreshortened, with admirable economy. When, early in the book, the second stage of Heyst's re-education opens we find him among the forlorn vestiges of the Tropical Coal Belt Company, the optimistic commercial enterprise that his combined generosity, indifference, and inexperience of mutuality in personal relations have made him unable to resist being drawn into. He is troubled with a sense of remorse over Morrison's death, which was the merest matter of ill-chance, and this sense associates intimately with a hurt feeling of having betrayed his own life, 'which ought to have been a masterpiece of aloofness.' In fact, his long-established equilibrium has been permanently upset; his uneasiness is an obscure recognition of radical discrepancies between his 'scheme' and the necessities of his own nature. Having resolved to keep himself out of reach of further involvements, he discovers with surprise that he now feels lonely:

'Where could he have gone to after all these years? Not a single soul belonging to him lived anywhere on earth. Of this fact—not such a remote one, after all—he had only lately become aware; for it is failure that makes a man enter into himself and reckon up his resources. And though he had made up his mind to retire from the world in hermit fashion, yet he was irrationally moved by this sense of loneliness which had come to him in the hour of renunciation. It hurt him. Nothing is more painful than the shock of contradictions that lacerate our intelligence and our feelings.'

It is in this state that Heyst, making a winding-up call at Sourabaya, finds himself exposed once more to a claim on his humanity. The inevitability of the plunge that he once more takes, this time before our eyes, is brought poignantly home to us. The whole episode, with its circumstances and setting, is rendered in irresistible immediacy: the torrid desolation of the hotel, the malicious asininity of the manly bearded Schomberg, hotel-keeper and Officer of the Reserve, the limp subjection of his poor charmless rag of a wife, the squalidly sinister Zangiacomos,

with their travelling concert-party, and the hopeless isolation of the girl-member who has the ill-luck to touch off
Schomberg's inflamed importunities—the present reality of
all this gives us at the same time the contained sensitiveness and aloof distinction of Heyst who registers it all, and
his action comes as the one possible issue of the pressures
evoked. He carries the girl off to the island that was to
have been his hermitage.

> 'He had no illusions about her, but his sceptical mind
> was dominated by his heart.'

—That is the account of his relations with her that he
gives himself at the outset. The development of those relations and of his sense of them is the process of self-discovery. In spite of the limiting suggestion of the account
just quoted, the tenderness he feels towards the girl carries
with it, we have seen, 'a greater sense of his own reality
than he had ever known in all his life.' And on this
follows a discovery that he is not so self-sufficient morally
as he had supposed. To the delicately solicitous Davidson
he has said:

> '"I took this course of signalling to you, because to
> preserve appearances might be of the utmost impor-
> tance. Not to me, of course. I don't care what people
> may say, and of course no one can hurt me. I suppose I
> have done a certain amount of harm, since I allowed
> myself to be tempted into action. It seemed innocent
> enough, but all action is bound to be harmful. It is
> devilish. That is why the world is evil upon the whole.
> But I have done with it! I shall never lift a little finger
> again."'

He is to discover, not only that he has not done with the
world and with action, but that he cares so much what
the world may say as to limit his capacity for action when
the urgent need confronts him. Unarmed, and menaced
by the sinister intruders upon the island, he deliberates:

> '"But what about that crowbar? Suppose I had it!

Could I stand in ambush at the side of the door—this door—and smash the first protruding head. . . . ? Could I? On suspicion, without compunction, with a firm and determined purpose? No, it is not in me. . . ."'

Then:

'"Do you know what the world would say?"
'"It would say that I—that Swede—after luring my friend and partner to his death from mere greed of money, have murdered those unoffending shipwrecked strangers from mere funk. That would be the story whispered—perhaps shouted—certainly spread out, and believed—and *believed*, my dear Lena!"'

That is the effect on Heyst of having learnt earlier from Lena, the girl, Schomberg's slanderous account of the death of Morrison. True, he says that the ruthless action ('And who knows if it isn't really my duty?') isn't 'in' him; but that he should associate his own scruple and inhibition with what people might say and believe is significant of the development he is undergoing.

Melodramatic as is the action of the latter part of the book (and so *seen*—and this is true of the whole book—as to invite the cinematographer), the focus of interest rests upon the subtleties of Heyst's relations with Lena. He finds himself committed to the establishment of a mutuality that is alien to the habit of a life-time—a habit concretely present in his voice and speech, which we hear as if we knew him:

'Heyst's tone was light, with the flavour of playfulness which seasoned all his speeches and seemed to be of the very essence of his thought.'

This tone and manner baffle and alarm the girl; but Heyst is the prisoner of his habit, and his efforts to escape constitute a poignant comedy. Attempting intimacy, he tells her about Morrison (this is before her shattering disclosure of Schomberg's account):

' "You saved a man for fun—is that what you mean? Just for fun?"

' "Why this tone of suspicion?" remonstrated Heyst. "I suppose the sight of this particular distress was disagreeable to me. What you call fun came afterwards, when it dawned on me that I was for him a walking, breathing, incarnate proof of the efficacy of prayer. I was a little fascinated by it—and then, could I have argued with him? You don't argue against such evidence, and besides, it would have looked as if I wanted to claim the merit. Already his gratitude was simply frightful. Funny position, wasn't it? The boredom came later, when we lived together on board his ship. I had, in a moment of inadvertence, created for myself a tie. How to define it precisely I don't know. One gets attached in a way to people one has done something for. But is that friendship? I am not sure what it was. I only know that he who forms a tie is lost. The germ of corruption has entered into his soul." '

In so far as she understands, this can serve only to heighten Lena's painful sense of insecurity—her doubt regarding his side of their relations with one another: he is a gentleman, he acted from pity—on what, then, can she build? His difficulty is not merely one of finding a suitable mode of expression; that he can talk like this in attempting intimacy gives us a measure of his inability to keep her realized as a concrete individual sentience to be communicated with—he is the old self-communing if sympathetic Heyst of 'kindness and scorn':

' "I don't even understand what I have done or left undone to distress you like this."

'He stopped, struck afresh by the physical and moral sense of the imperfection of their relations—a sense which made him desire her constant nearness, before his eyes, under his hand, and which, when she was out of his sight, made her so vague, so illusive and illusory, a promise that could not be embraced and held.

' "No! I don't see clearly what you mean. Is your mind

turned towards the future?" he interpellated her with
marked playfulness, because he was ashamed to let such
a word pass his lips. But all his cherished negatives
were falling from him one by one.'

Upon this situation supervenes, as if precipitated by his
'Nothing can break in on us here,' the sinister invasion—
the visit of the world, represented by the languid Jones,
his 'secretary' Ricardo and the anthropoid follower:

> ' "Here they are, the envoys of the outer world. Here
> they are before you—evil intelligence, instinctive savag-
> ery, arm in arm. The brute force is at the back." '

If doubts should arise about the melodramatic boldness
of this art (it is deliberately conceived—

> ' "No! Let it come!" Ricardo said viciously [of the
> thunderstorm that coincides with the dramatic crisis].
> "I am in the humour for it!" '),

it seems in place to refer back to considerations thrown
out above regarding the 'Elizabethan' qualities of Conrad's
art in *Nostromo*. It is true that *Victory,* which doesn't
pretend to the weight and scope of *Nostromo,* has nothing
corresponding to its packed and patterned structure of significances. Heyst is studied at length; yet it may be argued
that, convincing as he is, the extreme case that he is offered
as being really amounts to a kind of Morality representation of the human potentialities he embodies, so that he is
fittingly brought up against these embodiments of coun-
ter-potentialities. (Of Ricardo we are told that to Lena
'He was the embodied evil of the world.') And they too
are convincing (except for Ricardo's love-talk, and a
speech of Jones's); they belong to that aspect of Conrad's
art which makes us think of Dickens—a Dickens qualified
by a quite un-Dickensian maturity: they exist in strict
subservience to Conrad's quite un-Dickensian theme and
to their function, which is to precipitate Heyst's predicament to an issue in a conclusive action. At the worst we
might say about the resolution thus brought about that

it hasn't the finer inevitability—that which is never lacking
in the incomparably more complex and ambitious *Nostromo*: it is possible to reflect, on the one hand, that Heyst
had shocking bad luck in the coincidence of Jones and
Ricardo with Schomberg; and, on the other, that the antithesis of lust in Ricardo and woman-loathing in Jones
on which the *dénouement* depends has no irresistible significance in relation to Conrad's main theme.

But in any case the upshot of the action is to bring that
theme to a poignant crystallization. Lena, mortally
wounded (though unaware of it), but in triumphant possession of the dagger of which she has disarmed Ricardo,
dies 'convinced of the reality of her victory over death.'
Her relation with Heyst, whom she doesn't understand
and who doesn't understand her, has been enough to nerve
her for her dealings with the killer; 'she was no longer
alone now . . . she was no longer deprived of moral support.' Heyst, who knows her so little that he can
immediately before the end assume her to have betrayed
him, seduced by Ricardo's male fascinations, had nevertheless got from his relation with her that new sense of
reality, and now, after her death, makes to Davidson his
tragic pronouncement in favour of trust in life, before
firing the bungalow and himself dying in the flames. It is
an ironical victory for life, but unequivocally a victory.

The characteristic Conradian sensibility is that of the
creator of Heyst; that of the writer so intimately experienced in the strains and starvations of the isolated consciousness, and so deeply aware of the sense in which
reality is social, something established and sustained in a
kind of collaboration ('I have lived too long within myself,'
says Heyst, 'watching the mere shadows and shades of
life'). And complementary to Heyst, we realize, are Morrison and Davidson, upright, sensitive and humane individuals, in whom seems to be present a whole
background of routine sanity and decency—'we sailors,' the
feeling is; for Conrad is as much and as significantly *there*
as in Heyst. It is this background (which is reinforced, in
his own way, by Wang, the Chinaman) which makes the

intention of the 'victory' unequivocal. The voice that winds up the story in a brief account of the tragic end is Davidson's—Davidson's 'placid voice.'

If a work of so decidedly a lesser order than *Nostromo* has been given what may seem a disproportionate amount of space, that is because of the relation of Heyst to Decoud and to the distinctive tone of the great masterpiece, and the consequent advantage afforded the critic for the analysis of Conrad's sensibility. *Victory* is, at the same time, among those of Conrad's works which deserve to be current as representing his claim to classical standing; and of the novels (as distinguished from *nouvelles* and tales) in that class it is the one that answers most nearly to the stock notion of his genius—though even *Victory* is neither about the Malayan jungle nor about the sea.

The Secret Agent, the one I come to next (not chronologically, of course—it appeared in 1907, and *Victory* in 1915), is much more indubitably a classic and a masterpiece, and it doesn't answer to the notion at all—which is perhaps why it appears to have had nothing like due recognition. If we call it an ironic novel, it is with the same intention of the adjective as when *Jonathan Wild* is called an ironic novel. To note this is to be reminded, with a fresh shock, of the inertia of conventional valuation that makes *Jonathan Wild* a masterpiece and the classic of its *genre*. For *The Secret Agent* is truly classical in its maturity of attitude and the consummateness of the art in which this finds expression; in the contrast there is nothing for it but to see *Jonathan Wild* as the clumsy piece of hobbledehoydom, artistic and intellectual, that it is. The irony of *The Secret Agent* is not a matter of an insistent and obvious 'significance' of tone, or the endless repetition of a simple formula. The tone is truly subtle— subtle with the subtlety of the theme; and the theme develops itself in a complex organic structure. The effect depends upon an interplay of contrasting moral perspectives, and the rich economy of the pattern they make relates *The Secret Agent* to *Nostromo*: the two works, for all the great differences between them in range and temper, are triumphs of the same art—the aim of *The Secret Agent*, of course, confines the range, and the kind of irony involves a limiting detachment (we don't look for the secrets of Conrad's soul in *The Secret Agent*).

The matter, the 'story,' is that of a thriller—terrorist conclaves, embassy machinations, bomb-outrage, detection, murder, suicide; and to make, in treating such matter with all the refinements of his craft, a sophisticated moral interest the controlling principle is, we recognize, characteristic Conrad. His irony bears on the egocentric naïveties of moral conviction, the conventionality of conventional moral attitudes, and the obtuse assurance with which habit and self-interest assert absolute rights and wrongs. The pattern of the book is contrived to make us feel the different actors or lives as insulated currents of feeling and purpose—insulated, but committed to co-existence and interaction in what they don't question to be a common world, and sometimes making disconcerting contacts through the insulation.

The Verlocs, husband and wife, take their mutual insulation so for granted as to be mainly unconscious of it. What Mr. Verloc is becomes plain to us very early on. We see him leaving behind him the shop, fly-staled and dusty, with its display of revolutionary literature and pornographic goods, and making his way westward towards the Embassy of a Foreign Power. Conrad's London bears something of the same kind of relation to Dickens as Henry James's does in *The Princess Casamassima*. The direct influence of Dickens is unmistakable in certain minor lapses into facetious humour (see, for instance, in the account of Verloc's walk, the bit about No. 1 Chesham Square) from the characteristic astringent dryness. There is also, later, a major instance of obvious and unfortunate indebtedness to Dickens in the fantastic slow-motion macabre of the cab-journey to the almshouse. But *The Secret Agent* (unlike *The Princess Casamassima*) is one of the author's most successful works; its strength is something so utterly outside Dickens's compass as to have enabled Conrad to be influenced by him to purely Conradian ends.

And the essential relation to Dickens, it should be plain, is not a matter of being influenced for good or ill, but lies in that energy of vision and characterization which, we have seen, is sometimes as apt to make us say 'Shakespearean' as 'Dickensian.'

We have it in the interview between Verloc and Mr. Vladimir, First Secretary of the Embassy. The dialogue—and this is so throughout the book, for all the uncertainty about points of English usage apparent on practically every page of Conrad to the end—is consummate in its blend of inevitable naturalness with strict economy of relevance, and the whole is so dramatically realized that we are hardly aware of shifts to description, stage directions or reported thought: it all seems to be enacted before us.

'In the pause Mr. Vladimir formulated in his mind a series of disparaging remarks concerning Mr. Verloc's face and figure. The fellow was unexpectedly vulgar, heavy and impudently unintelligent. He looked uncommonly like a master plumber come to present his bill. The First Secretary of the Embassy, from his occasional excursions into the field of American humour, had formed a special notion of that class of mechanic as the embodiment of fraudulent laziness and incompetency.'

Mr. Vladimir himself we see with a vision heightened by Verloc's consternation and disgust:

'This anger was complicated by incredulity. And suddenly it dawned upon him that all this was an elaborate joke. Mr. Vladimir exhibited his white teeth in a smile, with dimples on his round, full face posed with a complacent inclination above the bristling bow of his necktie. The favourite of intelligent society women had assumed his drawing-room attitude accompanying the delivery of delicate witticisms. Sitting well forward, his white hand upraised, he seemed to hold delicately between his thumb and forefinger the subtlety of his suggestion.'

What he has enjoined upon Verloc, not as a joke but seriously, as a means of waking up the English police to a sense of their European responsibilities, is a bomb-attack upon Greenwich Observatory. Verloc, threatened in his routine comfort and indolence, feels not only helpless anger but a sense of moral outrage too:

'"It will cost money," Mr. Verloc said, by a sort of instinct.

'"That cock won't fight," Mr. Vladimir retorted, with an amazingly genuine English accent. "You'll get your screw every month, and no more till something happens. And if nothing happens very soon you won't get even that. What's your ostensible occupation? What are you supposed to live by?"

'"I keep a shop," answered Mr. Verloc.

'"A shop! What sort of shop?"

'"Stationery, newspapers. My wife—"

'"Your what?" interrupted Mr. Vladimir in his guttural Central Asian tones.

'"My wife," Mr. Verloc raised his husky voice slightly. "I am married."

'"That be damned for a yarn," exclaimed the other in unfeigned astonishment. "Married! And you a professed anarchist, too! What is this confounded nonsense? But I suppose it's merely a matter of speaking. Anarchists don't marry. It's well known. They can't. It would be apostasy."'

Actually Verloc is most respectably married. It is a triumph of the irony that we not only see him as a sympathetic character compared with Mr. Vladimir, but find ourselves on the point of saying that he is in all essentials an ordinary respectable citizen, concerned like any other to maintain himself and his wife in security and comfort: the shop, with its squalid trade and anarchistic frequentation, and the complicated treacheries of his profession, we see with him as matters of habit and routine, means to the end. In the final scene with his wife, when he tries to make her understand the full enormity of Mr. Vladimir's conduct, he says with righteous exasperation and with all the unction of an outraged moral sense:

' "There isn't a murdering plot for the last eleven years that I haven't had my finger in at the risk of my life. There's scores of these revolutionaries I've sent off, with their bombs in their blamed pockets, to get themselves caught on the frontier. The old Baron knew what I was worth to his country. And here suddenly a swine comes along—ignorant, overbearing swine." '

What Mrs. Verloc is comes out only bit by bit—the perfection of the structure of the book shows itself notably in the way in which we are put in possession of the necessary knowledge about her at the right time. We see her serving in the shop with intimidating aplomb, taking the frequentations of the revolutionists as a matter of course, and, placid good wife to a good husband, being tactfully solicitous about his health and comfort. His business, she knows, entails these and other associates, late absences from home, and occasional trips to the Continent; further, she doesn't inquire:

'Mrs. Verloc wasted no portion of this transient life in seeking for fundamental information. This is a sort of economy having all the appearances and some of the advantages of prudence. Obviously it may be good for one not to know too much. And such a view accords very well with constitutional indolence.'

Her mother, who lives with them, and who isn't given to asking questions either, sometimes wonders why Winnie, an attractive girl, married Mr. Verloc. It was, as a matter of fact, for the very reason that leads the mother to withdraw to an almshouse, there to spend in loneliness the remainder of her life: concern for the future of Stevie, the half-witted younger brother. One of the most poignant touches of irony in the book is when Winnie says:

' "That poor boy will miss you something cruel. I wish you had thought a little of that, mother." '

They had both, as a matter of fact, sacrificed themselves for Stevie. And Winnie now, with concealed anxiety, sets to work to impress Verloc with Stevie's devotion to him. Verloc is lost in the obsessing dreads and perplexities associated with the face of Mr. Vladimir; but, with Stevie's existence thus forced on his notice, he realizes Stevie's useful potentialities and is inspired with a timely idea. The result is the violent disintegration of Stevie when he stumbles with the bomb in Greenwich Park, and the immediate bringing home of the responsibility to Verloc by reason of the label, discovered among the rags and fragments by the police, that Winnie has sewn under the collar of Stevie's overcoat in case he should get lost.

There follows one of the most astonishing triumphs of genius in fiction, the final scene between Verloc and his wife. To put it in this way, however, is misleading, since the effect of the scene depends upon what comes before—depends upon the cunning organization of the whole book. We have been put in a position in which we can't fail to realize that, by the sudden knowledge of the death into which Verloc had led Stevie ('might be father and son,' she had fondly remarked, seeing them go off together), Winnie's 'moral nature had been subjected to a shock of which, in the physical order, the most violent earthquake of history could only be a faint and languid rendering.' And we appreciate to the full the moral insulation that has kept the Verlocs, in their decent marital domesticity, strangers to each other.

'"Do be reasonable, Winnie. What would it have been if you had lost me!"'

—Here we have the assumption on which Verloc, with magnanimous restraint (for did she not, without telling him, sew in that label which has done the mischief?), undertakes to help his wife to achieve a more reasonable attitude towards the misadventure.

'In his affairs of the heart Mr. Verloc had always been

carelessly generous, yet always with no other idea than that of being loved for himself. Upon this matter, his ethical notions being in agreement with his vanity, he was completely incorrigible. That this should be so in the case of his virtuous and legal connection he was perfectly certain. He had grown older, fatter, heavier, in the belief that he lacked no fascination for being loved for his own sake.'

It is extraordinary ironic comedy; the tension is deadly and is to end in murder, but the ways in which Verloc's moral feeling exhibits the naïveties of its relation with his egotism are irresistibly comic. He has intense righteous indignation to work off:

'"It wasn't the old Baron who would have had the wicked folly of getting me to call on him at eleven in the morning. There are two or three in this town that, if they had seen me going in, would have made no bones about knocking me on the head sooner or later. It was a silly, murderous trick to expose for nothing a man—like me."'

The development is rich, surprising and inevitable, and disturbing in its reality:

'For the first time in his life he was taking that incurious woman into his confidence. The singularity of the event, the force and importance of the personal feelings aroused in the course of this confession, drove Stevie's fate clean out of Mr. Verloc's mind. The boy's stuttering existence of fears and indignations, together with the violence of his end, had passed out of Mr. Verloc's mental sight for a time. For that reason, when he looked up he was startled by the inappropriate character of his wife's stare. It was not a wild stare, and it was not inattentive, but its attention was peculiar and not satisfactory, inasmuch that it seemed concentrated upon some point beyond Mr. Verloc's person. The impression was so strong that Mr. Verloc glanced over his shoulder. There was nothing behind him: there was just the whitewashed wall. The excellent husband of Winnie Verloc saw no writing on the wall. He turned to his wife again. . . .'

It is 'the note of wooing' ('"Come here," he said in a peculiar tone from his relaxed posture on the sofa') that finally gives the signal for the plunge of the knife between his ribs. That knife and its use, by the way, provide an illustration of the economy of form and pattern that gives every detail its significance. Not only does Verloc make (from his wife's point of view—'This man took the boy away to murder him' is the refrain running through her head) offensively insensitive use of it when, during the scene, he carves and grossly devours lumps of cold meat; he actually refers to the possibility of a 'stab in the back' and so prompts her obsessed mind to the action. And early in the book Winnie, whose likeness to Stevie is significantly touched on from time to time, has had to 'take the carving knife away from the boy,' who 'can't stand the notion of any cruelty' and has been excited by the atrocity literature kept for sale.

Upon the stabbing follows a gruesomely farcical coda in which the gallows-haunted Winnie, whose turn it now is to suppose herself loved for her own sake, clings round the neck of the gallant Comrade Ossipon, who is quite prepared to succeed to Comrade Verloc's bank-account, but is terrified when he discovers to what possibilities of suspicion he has laid himself open.

The scene between Verloc and his wife is balanced (to simplify with an inevitable crudeness, for the pattern is richly packed as well as subtle, and there can be no pretence of suggesting it fairly in summary) by the earlier scene between Chief Inspector Heat of the Special Crimes Department and the Assistant Commissioner. Heat is a magnificently done type, the higher-grade policeman, representative *par excellence* of Law and Order. 'Why not leave it to Heat?' asks Sir Ethelred, the great Personage, of the Assistant Commissioner.

'"Because he is an old departmental hand. They have

their own morality. My line of inquiry would appear to him an awful perversion of duty. For him the plain duty is to fix the guilt upon as many prominent anarchists as he can on some slight indications he had picked up in the course of his investigations on the spot; whereas I, he would say, am bent upon vindicating their innocence."'

Actually the Chief Inspector's morality is more interesting than that. When the discovery of the label on the singed rag brings the Greenwich bomb-affair home to Verloc, Heat is faced with a problem: luck having years before put Verloc in his way, he has been using this valuable source of information privately, and with great profit in respect of reputation and promotion. To follow up the clue would bring out all kinds of things and certainly destroy the source.

The incomplete explicitness of the motives in play—an incompleteness that may be said to take the positive form of a kind of resonance of righteous feeling—is rendered with fine ironic subtlety:

'He no longer considered it eminently desirable all round to establish publicly the identity of the man who had blown himself up that morning with such horrible completeness. But he was not certain of the view his department would take. A department is to those it employs a complex personality with ideas and fads of its own. It depends on the loyal devotion of its servants, and the devoted loyalty of trusted servants is associated with a certain amount of affectionate contempt, which keeps it sweet, as it were. By a benevolent provision of Nature no man is a hero to his valet, or else the heroes would have to brush their own clothes. Likewise no department appears perfectly wise to the intimacy of its workers. A department does not know so much as some of its servants. Being a dispassionate organism, it can never be perfectly informed. It would not be good for its efficiency to know too much. Chief Inspector Heat got out of the train in a state of thoughtfulness entirely untainted with disloyalty, but not quite free of that jealous mistrust which so often springs on the ground of perfect devotion, whether to women or to institutions.'

During his interview with his chief, the Assistant Commissioner, to whom he listens 'with outward deference (which means nothing, being a matter of duty) and inwardly with benevolent toleration,' he settles down to the resolution of bringing the trail of suspicion home to Michaelis, a ticket-of-leave ex-convict who happens to be the only thoroughly sympathetic member of the revolutionary group:

' "There will be no difficulty in getting up sufficient evidence against *him*," he said with virtuous complacency. "You may trust me for that, sir." '

He can take this line with the complete assurance of his moral judgment.

'It was perfectly legal to arrest that man on the barest suspicion. It was legal and expedient on the face of it. His two former chiefs would have seen the point at once; whereas this one, without saying either yes or no, sat there, as if lost in a dream. Moreover, besides being legal and expedient, the arrest of Michaelis solved a little personal difficulty which worried Chief Inspector Heat somewhat. This difficulty had its bearing upon his reputation, upon his comfort, and even upon the efficient performance of his duties. For if Michaelis no doubt knew something about this outrage, the Chief Inspector was fairly certain that he did not know too much. This was just as well. He knew much less—the Chief Inspector was positive—than certain other individuals he had in his mind, but whose arrest seemed to him inexpedient, besides being a more complicated matter, on account of the rules of the game. The rules of the game did not protect so much Michaelis who was an ex-convict. It would be stupid not to take advantage of legal facilities. . . .'

When the Assistant Commissioner disconcerts him with an undepartmental scepticism ('Now what is it you've got up your sleeve?'), Heat is not only very annoyed ('"You, my boy," he said to himself . . . "you, my boy, you don't know your place, and your place won't know you very long either, I bet"'), he is morally outraged:

> 'He had discovered in this affair a delicate and perplexing side, forcing upon the discoverer a certain amount of insincerity which, under the names of skill, prudence, discretion, turns up at one point or another in most human affairs. He felt at the moment like a tight-rope artist might feel if suddenly, in the middle of the performance, the manager of the Music Hall were to rush out of the proper managerial seclusion and begin to shake the rope.'

His indignation responds musically, as it were, to that of Comrade Ossipon (along with a great deal else) when he hears of the bomb-explosion, and exclaims that 'under the present circumstances it's nothing short of criminal.'

Heat has a further reason for not following up the clue. He has just, in one of the most memorable of the many vivid and pregnant scenes and episodes in the book, had his chance meeting in the narrow by-street with the Professor, who made the bomb. The Chief Inspector is not in any case in his element where revolutionists are concerned:

> 'At the beginning of his career Chief Inspector Heat had been concerned with the more energetic forms of thieving. He had gained his spurs in that sphere, and naturally enough had kept for it, after his promotion to another department, a feeling not very far removed from affection. Thieving was not a sheer absurdity. It was a form of human industry, perverse indeed, but still an industry exercised in an industrious world; it was work undertaken for the same reason as the work in potteries, in coal mines, in fields, in tool-grinding shops. It was labour, whose practical difference from the

other forms of labour consisted in the nature of its risk, which did not lie in ankylosis, or lead-poisoning, or fire-damp, or gritty dust, but in what may be briefly defined in its own special phraseology as "Seven years hard." Chief Inspector Heat was, of course, not insensible to the gravity of moral differences. But neither were the thieves he had been looking after. They submitted to the severe sanctions of a morality familiar to Chief Inspector Heat with a certain resignation. They were his fellow-citizens gone wrong because of imperfect education Chief Inspector Heat believed; but allowing for that difference, he could understand the mind of a burglar, because, as a matter of fact, the mind and the instincts of a burglar are of the same kind as the mind and the instincts of a police officer. Both recognize the same conventions and have a working knowledge of each other's methods and of the routine of their respective trades. They understand each other, which is advantageous to both, and establishes a sort of amenity in their relations. Products of the same machine, one classed as useful and the other as noxious, they take the machine for granted in different ways, but with a seriousness essentially the same.'

The Professor, physically insignificant, but happy in the superiority given him by the bomb he always carries on his person and by his reputation for a reckless readiness to touch it off rather than be arrested, represents revolutionary abnormality in its most disconcerting and repugnant form:

'After paying this tribute to what is normal in the constitution of society (for the idea of thieving appeared to his instinct as normal as the idea of property), Chief Inspector Heat felt very angry with himself for having stopped. . . .

'The encounter did not leave behind with Inspector Heat that satisfactory sense of superiority the members of the police force get from the unofficial but intimate side of their intercourse with the criminal classes, by which the vanity of power is soothed, and the vulgar love of domination over our fellow-creatures is flattered as worthily as it deserves.

'The perfect anarchist was not recognized as a fellow-creature by Chief Inspector Heat. He was impossible— a mad dog to be left alone. . . . This being the strong feeling of Inspector Heat, it appeared to him just and proper that this affair should be shunted off its obscure and inconvenient track, leading goodness knows where, into a quiet (and lawful) siding called Michaelis.'

Conrad himself shows an unmistakable dislike of revolutionists. In *The Secret Agent* he explains them mainly in terms of indolence (though the Professor and Michaelis are contrasting and complementary special cases). In *Under Western Eyes* (1911), which comes up for notice next, his revolutionists are Russians, and, while his presentment is hardly more flattering, his general reflections are on different lines:

'". . . in a real revolution—not a simple dynastic change or a mere reform of institutions—in a real revolution the best characters do not come to the front. A violent revolution falls into the hands of narrow-minded fanatics and of tyrannical hypocrites at first. Afterwards comes the turn of all the pretentious intellectual failures of the time. Such are the chiefs and the leaders. You will notice that I have left out the mere rogues. The scrupulous and the just, the noble, humane, and devoted natures; the unselfish and the intelligent may begin a movement—but it passes away from them. They are not the leaders of a revolution. They are its victims: the victims of disgust, of disenchantment— often of remorse. Hopes grotesquely betrayed, ideals caricatured—that is the definition of revolutionary successes. There have been in every revolution hearts broken by such successes."'

The old teacher of languages, the presence in the story of 'western eyes,' is here warning Natalia, sister of

Haldin the heroic assassin; and the revolutionists we are shown—

> ' "Bearers [comments Razumov] of the spark to start an explosion which is meant to change fundamentally the lives of so many millions in order that Peter Ivanovitch should be the head of a state" '

—leave no room for doubt that he speaks for Conrad. In Peter Ivanovitch, 'the heroic fugitive,' eloquent, woman-exploiting egoist, and 'Russian Mazzini,' we have, we suspect, an actual historical person.

The space given to *The Secret Agent* doesn't leave much for *Under Western Eyes*. But *The Secret Agent* is one of Conrad's two supreme masterpieces, one of the two unquestionable classics of the first order that he added to the English novel, and, in its own way, it is like *Nostromo* in the subtle and triumphant complexity of its art—like, too, in not having had due critical recognition. *Under Western Eyes* cannot be claimed with the same confidence for that order, though it is a most distinguished work, and must be counted among those upon which Conrad's status as one of the great English masters securely rests. It is related to *The Secret Agent* not only by the revolutionists, but by the theme of isolation (for this figures a great deal in that book—Winnie Verloc jumps to her death from the night Channel-steamer at least as much to escape the void in which Stevie's death followed by Ossipon's desertion has left her as from fear of the gallows). *Under Western Eyes* has for theme moral isolation as represented by the case of the Russian student Razumov.

Never having known parents, and without connexions, Razumov even at the outset of the history is 'as lonely in the world as a fish swimming in the sea.' He is wholly bent on his career, and we are told characteristically:

> 'There was nothing strange in the student Razumov's wish for distinction. A man's real life is that accorded to him in the thoughts of other men by reason of respect or natural love.'

His prospects are destroyed by the uninvited confidence shown in him by Haldin, a student revolutionist, who, having brought off a political assassination, takes refuge in Razumov's rooms. From the moment of finding him there Razumov is doomed to endure a trapped and tormented conscience in utter loneliness:

'Who knows what true loneliness is—not the conventional word, but the naked terror? To the lonely themselves it wears a mask. The most miserable outcast hugs some memory or some illusion. Now and then a fatal conjunction of events may lift the veil for an instant. For an instant only. No human being could bear a steady view of moral solitude without going mad. 'Razumov had reached that point of vision.'

This is his state as he tramps the streets in the winter night, crystallizing his decision to give Haldin up.

'Indeed, it could hardly be called a decision. He had simply discovered what he had meant to do all along. And yet he felt the need of some other mind's sanction.'

Giving Haldin up doesn't save Razumov's career. He is involved, and the police have a use for him. He seeks to terminate his interview with Councillor Mikulin, a creepily convincing Russian bureaucrat, by asserting his 'right to be done once for all with that man,' and 'to retire—simply to retire':

'An unhurried voice said—
'"Kirylo Sidorovitch."
'Razumov at the door turned his head.
'"To retire," he repeated.
'"Where to?" asked Councillor Mikulin softly.'

Razumov's mental conflicts and stresses during the Part I that ends on this note are rendered from the inside with extraordinary power. We are thus put in a position to appreciate the observations from the outside recorded through the English teacher of languages at Geneva, where Razumov, now a spy among the revolutionists, complicates his problem by falling in love with Haldin's sister. The earlier inside account of his tormented consciousness shows the influence of Dostoievsky, and the effect is to bring out the antipathetic detachment of Conrad's radical attitude from all that Dostoievsky stands for. If Conrad knows his Dostoievsky, he sees him through 'western eyes,' and sees him, along with 'the lawlessness of autocracy and lawlessness of revolution,' as among the 'moral conditions ruling over a large part of this earth's surface' that the old language teacher, in telling Razumov's story, perceives himself to be rendering.

Having, by confession to Haldin's sister and to the revolutionists, escaped at last from the worst of his moral isolation, Razumov ends, a cripple, his ear-drums deliberately burst by the champion revolutionary killer, in the less intolerable isolation of stone deafness.

Moral isolation is again the theme of *Chance* (1914), which is, again, a very different kind of book—different from *Under Western Eyes* and from the other novels. Flora de Barral, daughter of the great de Barral, grand-style financial adventurer, suffers first, at the time of her father's *débâcle,* the shock of a fiendish moral assault from her governess (Flora having no mother—having no one but her father); then, her father in jail, suffers further bad luck in the form of odious relatives, and has bad luck again even in her good luck: her rescue by the chivalrous Captain Anthony, 'son of the poet.'

We have, in fact, a variant of the Heyst-Lena situation: while each needs, neither knows, the other, and the nature and circumstances of the rescue leave each exquisitely and inhibitingly scrupulous about taking advantage of the other's helplessness or chivalry. The woman is not, this time, the minor focus of interest, but rather the reverse—Flora is the central character of the book; and Anthony, on the other hand, reintroduces the Lord Jim theme:

'The inarticulate son had set up a standard for himself with that need for embodying in his conduct the dreams, the passion, the impulses the poet puts into the arrangements of verses, which are dearer to him than his own self—and may make his own self appear sublime in the eyes of other people, and even in his own eyes.

'Did Anthony wish to appear sublime in his own eyes?'

Again:

'If Anthony's love had been as egoistic as love generally is it would have been greater than the egoism of his vanity—or of his generosity, if you like.'

In any case, 'She beat him at his own honourable game.' The question about her is given here (the pilgrimage is a rendezvous with Anthony in the East End):

'She had had an ugly pilgrimage, but whether of love or necessity, who could tell.'

The technical distinction of *Chance* has not lacked recognition. That no doubt is because *Chance* invites the description 'technical triumph' in a way which *Nostromo* and *The Secret Agent* do not. One's sense that the 'doing' (see the significant terms of Henry James's appreciation in the essay called *The New Novel, 1914*, to be found in *Notes on Novelists*) was not so strictly as in their case a preoccupation with getting the essential theme or themes 'done' is perhaps not fair—not fair, expressed so. The fact is that Conrad's essential interest here didn't yield him anything like so rich a pattern as in either of those two books, and the theme indicated by the title, ingeniously exploited as it is in the mode of presentation, has no essential relation with the main theme: chance plays no notably different part from that it must play in any story offering a novelist a study of human nature, and Conrad (it may be suggested) by calling the novel *Chance*—and insisting a great deal on the word—implicitly concedes the critical point in question: the point regarding the difference between *Chance* and the other two.

One tends to make the point a little unfairly because of

irritation with Marlow, who is essential to the presentation—

'"But we, my dear Marlow, have the inestimable advantage of understanding what is happening to others"'

—but is also, in a way touched on earlier, too easy a convenience:

'Marlow emerged out of the shadow of the book-case to get himself a cigar from a box which stood on a little table by my side. In the full light of the room I saw in his eyes that slightly mocking expression with which he habitually covers up his sympathetic impulses of mirth and pity before the unreasonable complications the idealism of mankind puts into the simple but poignant problem of conduct on this earth.'

This suggests well enough the kind of direct injection of tone and attitude that Marlow licenses, and the consequent cheapening effect. Nevertheless, the view from the outside, the correlated glimpses from different angles, the standing queries and suspended judgments—this treatment, applied by means of Marlow and the complication of witnesses, is, quite plainly, the kind demanded by the essential undertaking of the book. And it is applied successfully; even the most difficult part of all, the rendering of the 'tension of the false situation' on board the *Ferndale*, comes off pretty well (though there is a touch of sentimentality about the handling of Flora).

The genius is amply apparent in *Chance*. It is most apparent in the force of realization with which the characters are evoked, and which has led above to the mention of Dickens. That which suggests Dickens in *Chance*—and there is a great deal of it—is all strongly characteristic Conrad. There is the Shipping Office and old Powell-Socrates, with his 'tall hat very far at the back of his head . . . a full unwrinkled face, and such clear-shining eyes that his grey beard looked quite false on him, stuck on for a disguise'; there are the Fynes—the comedy of Marlow's

intercourse with them is characteristic and good; the great
de Barral himself; Flora's odious relative, the cardboard
box manufacturer, who 'had all the civic virtues in their
meanest form'; Franklin the mate—

> 'The mate who, on account of his peculiar build,
> could not turn his head quite freely, twisted his thick
> trunk slightly, and ran his black eyes in the corners
> towards the steward.'

There we have an illustration of the vivid particularity
with which things are *seen*. For another, here is the sinister old de Barral:

> 'gliding away with his walk which Mr. Powell de-
> scribed to me as being as level and wary as his voice. He
> walked as if he were carrying a glass full of water on
> his head.'

The solemn little Fyne, irreproachable Civil Servant, is
epitomized in the picture of him escaping with his gravity
from under the noses of the dray-horses:

> 'He skipped wildly out of the way and up on the
> curbstone with a purely instinctive precision; his mind
> had nothing to do with his movements. In the middle
> of his leap, and while in the act of sailing gravely
> through the air, he continued to relieve his outraged
> feelings.'

The distinction of mind is as apparent in *Chance* as this
kind of vitality; it is certainly a remarkable novel.

There is no other that need be discussed. *The Rover*,
the latest one finished, with its pathos of retrospect and
its old man's sense of the unreality of life, comes plainly
from a mind conscious of being at the end of its own days:
it has a remote vividness, but no central energy. The
unfinished *Suspense* so little lives up to its title that the
published part of it is hard to get through. But *Nostromo*,
The Secret Agent, *Under Western Eyes*, *Chance*, *Victory*
—it is an impressive enough tale of books (all produced

within a decade and a half) for any man to have to his credit. And—not to the credit of English literary culture or English criticism—it went, the evidence obliges us to conclude, without recognition. True, Conrad enjoyed a vogue in the early nineteen-twenties, when he was bringing out a series of inferior novels; and he had been for some time an established name. But—for all the odd success of *Chance*—he had too good reason to feel that he was regarded as the author of *Lord Jim;* the writer of stories about the sea, the jungle and the islands, who had made some curious ventures outside his beat, but would yet, one hoped, return to it. Perhaps what may be found against his name in the new *Concise Cambridge History of English Literature* gives what is still the prevalent view.

But he was not only by far the greatest of the Edwardians; there is more to be said than that. Scott, Thackeray, Meredith and Hardy are commonly accounted great English novelists: if the criterion is the achievement in work addressed to the adult mind, and capable as such of engaging again and again its full critical attention, then Conrad is certainly a greater novelist than the four enumerated. This, which may seem a more striking claim to some critics than to others, is merely a way of insisting on the force of the judgment that Conrad is among the very greatest novelists in the language—or any language.

V. 'HARD TIMES'

An Analytic Note

"HARD TIMES" is not a difficult work; its intention and nature are pretty obvious. If, then, it is the masterpiece I take it for, why has it not had general recognition? To judge by the critical record, it has had none at all. If there exists anywhere an appreciation, or even an acclaiming reference, I have missed it. In the books and essays on Dickens, so far as I know them, it is passed over as a very minor thing; too slight and insignificant to distract us for more than a sentence or two from the works worth critical attention. Yet, if I am right, of all Dickens's works it is the one that has all the strength of his genius, together with a strength no other of them can show—that of a completely serious work of art.

The answer to the question asked above seems to me to bear on the traditional approach to 'the English novel.' For all the more sophisticated critical currency of the last decade or two, that approach still prevails, at any rate in the appreciation of the Victorian novelists. The business of the novelist, you gather, is to 'create a world,' and the mark of the master is external abundance—he gives you lots of 'life.' The test of life in his characters (he must above all create 'living' characters) is that they go on living outside the book. Expectations as unexacting as these are not when they encounter significance, grateful for it, and when it meets them in that insistent form where nothing is very engaging as 'life' unless its relevance is fully taken, miss it altogether. This is the only way in which I can account for the neglect suffered by Henry James's *The Europeans*, which may be classed with *Hard Times* as a moral fable—though one might have supposed that James would enjoy the advantage of being approached with expectations of subtlety and closely calculated relevance. Fashion, however, has not recommended his earlier work, and this (whatever appreciation may be enjoyed by *The Ambassadors*) still suffers from the prevailing expectation of redundant and irrelevant 'life.'

I need say no more by way of defining the moral fable than that in it the intention is peculiarly insistent, so that the representative significance of everything in the fable—character, episode, and so on—is immediately apparent as we read. Intention might seem to be insistent enough in the opening of *Hard Times*, in that scene in Mr. Gradgrind's school. But then, intention is often very insistent in Dickens, without its being taken up in any inclusive significance that informs and organizes a coherent whole; and, for lack of any expectation of an organized whole, it has no doubt been supposed that in *Hard Times* the satiric irony of the first two chapters is merely, in the large and genial Dickensian way, thrown together with melodrama, pathos and humour—and that we are given these ingredients more abundantly and exuberantly elsewhere. Actually, the Dickensian vitality is there, in its varied characteristic modes, which have the more force because they are free of redundance: the creative exuberance is controlled by a profound inspiration.

The inspiration is what is given in the title, *Hard Times*. Ordinarily Dickens's criticisms of the world he lives in are casual and incidental—a matter of including among the ingredients of a book some indignant treatment of a particular abuse. But in *Hard Times* he is for once possessed by a comprehensive vision, one in which the inhumanities of Victorian civilization are seen as fostered and sanctioned by a hard philosophy, the aggressive formulation of an inhumane spirit. The philosophy is represented by Thomas Gradgrind, Esquire, Member of Parliament for Coketown, who has brought up his children on the lines of the experiment recorded by John Stuart Mill as carried out on himself. What Gradgrind stands for is, though repellent, nevertheless respectable; his Utilitarianism is a theory sincerely held and there is intellectual disinterestedness in its application. But Gradgrind marries his eldest daughter to Josiah Bounderby, 'banker, merchant, manfacturer,' about whom there is no disinterestedness whatever, and nothing to be respected. Bounderby is Victorian 'rugged individualism' in its grossest and most intransigent form. Concerned with nothing but self-assertion and power and material success, he has no interest in ideals or ideas—except the idea of being the completely self-made man (since, for all his brag, he is not that in fact). Dickens here makes a just observation about the affinities and practical tendency of Utilitarianism, as, in his presentment of the Gradgrind home and the Gradgrind elementary school, he does about the Utilitarian spirit in Victorian education.

All this is obvious enough. But Dickens's art, while remaining that of the great popular entertainer, has in *Hard Times*, as he renders his full critical vision, a stamina, a flexibility combined with consistency, and a depth that he seems to have had little credit for. Take that opening scene in the school-room:

'"Girl number twenty," said Mr. Gradgrind, squarely pointing with his square forefinger, "I don't know that girl. Who is that girl?"

'"Sissy Jupe, sir," explained number twenty, blushing, standing up, and curtsying.

'"Sissy is not a name," said Mr. Gradgrind. "Don't call yourself Sissy. Call yourself Cecilia."

'"It's father as call me Sissy, sir," returned the young girl in a trembling voice, and with another curtsy.

'"Then he has no business to do it," said Mr. Gradgrind. "Tell him he mustn't. Cecilia Jupe. Let me see. What is your father?"

'"He belongs to the horse-riding, if you please, sir."

'Mr. Gradgrind frowned, and waved off the objectionable calling with his hand.

'"We don't want to know anything about that here. You mustn't tell us about that here. Your father breaks horses, don't he?"

' "If you please, sir, when they can get any to break, they do break horses in the ring, sir."

' "You mustn't tell us about the ring here. Very well, then. Describe your father as a horse-breaker. He doctors sick horses, I dare say?"

' "Oh, yes, sir!"

' "Very well, then. He is a veterinary surgeon, a farrier, and horse-breaker. Give me your definition of a horse."

(Sissy Jupe thrown into the greatest alarm by this demand.)

' "Girl number twenty unable to define a horse!" said Mr. Gradgrind, for the general benefit of all the little pitchers. "Girl number twenty possessed of no facts in reference to one of the commonest animals! Some boy's definition of a horse. Bitzer, yours."

· · · · · · · ·

' "Quadruped. Graminivorous. Forty teeth, namely, twenty-four grinders, four eye-teeth, and twelve incisive. Sheds coat in the spring; in marshy countries, sheds hoofs too. Hoofs hard, but requiring to be shod with iron. Age known by marks in mouth." Thus (and much more) Bitzer.'

Lawrence himself, protesting against harmful tendencies in education, never made the point more tellingly. Sissy has been brought up among horses, and among people whose livelihood depends upon understanding horses but 'we don't want to know anything about that here.' Such knowledge isn't real knowledge. Bitzer, the model pupil, on the button's being pressed, promptly vomits up the genuine article, 'Quadruped. Graminivorous,' etc.; and 'Now, girl number twenty, you know what a horse is.' The irony, pungent enough locally, is richly developed in the subsequent action. Bitzer's aptness has its evaluative comment in his career. Sissy's incapacity to acquire this kind of 'fact' or formula, her unaptness for education, is manifested to us, on the other hand, as part and parcel of her sovereign and indefeasible humanity: it is the virtue that makes it impossible for her to understand, or acquiesce in, an ethos for which she is 'girl number twenty,' or to think of any other human being as a unit for arithmetic.

This kind of ironic method might seem to commit the author to very limited kinds of effect. In *Hard Times*, however, it associates quite congruously, such is the flexibility of Dickens's art, with very different methods; it co-operates in a truly dramatic and profoundly poetic whole. Sissy Jupe, who might be taken here for a merely conventional *persona*, has already, as a matter of fact, been established in a potently symbolic rôle: she is part of the poetically-creative operation of Dickens's genius in *Hard Times*. Here is a passage I omitted from the middle of the excerpt quoted above:

'The square finger, moving here and there, lighted suddenly on Bitzer, perhaps because he chanced to sit in the same ray of sun-light which, darting in at one of the bare windows of the intensely whitewashed room, irradiated Sissy. For the boys and girls sat on the face of an inclined plane in two compact bodies, divided up the centre by a narrow interval; and Sissy, being at the corner of a row on the sunny side, came in for the beginning of a sunbeam, of which Bitzer, being at the corner of a row on the other side, a few rows in advance, caught the end. But, whereas the girl was so dark-eyed and dark-haired that she seemed to receive a deeper and more lustrous colour from the sun when it shone upon her, the boy was so light-eyed and light-haired that the self-same rays appeared to draw out of him what little colour he ever possessed. His cold eyes would hardly have been eyes, but for the short ends of lashes which, by bringing them into immediate contrast with something paler than themselves, expressed their form. His short-cropped hair might have been a mere continuation of the sandy freckles on his forehead and face. His skin was so unwholesomely deficient in the natural tinge, that he looked as though, if he were cut, he would bleed white.'

There is no need to insist on the force—representative

of Dickens's art in general in *Hard Times*—with which the moral and spiritual differences are rendered here in terms of sensation, so that the symbolic intention emerges out of metaphor and the vivid evocation of the concrete. What may, perhaps, be emphasized is that Sissy stands for vitality as well as goodness—they are seen, in fact, as one; she is generous, impulsive life, finding self-fulfilment in self-forgetfulness—all that is the antithesis of calculating self-interest. There is an essentially Laurentian suggestion about the way in which 'the dark-eyed and dark-haired' girl, contrasting with Bitzer, seemed to receive a 'deeper and more lustrous colour from the sun,' so opposing the life that is lived freely and richly from the deep instinctive and emotional springs to the thin-blooded, quasi-mechanical product of Gradgrindery.

Sissy's symbolic significance is bound up with that of Sleary's Horse-riding, where human kindness is very insistently associated with vitality. Representing human spontaneity, the circus-athletes represent at the same time highly-developed skill and deftness of kinds that bring poise, pride and confident ease—they are always buoyant, and, ballet-dancer-like, in training:

> 'There were two or three handsome young women among them, with two or three husbands, and their two or three mothers, and their eight or nine little children, who did the fairy business when required. The father of one of the families was in the habit of balancing the father of another of the families on the top of a great pole; the father of the third family often made a pyramid of both those fathers, with Master Kidderminster for the apex, and himself for the base; all the fathers could dance upon rolling casks, stand upon bottles, catch knives and balls, twirl hand-basins, ride upon anything, jump over everything, and stick at nothing. All the mothers could (and did) dance upon the slack wire and the tight-rope, and perform rapid acts on bare-backed steeds; none of them were at all particular in respect of showing their legs; and one of them, alone in a Greek

chariot, drove six-in-hand into every town they came to. They all assumed to be mighty rakish and knowing, they were not very tidy in their private dresses, they were not at all orderly in their domestic arrangements, and the combined literature of the whole company would have produced but a poor letter on any subject. Yet there was a remarkable gentleness and childishness about these people, a special inaptitude for any kind of sharp practice, and an untiring readiness to help and pity one another, deserving often of as much respect, and always of as much generous construction, as the every-day virtues of any class of people in the world.'

Their skills have no value for the Utilitarian calculus, but they express vital human impulse, and they minister to vital human needs. The Horse-riding, frowned upon as frivolous and wasteful by Gradgrind and malignantly scorned by Bounderby, brings the machine-hands of Coketown (the spirit-quenching hideousness of which is hauntingly evoked) what they are starved of. It brings to them, not merely amusement, but art, and the spectacle of trimuphant activity that, seeming to contain its end within itself, is, in its easy mastery, joyously self-justified. In investing a travelling circus with this kind of symbolic value Dickens expresses a profounder reaction to industrialism than might have been expected of him. It is not only pleasure and relaxation the Coketowners stand in need of; he feels the dreadful degradation of life that would remain even if they were to be given a forty-four hour week, comfort, security and fun. We recall a characteristic passage from D. H. Lawrence.

'The car ploughed uphill through the long squalid straggle of Tevershall, the blackened brick dwellings, the black slate roofs, glistening their sharp edges, the mud black with coal-dust, the pavements wet and black. It was as if dismalness had soaked through and through everything. The utter negation of natural beauty, the utter negation of the gladness of life, the utter absence of the instinct for shapely beauty which every bird and beast has, the utter death of the human intuitive faculty was appalling. The stacks of soap in the grocers' shops, the rhubarb and lemons in the greengrocers'! the awful hats in the milliners all went by ugly, ugly, ugly, followed by the plaster and gilt horror of the cinema with its wet picture anouncements, "A Woman's Love," and the new big Primitive chapel, primitive enough in its stark brick and big panes of greenish and raspberry glass in the windows. The Wesleyan chapel, higher up, was of blackened brick and stood behind iron railings and blackened shrubs. The Congregational chapel, which thought itself superior, was built of rusticated sandstone and had a steeple, but not a very high one. Just beyond were the new school buildings, expensive pink brick, and gravelled playground inside iron railings, all very imposing, and mixing the suggestion of a chapel and a prison. Standard Five girls were having a singing lesson, just finishing the la-me-do-la exercises and beginning a "sweet children's song." Anything more unlike song, spontaneous song, would be impossible to imagine: a strange bawling yell followed the outlines of a tune. It was not like animals: animals *mean* something when they yell. It was like nothing on earth, and it was called singing. Connie sat and listened with her heart in her boots, as Field was filling petrol. What could possibly become of such a people, a people in whom the living intuitive faculty was dead as nails, and only queer mechanical yells and uncanny will-power remained?'

Dickens couldn't have put it in just those terms, but the way in which his vision of the Horse-riders insists on their gracious vitality implies that reaction.

Here an objection may be anticipated—as a way of making a point. Coketown, like Gradgrind and Bounderby, is real enough; but it can't be contended that the Horseriding is real in the same sense. There would have been some athletic skill and perhaps some bodily grace among the people of a Victorian travelling circus, but surely so much squalor, grossness and vulgarity that we must find

Dickens's symbolism sentimentally false? And 'there was a remarkable gentleness and childishness about these people, a special inaptitude for any kind of sharp practice'—that, surely, is going ludicrously too far?

If Dickens, intent on an emotional effect, or drunk with moral enthusiasm, had been deceiving himself (it couldn't have been innocently) about the nature of the actuality, he would then indeed have been guilty of sentimental falsity, and the adverse criticism would have held. But the Horse-riding presents no such case. The virtues and qualities that Dickens prizes do indeed exist, and it is necessary for his critique of Utilitarianism and industrialism, and for (what is the same thing) his creative purpose, to evoke them vividly. The book can't, in my judgment, be fairly charged with giving a misleading representation of human nature. And it would plainly not be intelligent criticism to suggest that anyone could be misled about the nature of circuses by *Hard Times*. The critical question is merely one of tact: was it well-judged of Dickens to try to do *that*—which had to be done somehow—with a travelling circus?

Or, rather, the question is: by what means has he succeeded? For the success is complete. It is conditioned partly by the fact that, from the opening chapters, we have been tuned for the reception of a highly conventional art—though it is a tuning that has no narrowly limiting effect. To describe at all cogently the means by which this responsiveness is set up would take a good deal of 'practical criticism' analysis—analysis that would reveal an extraordinary flexibility in the art of *Hard Times*. This can be seen very obviously in the dialogue. Some passages might come from an ordinary novel. Others have the ironic pointedness of the school-room scene in so insistent a form that we might be reading a work as stylized as Jonsonian comedy: Gradgrind's final exchange with Bitzer (quoted below) is a supreme instance. Others again are 'literary,' like the conversation between Gradgrind and Louisa on her flight home for refuge from Mr. James Harthouse's attentions.

To the question how the reconciling is done—there is much more diversity in *Hard Times* than these references to dialogue suggest—the answer can be given by pointing to the astonishing and irresistible richness of life that characterizes the book everywhere. It meets us everywhere, unstrained and natural, in the prose. Out of such prose a great variety of presentations can arise congenially with equal vividness. There they are, unquestionably 'real.' It goes back to an extraordinary energy of perception and registration in Dickens. 'When people say that Dickens exaggerates,' says Mr. Santayana, 'it seems to me that they can have no eyes and no ears. They probably have only *notions* of what things and people are; they accept them conventionally, at their diplomatic value.' Settling down as we read to an implicit recognition of this truth, we don't readily and confidently apply any criterion we suppose ourselves to hold for distinguishing varieties of relation between what Dickens gives us and a normal 'real.' His flexibility is that of a richly poetic art of the word. He doesn't write 'poetic prose'; he writes with a poetic force of evocation, registering with the responsiveness of a genius of verbal expression what he so sharply sees and feels. In fact, by texture, imaginative mode, symbolic method, and the resulting concentration, *Hard Times* affects us as belonging with formally poetic works.

There is, however, more to be said about the success that attends. Dickens's symbolic intention in the Horse-riding; there is an essential quality of his genius to be emphasized. There is no Hamlet in him, and he is quite unlike Mr. Eliot.

> *The red-eyed scavengers are creeping*
> *From Kentish Town and Golders Green*

—there is nothing of that in Dickens's reaction to life. He observes with gusto the humanness of humanity as exhibited in the urban (and suburban) scene. When he sees, as he sees so readily, the common manifestations of human kindness, and the essential virtues, asserting themselves in the midst of ugliness, squalor and banality, his

warmly sympathetic response has no disgust to overcome.
There is no suggestion, for instance, of recoil—or of dis-
tance-keeping—from the game-eyed, brandy-soaked, flabby-
surfaced Mr. Sleary, who is successfully made to figure for
us a humane, anti-Utilitarian positive. This is not sentimentality in Dickens, but genius, and a genius that should
be found peculiarly worth attention in an age when, as
D. H. Lawrence (with, as I remember, Mr. Wyndham
Lewis immediately in view) says, 'My God! they stink,'
tends to be an insuperable and final reaction.

Dickens, as everyone knows, is very capable of sentimentality. We have it in *Hard Times* (though not to any
seriously damaging effect) in Stephen Blackpool, the good,
victimized working-man, whose perfect patience under in-
fliction we are expected to find supremely edifying and
irresistibly touching as the agonies are piled on for his
martyrdom. But Sissy Jupe is another matter. A general
description of her part in the fable might suggest the
worst, but actually she has nothing in common with Little
Nell: she shares in the strength of the Horse-riding. She
is wholly convincing in the function Dickens assigns to
her. The working of her influence in the Utilitarian home
is conveyed with a fine tact, and we do really feel her as a
growing potency. Dickens can even, with complete success, give her the stage for a victorious *tête-à-tête* with the
well-bred and languid elegant, Mr. James Harthouse, in
which she tells him that his duty is to leave Coketown
and cease troubling Louisa with his attentions:

'She was not afraid of him, or in any way disconcerted; she seemed to have her mind entirely preoccupied with the occasion of her visit, and to have
substituted that consideration for herself.'

The quiet victory of disinterested goodness is wholly convincing.

At the opening of the book Sissy establishes the essential
distinction between Gradgrind and Bounderby. Gradgrind, by taking her home, however ungraciously, shows

himself capable of humane feeling, however unacknowl-
edged. We are reminded, in the previous school-room
scene, of the Jonsonian affinities of Dickens's art, and
Bounderby turns out to be consistently a Jonsonian character in the sense that he is incapable of change. He remains the blustering egotist and braggart, and responds in
character to the collapse of his marriage:

> ' "I'll give *you* to understand, in reply to that, that
> there unquestionably is an incompatibility of the first
> magnitude—to be summed up in this—that your daugh-
> ter don't properly know her husband's merits, and is not
> impressed with such a sense as would become her, by
> George! of the honour of his alliance. That's plain
> speaking, I hope." '

He remains Jonsonianly consistent in his last testament
and death. But Gradgrind, in the nature of the fable, has
to *experience* the confutation of his philosophy, and to be
capable of the change involved in admitting that life has
proved him wrong. (Dickens's art in *Hard Times* differs
from Ben Jonson's not in being inconsistent, but in being
so very much more flexible and inclusive—a point that
seemed to be worth making because the relation between
Dickens and Jonson has been stressed of late, and I have
known unfair conclusions to be drawn from the comparison, notably in respect of *Hard Times*.)

The confutation of Utilitarianism by life is conducted
with great subtlety. That the conditions for it are there in
Mr. Gradgrind he betrays by his initial kindness, ungenial
enough, but properly rebuked by Bounderby, to Sissy.
'Mr. Gradgrind,' we are told, 'though hard enough, was
by no means so rough a man as Mr. Bounderby. His character was not unkind, all things considered; it might have
been very kind indeed if only he had made some mistake
in the arithmetic that balanced it years ago.' The inadequacy of the calculus is beautifully exposed when he
brings it to bear on the problem of marriage in the consummate scene with his eldest daughter:

'He waited, as if he would have been glad that she said something. But she said never a word.

'"Louisa, my dear, you are the subject of a proposal of marriage that has been made to me."

'Again he waited, and again she answered not one word. This so far surprised him as to induce him gently to repeat, "A proposal of marriage, my dear." To which she returned, without any visible emotion whatever:

'"I hear you, father. I am attending, I assure you."

'"Well!" said Mr. Gradgrind, breaking into a smile, after being for the moment at a loss, "you are even more dispassionate than I expected, Louisa. Or, perhaps, you are not unprepared for the announcement I have it in charge to make?"

'"I cannot say that, father, until I hear it. Prepared or unprepared, I wish to hear it all from you. I wish to hear you state it to me, father."

'Strange to relate, Mr. Gradgrind was not so collected at this moment as his daughter was. He took a paper knife in his hand, turned it over, laid it down, took it up again, and even then had to look along the blade of it, considering how to go on.

'"What you say, my dear Louisa, is perfectly reasonable. I have undertaken, then, to let you know that—in short, that Mr. Bounderby . . ."'

His embarrassment—by his own avowal—is caused by the perfect rationality with which she receives his overture. He is still more disconcerted when, with a completely dispassionate matter-of-factness that does credit to his *régime*, she gives him the opportunity to state in plain terms precisely what marriage should mean for the young Houyhnhnm:

'Silence between them. The deadly statistical clock very hollow. The distant smoke very black and heavy.

'"Father," said Louisa, "do you think I love Mr. Bounderby?"

'Mr. Gradgrind was extremely discomforted by this

unexpected question. "Well, my child," he returned, "I
—really—cannot take upon myself to say."

'"Father," pursued Louisa in exactly the same voice
as before, "do you ask me to love Mr. Bounderby?"

'"My dear Louisa, no. I ask nothing."

'"Father," she still pursued, "does Mr. Bounderby ask
me to love him?"

'"Really, my dear," said Mr. Gradgrind, "it is difficult
to answer your question—"

'"Difficult to answer it, Yes or No, father?"

'"Certainly, my dear. Because"—here was something
to demonstrate, and it set him up again—"because the
reply depends so materially, Louisa, on the sense in
which we use the expression. Now, Mr. Bounderby
does not do you the injustice, and does not do himself
the injustice, of pretending to anything fanciful, fantastic, or (I am using synonymous terms) sentimental. Mr.
Bounderby would have seen you grow up under his eye
to very little purpose, if he could so far forget what is
due to your good sense, not to say to his, as to address
you from any such ground. Therefore, perhaps, the expression itself—I merely suggest this to you, my dear—
may be a little misplaced."

'"What would you advise me to use in its stead, father?"

'"Why, my dear Louisa," said Mr. Gradgrind, completely recovered by this time, "I would advise you
(since you ask me) to consider the question, as you
have been accustomed to consider every other question,
simply as one of tangible Fact. The ignorant and the
giddy may embarrass such subjects with irrelevant fan-
cies, and other absurdities that have no existence, properly viewed—really no existence—but it is no
compliment to you to say that you know better. Now,
what are the Facts of this case? You are, we will say in
round numbers, twenty years of age; Mr. Bounderby is,
we will say in round numbers, fifty. There is some dis-
parity in your respective years, but . . ."'

—And at this point Mr. Gradgrind seizes the chance for a happy escape into statistics. But Louisa brings him firmly back:

'"What do you recommend, father?" asked Louisa, her reserved composure not in the least affected by these gratifying results, "that I should substitute for the term I used just now? For the misplaced expression?"

'"Louisa," returned her father, "it appears to me that nothing can be plainer. Confining yourself rigidly to Fact, the question of Fact you state to yourself is: Does Mr. Bounderby ask me to marry him? Yes, he does. The sole remaining question then is: Shall I marry him? I think nothing can be plainer than that."

'"Shall I marry him?" repeated Louisa with great deliberation.

'"Precisely."'

It is a triumph of ironic art. No logical analysis could dispose of the philosophy of fact and calculus with such neat finality. As the issues are reduced to algebraic formulation they are patently emptied of all real meaning. The instinct-free rationality of the emotionless Houyhnhnm is a void. Louisa proceeds to try and make him understand that she is a living creature and therefore no Houyhnhnm, but in vain ('to see it, he must have overleaped at a bound the artificial barriers he had for many years been erecting between himself and all those subtle essences of humanity which will elude the utmost cunning of algebra, until the last trumpet ever to be sounded will blow even algebra to wreck').

'Removing her eyes from him, she sat so long looking silently towards the town, that he said at length: "Are you consulting the chimneys of the Coketown works, Louisa?"

'"There seems to be nothing there but languid and monotonous smoke. Yet, when the night comes, Fire bursts out, father!" she answered, turning quickly.

'"Of course I know that, Louisa. I do not see the

application of the remark." To do him justice, he did
not at all.

'She passed it away with a slight motion of her hand,
and concentrating her attention upon him again, said,
"Father, I have often thought that life is very short."
—This was so distinctly one of his subjects that he in-
terposed:

'"It is short, no doubt, my dear. Still, the average
duration of human life is proved to have increased of
late years. The calculations of various life assurance and
annuity offices, among other figures which cannot go
wrong, have established the fact."

'"I speak of my own life, father."

'"Oh, indeed! Still," said Mr. Gradgrind, "I need not
point out to you, Louisa, that it is governed by the laws
which govern lives in the aggregate."

'"While it lasts, I would wish to do the little I can, and
the little I am fit for. What does it matter?"

'Mr. Gradgrind seemed rather at a loss to understand
the last four words; replying, "How, matter? What matter, my dear?"

'"Mr. Bounderby," she went on in a steady, straight
way, without regarding this, "asks me to marry him.
The question I have to ask myself is, shall I marry him?
That is so, father, is it not? You have told me so, father.
Have you not?"

'"Certainly, my dear."

'"Let it be so."'

The psychology of Louisa's development and of her
brother Tom's is sound. Having no outlet for her emotional
life except in her love for her brother, she lives for him,
and marries Bounderby—under pressure from Tom—for
Tom's sake ('What does it matter?'). Thus, by the constrictions and starvations of the Gradgrind *régime,* are natural affection and capacity for disinterested devotion
turned to ill. As for Tom, the *régime* has made of him a
bored and sullen whelp, and 'he was becoming that not
unprecedented triumph of calculation which is usually at

work on number one'—the Utilitarian philosophy has done
that for him. He declares that when he goes to live with
Bounderby as having a post in the bank, 'he'll have his
revenge.'—'I mean, I'll enjoy myself a little, and go about
and see something and hear something. I'll recompense
myself for the way in which I've been brought up.' His
descent into debt and bank-robbery is natural. And it is
natural that Louisa, having sacrificed herself for this unrepaying object of affection, should be found not altogether unresponsive when Mr. James Harthouse, having
sized up the situation, pursues his opportunity with well-
bred and calculating tact. His apologia for genteel cyni-
cism is a shrewd thrust at the Gradgrind philosophy:

> ' "The only difference between us and the professors
> of virtue or benevolence, or philanthropy—never mind
> the name—is, that we know it is all meaningless, and
> say so; while they know it equally, and will never say
> so."
> 'Why should she be shocked or warned by this reiter-
> ation? It was not so unlike her father's principles, and
> her early training, that it need startle her.'

When, fleeing from temptation, she arrives back at her
father's house, tells him her plight, and, crying, 'All I
know is, your philosophy and your teaching will not save
me,' collapses, he sees 'the pride of his heart and the triumph of his system lying an insensible heap at his feet.'
The fallacy now calamitously demonstrated can be seen
focussed in that 'pride,' which brings together in an illusory oneness the pride of his system and his love for his
child. What that love is Gradgrind now knows, and he
knows that it matters to him more than the system, which
is thus confuted (the educational failure as such being
a lesser matter). There is nothing sentimental here; the
demonstration is impressive, because we are convinced of
the love, and because Gradgrind has been made to exist
for us as a man who has 'meant to do right':

> 'He said it earnestly, and, to do him justice, he had.

In gauging fathomless deeps with his little mean excise rod, and in staggering over the universe with his rusty stiff-legged compasses, he had meant to do great things. Within the limits of his short tether he had tumbled about, annihilating the flowers of existence with greater singleness of purpose than many of the blatant personages whose company he kept.'

The demonstration still to come, that of which the other 'triumph of his system,' Tom, is the centre, is sardonic comedy, imagined with great intensity and done with the sure touch of genius. There is the pregnant scene in which Mr. Gradgrind, in the deserted ring of a third-rate travelling circus, has to recognize his son in a comic negro servant; and has to recognize that his son owes his escape from Justice to a peculiarly disinterested gratitude—to the opportunity given him by the non-Utilitarian Mr. Sleary, grateful for Sissy's sake, to assume such a disguise:

'In a preposterous coat, like a beadle's, with cuffs and flaps exaggerated to an unspeakable extent; in an immense waistcoat, knee breeches, buckled shoes, and a mad cocked-hat; with nothing fitting him, and everything of coarse material, moth-eaten, and full of holes; with seams in his black face, where fear and heat had started through the greasy composition daubed all over it; anything so grimly, detestably, ridiculously shameful as the whelp in his comic livery, Mr. Gradgrind never could by any other means have believed in, weighable and measurable fact though it was. And one of his model children had come to this!

'At first the whelp would not draw any nearer but persisted in remaining up there by himself. Yielding at length, if any concession so sullenly made can be called yielding, to the entreaties of Sissy—for Louisa he disowned altogether—he came down, bench by bench, until he stood in the sawdust, on the verge of the circle, as far as possible, within its limits, from where his father sat.

' "How was this done?" asked the father.

'"How was what done?" moodily answered the son.

'"This robbery," said the father, raising his voice upon the word.

'"I forced the safe myself overnight, and shut it up ajar before I went away. I had had the key that was found made long before. I dropped it that morning, that it might be supposed to have been used. I didn't take the money all at once. I pretended to put my balance away every night, but I didn't. Now you know all about it."

'"If a thunderbolt had fallen on me," said the father, "it would have shocked me less than this!"

'"I don't see why," grumbled the son. "So many people are employed in situations of trust; so many people, out of so many, will be dishonest. I have heard you talk, a hundred times, of its being a law. How can *I* help laws? You have comforted others with such things, father. Comfort yourself!"

'The father buried his face in his hands, and the son stood in his disgraceful grotesqueness, biting straw: his hands, with the black partly worn away inside, looking like the hands of a monkey. The evening was fast closing in; and, from time to time, he turned the whites of his eyes restlessly and impatiently towards his father. They were the only parts of his face that showed any life or expression, the pigment upon it was so thick.'

Something of the rich complexity of Dickens's art may be seen in this passage. No simple formula can take account of the various elements in the whole effect, a sardonic-tragic in which satire consorts with pathos. The excerpt in itself suggests the justification for saying that *Hard Times* is a poetic work. It suggests that the genius of the writer may fairly be described as that of a poetic dramatist, and that, in our preconceptions about 'the novel,' we may miss, within the field of fictional prose, possibilities of concentration and flexibility in the interpretation of life such as we associate with Shakespearean drama.

The note, as we have it above in Tom's retort, of ironic-satiric discomfiture of the Utilitarian philosopher by the rebound of his formulae upon himself is developed in the ensuing scene with Bitzer, the truly successful pupil, the real triumph of the system. He arrives to intercept Tom's flight:

'Bitzer, still holding the paralysed culprit by the collar, stood in the Ring, blinking at his old patron through the darkness of the twilight.

' "Bitzer," said Mr. Gradgrind, broken down, and miserably submissive to him, "have you a heart?"

' "The circulation, sir," returned Bitzer, smiling at the oddity of the question, "couldn't be carried on without one. No man, sir, acquainted with the facts established by Harvey relating to the circulation of the blood, can doubt that I have a heart."

' "Is it accessible," cried Mr. Gradgrind, "to any compassionate influence?"

' "It is accessible to Reason, sir," returned the excellent young man. "And to nothing else."

'They stood looking at each other; Mr. Gradgrind's face as white as the pursuer's.

' "What motive—even what motive in reason—can you have for preventing the escape of this wretched youth," said Mr. Gradgrind, "and crushing his miserable father? See his sister here. Pity us!"

' "Sir," returned Bitzer in a very business-like and logical manner, "since you ask me what motive I have in reason for taking young Mr. Tom back to Coketown, it is only reasonable to let you know . . . I am going to take young Mr. Tom back to Coketown, in order to deliver him over to Mr. Bounderby. Sir, I have no doubt whatever that Mr. Bounderby will then promote me to young Mr. Tom's situation. And I wish to have his situation, sir, for it will be a rise to me, and will do me good."

' "If this is solely a question of self-interest with you—" Mr. Gradgrind began.

'"I beg your pardon for interrupting you, sir," returned Bitzer, "but I am sure you know that the whole social system is a question of self-interest. What you must always appeal to is a person's self-interest. It's your only hold. We are so constituted. I was brought up in that catechism when I was very young, sir, as you are aware."

'"What sum of money," said Mr. Gradgrind, "will you set against your expected promotion?"

'"Thank you, sir," returned Bitzer, "for hinting at the proposal; but I will not set any sum against it. Knowing that your clear head would propose that alternative, I have gone over the calculations in my mind; and I find that to compound a felony, even on very high terms indeed, would not be as safe and good for me as my improved prospects in the Bank."

'"Bitzer," said Mr. Gradgrind, stretching out his hands as though he would have said, See how miserable I am! "Bitzer, I have but one chance left to soften you. You were many years at my school. If, in remembrance of the pains bestowed upon you there, you can persuade yourself in any degree to disregard your present interest and release my son, I entreat and pray you to give him the benefit of that remembrance."

'"I really wonder, sir," rejoined the old pupil in an argumentative manner, "to find you taking a position so untenable. My schooling was paid for; it was a bargain; and when I came away, the bargain ended."

'It was a fundamental principle of the Gradgrind philosophy, that everything was to be paid for. Nobody was ever on any account to give anybody anything, or render anybody help without purchase. Gratitude was to be abolished, and the virtues springing from it were not to be. Every inch of the existence of mankind, from birth to death, was to be a bargain across the counter. And if we didn't get to Heaven that way, it was not a politico-economical place, and we had no business there.

'"I don't deny," added Bitzer, "that my schooling was cheap. But that comes right, sir. I was made in the cheap-

est market, and have to dispose of myself in the dear-
est."'

Tom's escape is contrived, successfully in every sense,
by means belonging to Dickensian high-fantastic comedy.
And there follows the solemn moral of the whole fable, put
with the rightness of genius into Mr. Sleary's asthmatic
mouth. He, agent of the artist's marvellous tact, acquits
himself of it characteristically:

> ' "Thquire, you don't need to be told that dogth ith
> wonderful animalth."
> ' "Their instinct," said Mr. Gradgrind, "is surprising."
> ' "Whatever you call it—and I'm bletht if I know what
> to call it"—said Sleary, "it ith athtonithing. The way in
> which a dog'll find you—the dithtanthe he'll come!"
> ' "His scent," said Mr. Gradgrind, "being so fine."
> ' "I'm bletht if I know what to call it," repeated Sleary,
> shaking his head, "but I have had dogth find me,
> Thquire . . ."'

—And Mr. Sleary proceeds to explain that Sissy's truant
father is certainly dead because his performing dog, who
would never have deserted him living, has come back to
the Horse-riding:

> ' "he wath lame, and pretty well blind. He went
> round to our children, one after another, ath if he wath
> a theeking for a child he knowed; and then he come to
> me, and throwed hithelf up behind, and thtood on his
> two fore-legth, weak as he wath, and then he wagged
> hith tail and died. Thquire, that dog was Merrylegth."'

The whole passage has to be read as it stands in the text
(Book III, Chapter VIII). Reading it there we have to
stand off and reflect at a distance to recognize the potentialities that might have been realized elsewhere as Dickensian sentimentality. There is nothing sentimental in the
actual effect. The profoundly serious intention is in control, the touch sure, and the structure that ensures the
poise unassertively complex. Here is the formal moral:

' "Tho, whether her father bathely detherted her; or whether he broke hith own heart alone, rather than pull her down along with him; never will be known now, Thquire, till—no, not till we know how the dogth findth uth out!"

' "She keeps the bottle that he sent her for, to this hour; and she will believe in his affection to the last moment of her life," said Mr. Gradgrind.

' "It theemth to prethent two thingth to a perthon, don't it, Thquire?" said Mr. Sleary, musing as he looked down into the depths of his brandy-and-water: "one, that there ith a love in the world, not all Thelf-interetht after all, but thomething very different; t'other, that it hath a way of ith own of calculating or not calculating, whith thomehow or another ith at leatht ath hard to give a name to, ath the wayth of the dogth ith!"

'Mr. Gradgrind looked out of the window, and made no reply. Mr. Sleary emptied his glass and recalled the ladies.'

It will be seen that the effect (I repeat, the whole passage must be read), apparently so simple and easily right, depends upon a subtle interplay of diverse elements, a multiplicity in unison of timbre and tone. Dickens, we know, was a popular entertainer, but Flaubert never wrote anything approaching this in subtlety of achieved art. Dickens, of course, has a vitality that we don't look for in Flaubert. Shakespeare was a popular entertainer, we reflect—not too extravagantly, we can surely tell ourselves, as we ponder passages of this characteristic quality in their relation, a closely organized one, to the poetic whole.

Criticism, of course, has its points to make against *Hard Times*. It can be said of Stephen Blackpool, not only that he is too good and qualifies too consistently for the martyr's halo, but that he invites an adaptation of the objection brought, from the negro point of view, against Uncle Tom, which was to the effect that he was a white man's good nigger. And certainly it doesn't need a working-class bias to produce the comment that when Dickens comes to

the Trade Unions his understanding of the world he offers
to deal with betrays a marked limitation. There were undoubtedly professional agitators, and Trade Union solidarity was undoubtedly often asserted at the expense of the
individual's rights, but it is a score against a work so insistently typical in intention that it should give the representative rôle to the agitator, Slackbridge, and make Trade
Unionism nothing better than the pardonable error of the
misguided and oppressed, and, as such, an agent in the
martyrdom of the good working man. (But to be fair we
must remember the conversation between Bitzer and Mrs.
Sparsit:

"'It is much to be regretted,' said Mrs. Sparsit, making her nose more Roman and her eyebrows more Co-
riolanian in the strength of her severity, "that the united
masters allow of any such class combination."

'"Yes, ma'am," said Bitzer.

'"Being united themselves, they ought one and all to
set their faces against employing any man who is united
with any other man," said Mrs. Sparsit.

'"They have done that, ma'am," returned Bitzer; "but
it rather fell through, ma'am."

'"I do not pretend to understand these things," said
Mrs. Sparsit with dignity. ". . . I only know that those
people must be conquered, and that it's high time it
was done, once for all."')

Just as Dickens has no glimpse of the part to be played
by Trade Unionism in bettering the conditions he de-
plores, so, though he sees there are many places of worship
in Coketown, of various kinds of ugliness, he has no notion of the part played by religion in the life
of nineteenth-century industrial England. The kind of
self-respecting steadiness and conscientious restraint that
he represents in Stephen did certainly exist on a large scale
among the working-classes, and this is an important historical fact. But there would have been no such fact if
those chapels described by Dickens had had no more relation to the life of Coketown than he shows them to
have.

Again, his attitude to Trade Unionism is not the only expression of a lack of political understanding. Parliament for him is merely the 'national dust-yard,' where the 'national dustmen' entertain one another 'with a great many noisy little fights among themselves,' and appoint commissions which fill blue-books with dreary facts and futile statistics—of a kind that helps Gradgrind to 'prove that the Good Samaritan was a bad economist.'

Yet Dickens's understanding of Victorian civilization is adequate for his purpose; the justice and penetration of his criticism are unaffected. And his moral perception works in alliance with a clear insight into the English social structure. Mr. James Harthouse is necessary for the plot; but he too has his representative function. He has come to Coketown as a prospective parliamentary candidate, for 'the Gradgrind party wanted assistance in cutting the throats of the Graces,' and they 'liked fine gentlemen; they pretended that they did not, but they did.' And so the alliance between the old ruling class and the 'hard' men figures duly in the fable. This economy is typical. There is Mrs. Sparsit, for instance, who might seem to be there merely for the plot. But her 'husband was a Powler,' a fact she reverts to as often as Bounderby to his mythical birth in a ditch; and the two complementary opposites, when Mr. James Harthouse, who in his languid assurance of class-superiority doesn't need to boast, is added, form a trio that suggests the whole system of British snobbery.

But the packed richness of *Hard Times* is almost incredibly varied, and not all the quoting I have indulged in suggests it adequately. The final stress may fall on Dickens's command of word, phrase, rhythm and image: in ease and range there is surely no greater master of English except Shakespeare. This comes back to saying that Dickens is a great poet: his endless resource in felicitously varied expression is an extraordinary responsiveness to life. His senses are charged with emotional energy, and his intelligence plays and flashes in the quickest and sharpest perception. That is, his mastery of 'style' is of the only kind that matters—which is not to say that he hasn't a conscious interest in what can be done with words; many

of his felicities could plainly not have come if there had
not been, in the background, a habit of such interest.
Take this, for instance:

> 'He had reached the neutral ground upon the out-
> skirts of the town, which was neither town nor country,
> but either spoiled . . .'

But he is no more a stylist than Shakespeare; and his
mastery of expression is most fairly suggested by stressing,
not his descriptive evocations (there are some magnificent
ones in *Hard Times*—the varied *décor* of the action is made
vividly present, you can feel the velvety dust trodden by
Mrs. Sparsit in her stealth, and feel the imminent storm),
but his strictly dramatic felicities. Perhaps, however,
'strictly' is not altogether a good pointer, since Dickens
is a master of his chosen art, and his mastery shows itself
in the way in which he moves between less direct forms
of the dramatic and the direct rendering of speech. Here
is Mrs. Gradgrind dying (a cipher in the Gradgrind system, the poor creature has never really been alive):

> 'She had positively refused to take to her bed; on the
> ground that, if she did, she would never hear the last
> of it.
> 'Her feeble voice sounded so far away in her bundle
> of shawls, and the sound of another voice addressing her
> seemed to take such a long time in getting down to her
> ears, that she might have been lying at the bottom of
> a well. The poor lady was nearer Truth than she ever
> had been: which had much to do with it.
> 'On being told that Mrs. Bounderby was there, she
> replied, at cross purposes, that she had never called him
> by that name since he had married Louisa; and that
> pending her choice of an objectionable name, she had
> called him J; and that she could not at present depart
> from that regulation, not being yet provided with a
> permanent substitute. Louisa had sat by her for some
> minutes, and had spoken to her often, before she arrived

at a clear understanding who it was. She then seemed to come to it all at once.

'"Well, my dear," said Mrs. Gradgrind, "and I hope you are going on satisfactorily to yourself. It was all your father's doing. He set his heart upon it. And he ought to know."

'"I want to hear of you, mother; not of myself."

'"You want to hear of me, my dear? That's something new, I am sure, when anybody wants to hear of me. Not at all well, Louisa. Very faint and giddy."

'"Are you in pain, dear mother?"

'"I think there's a pain somewhere in the room," said Mrs. Gradgrind, "but I couldn't positively say that I have got it."

'After this strange speech, she lay silent for some time.

. . . .

'"But there is something—not an Ology at all—that your father has missed, or forgotten, Louisa. I don't know what it is. I have often sat with Sissy near me, and thought about it. I shall never get its name now. But your father may. It makes me restless. I want to write to him, to find out, for God's sake, what it is. Give me a pen, give me a pen."

'Even the power of restlessness was gone, except from the poor head, which could just turn from side to side.

'She fancied, however, that her request had been complied with, and that the pen she could not have held was in her hand. It matters little what figures of wonderful no-meaning she began to trace upon her wrappers. The hand soon stopped in the midst of them; the light that had always been feeble and dim behind the weak transparency, went out; and even Mrs. Gradgrind, emerged from the shadow in which man walketh and disquieteth himself in vain, took upon her the dread solemnity of the sages and patriarchs.'

With this kind of thing before us, we talk not of style but of dramatic creation and imaginative genius.

Appendix

DANIEL DERONDA: A Conversation

By Henry James

THEODORA, one day early in the autumn, sat on her verandah with a piece of embroidery, the design of which she made up as she proceeded, being careful, however, to have a Japanese screen before her, to keep her inspiration at the proper altitude. Pulcheria, who was paying her a visit, sat near her with a closed book, in a paper cover, in her lap. Pulcheria was playing with the pug-dog, rather idly, but Theodora was stitching, steadily and meditatively. 'Well,' said Theodora at last, 'I wonder what he accomplished in the East.' Pulcheria took the little dog into her lap and made him sit on the book. 'Oh,' she replied, 'they had tea-parties at Jerusalem—exclusively of ladies—and he sat in the midst and stirred his tea and made high-toned remarks. And then Mirah sang a little, just a little, on account of her voice being so weak. Sit still, Fido,' she continued, addressing the little dog, 'and keep your nose out of my face. But it's a nice little nose, all the same,' she pursued, 'a nice little short snub nose and not a horrid big Jewish nose. Oh, my dear, when I think what a collection of noses there must have been at that wedding!' At this moment Constantius steps upon the verandah from within, hat and stick in hand and his shoes a trifle dusty. He has some distance to come before he reaches the place where the ladies are sitting, and this gives Pulcheria time to murmur, 'Talk of snub noses!' Constantius is presented by Theodora to Pulcheria, and he sits down and exclaims upon the admirable blueness of the sea, which lies in a straight band across the green of the little lawn; comments too upon the pleasure of having one side of one's verandah in the shade. Soon Fido, the little dog, still restless, jumps off Pulcheria's lap and reveals the book, which lies title upward. 'Oh', says Constantius, 'you have been finishing *Daniel Deronda*?' Then follows a conversation which it will be more convenient to present in another form.

THEODORA. Yes, Pulcheria has been reading aloud the last chapters to me. They are wonderfully beautiful.

CONSTANTIUS (after a moment's hesitation). Yes, they are very beautiful. I am sure you read well, Pulcheria, to give the fine passages their full value.

THEODORA. She reads well when she chooses, but I am sorry to say that in some of the fine passages of this last book she took quite a false tone. I couldn't have read them aloud myself; I should have broken down. But Pulcheria—would you really believe it?—when she couldn't go on it was not for tears, but for—the contrary.

CONSTANTIUS. For smiles? Did you really find it comical? One of my objections to *Daniel Deronda* is the absence of those delightfully humorous passages which enlivened the author's former works.

PULCHERIA. Oh, I think there are some places as amusing as anything in *Adam Bede* or *The Mill on the Floss*: for instance where, at the last, Deronda wipes Gwendolen's tears and Gwendolen wipes his.

CONSTANTIUS. Yes, I know what you mean. I can understand that situation presenting a slightly ridiculous image; that is, if the current of the story don't swiftly carry you past.

PULCHERIA. What do you mean by the current of the story? I never read a story with less current. It is not a river; it is a series of lakes. I once read of a group of little uneven ponds resembling, from a bird's-eye view, a looking-glass which had fallen upon the floor and broken, and was lying in fragments. That is what *Daniel Deronda* would look like, on a bird's-eye view.

THEODORA. Pulcheria found that comparison in a French novel. She is always reading French novels.

CONSTANTIUS. Ah, there are some very good ones.

PULCHERIA (perversely). I don't know; I think there are some very poor ones.

CONSTANTIUS. The comparison is not bad, at any rate.

I know what you mean by *Daniel Deronda* lacking current. It has almost as little as *Romola*.

PULCHERIA. Oh, *Romola* is unpardonably slow; it is a kind of literary tortoise.

CONSTANTIUS. Yes, I know what you mean by that. But I am afraid you are not friendly to our great novelist.

THEODORA. She likes Balzac and George Sand and other impure writers.

CONSTANTIUS. Well, I must say I understand that.

PULCHERIA. My favourite novelist is Thackeray, and I am extremely fond of Miss Austen.

CONSTANTIUS. I understand that too. You read over *The Newcomes* and *Pride and Prejudice.*

PULCHERIA. No, I don't read them over now; I think them over. I have been making visits for a long time past to a series of friends, and I have spent the last six months in reading *Daniel Deronda* aloud. Fortune would have it that I should always arrive by the same train as the new number. I am accounted a frivolous, idle creature; I am not a disciple in the new school of embroidery, like Theodora; so I was immediately pushed into a chair and the book thrust into my hand, that I might lift up my voice and make peace between all the impatiences that were snatching at it. So I may claim at least that I have read every word of the work. I never skipped.

THEODORA. I should hope not, indeed!

CONSTANTIUS. And do you mean that you really didn't enjoy it?

PULCHERIA. I found it protracted, pretentious, pedantic.

CONSTANTIUS. I see; I can understand that.

THEODORA. Oh, you understand too much! This is the twentieth time you have used that formula.

CONSTANTIUS. What will you have? You know I must try to understand; it's my trade!

THEODORA. He means he writes reviews. Trying *not* to understand is what I call that trade!

CONSTANTIUS. Say then I take it the wrong way; that is

why it has never made my fortune. But I do try to understand; it is my—my—(He pauses).

THEODORA. I know what you want to say. Your strong side.

PULCHERIA. And what is his weak side?

THEODORA. He writes novels.

CONSTANTIUS. I have written *one*. You can't call that a side. It's a little facet, at the most.

PULCHERIA. You talk as if you were a diamond. I should like to read it—not aloud!

CONSTANTIUS. You can't read it softly enough. But you, Theodora, you didn't find our book too 'protracted?'

THEODORA. I should have liked it to continue indefinitely; to keep coming out always; to be one of the regular things of life.

PULCHERIA. Oh, come here, little dog! To think that *Daniel Deronda* might be perpetual when you, little short-nosed darling, can't last at the most more than nine or ten years!

THEODORA. A book like *Daniel Deronda* becomes part of one's life; one lives in it, or alongside of it. I don't hesitate to say that I have been living in this one for the last eight months. It is such a complete world George Eliot builds up; it is so vast, so much-embracing! It has such a firm earth and such an ethereal sky. You can turn into it and lose yourself in it.

PULCHERIA. Oh, easily, and die of cold and starvation!

THEODORA. I have been very near to poor Gwendolen and very near to that sweet Mirah. And the dear little Meyricks also; I know them intimately well.

PULCHERIA. The Meyricks, I grant you, are the best thing in the book.

THEODORA. They are a delicious family; I wish they lived in Boston. I consider Herr Klesmer almost Shakespearean, and his wife is almost as good. I have been near to poor, grand Mordecai—

PULCHERIA. Oh, reflect, my dear; not too near!

THEODORA. And as for Deronda himself I freely confess that I am consumed with a hopeless passion for him. He is the most irresistible man in the literature of fiction.

PULCHERIA. He is not a man at all.

THEODORA. I remember nothing more beautiful than the description of his childhood, and that picture of his lying on the grass in the abbey cloister, a beautiful seraph-faced boy, with a lovely voice, reading history and asking his Scotch tutor why the Popes had so many nephews. He must have been delightfully handsome.

PULCHERIA. Never, my dear, with that nose! I am sure he had a nose, and I hold that the author has shown great pusillanimity in her treatment of it. She has quite shirked it. The picture you speak of is very pretty, but a picture is not a person. And why is he always grasping his coat-collar, as if he wished to hang himself up? The author had an uncomfortable feeling that she must make him do something real, something visible and sensible, and she hit upon that clumsy figure. I don't see what you mean by saying you have been *near* those people; that is just what one is not. They produce no illusion. They are described and analysed to death, but we don't see them nor hear them nor touch them. Deronda clutches his coat-collar, Mirah crosses her feet, Mordecai talks like the Bible; but that doesn't make real figures of them. They have no existence outside of the author's study.

THEODORA. If you mean that they are nobly imaginative I quite agree with you; and if they say nothing to your own imagination the fault is yours, not theirs.

PULCHERIA. Pray don't say they are Shakespearean again. Shakespeare went to work another way.

CONSTANTIUS. I think you are both in a measure right; there is a distinction to be drawn. There are in *Daniel Deronda* the figures based upon observation and the figures based upon invention. This distinction, I know, is rather a rough one. There are no figures in any novel that are pure observation, and none that are pure invention. But either element may preponderate, and in those cases in which invention has preponderated George Eliot seems to me to have achieved at the best but so many brilliant failures.

THEODORA. And are *you* turning severe? I thought you admired her so much.

CONSTANTIUS. I defy any one to admire her more, but one must discriminate. Speaking brutally, I consider *Daniel Deronda* the weakest of her books. It strikes me as very sensibly inferior to *Middlemarch*. I have an immense opinion of *Middlemarch*.

PULCHERIA. Not having been obliged by circumstances to read *Middlemarch* to other people, I didn't read it at all. I couldn't read it to myself. I tried, but I broke down. I appreciated Rosamond, but I couldn't believe in Dorothea.

THEODORA (very gravely). So much the worse for you, Pulcheria. I have enjoyed *Daniel Deronda because* I had enjoyed *Middlemarch*. Why should you throw *Middlemarch* up against her? It seems to me that if a book is fine it is fine. I have enjoyed *Deronda* deeply, from beginning to end.

CONSTANTIUS. I assure you, so have I. I can read nothing of George Eliot's without enjoyment. I even enjoy her poetry, though I don't approve of it. In whatever she writes I enjoy her intelligence; it has space and air like a fine landscape. The intellectual brilliancy of *Daniel Deronda* strikes me as very great, in excess of anything the author has done. In the first couple of numbers of the book this ravished me. I delighted in its deep, rich English tone, in which so many notes seemed melted together.

PULCHERIA. The tone is not English, it is German.

CONSTANTIUS. I understand that—if Theodora will allow me to say so. Little by little I began to feel that I cared less for certain notes than for others. I say it under my breath—I began to feel an occasional temptation to skip. Roughly speaking, all the Jewish burden of the story tended to weary me; it is this part that produces the poor illusion which I agree with Pulcheria in finding. Gwendolen and Grandcourt are admirable—Gwendolen is a masterpiece. She is known, felt and presented, psychologically, altogether in the grand manner. Beside her and beside her husband—a consummate picture of English brutality refined and distilled (for Grandcourt is before all things brutal), Deronda, Mordecai and Mirah are hardly more than shadows. They and their fortunes are all improvisation. I don't say anything against improvisation. When it succeeds it has a surpassing charm. But it must succeed. With George Eliot it seems to me to succeed, but a little less than one would expect of her talent. The story of Deronda's life, his mother's story, Mirah's story, are quite the sort of thing one finds in George Sand. But they are really not so good as they would be in George Sand. George Sand would have carried it off with a lighter hand.

THEODORA. Oh, Constantius, how can you compare George Eliot's novels to that woman's? It is sunlight and moonshine.

PULCHERIA. I really think the two writers are very much alike. They are both very voluble, both addicted to moralizing and philosophizing *à tout bout de champ*, both inartistic.

CONSTANTIUS. I see what you mean. But George Eliot is solid, and George Sand is liquid. When occasionally George Eliot liquefies—as in the history of Deronda's birth, and in that of Mirah—it is not to so crystalline a clearness as the author of *Consuelo* and *André*. Take Mirah's long narrative of her adventures, when she unfolds them to Mrs. Meyrick. It is arranged, it is artificial, *ancien jeu*, quite in the George Sand manner. But George Sand would have done it better. The false tone would have remained, but it would have been more persuasive. It would have been a fib, but the fib would have been neater.

THEODORA. I don't think fibbing neatly a merit, and I don't see what is to be gained by such comparisons. George Eliot is pure and George Sand is impure; how can you compare them? As for the Jewish element in Deronda, I think it a very fine idea; it's a noble subject. Wilkie Collins and Miss Braddon would not have thought of it, but that does not condemn it. It shows a large conception of what one may do in a novel. I heard you say, the other day, that most novels were so trivial—that they had no general ideas. Here is a general idea, the idea interpreted by Deronda. I have never disliked the Jews as some people do; I am not like Pulcheria, who sees a Jew in every bush. I wish there were one; I would cultivate shrubbery. I have known too many clever and charming Jews; I have known none that were not clever.

PULCHERIA. Clever, but not charming.

CONSTANTIUS. I quite agree with you as to Deronda's going in for the Jews and turning out a Jew himself being a fine subject, and this quite apart from the fact of whether such a thing as a Jewish revival be at all a possibility. If it be a possibility, so much the better—so much the better for the subject, I mean.

PULCHERIA. *A la bonne heure!*

CONSTANTIUS. I rather suspect it is not a possibility; that the Jews in general take themselves much less seriously than that. They have other fish to fry. George Eliot takes them as a person outside of Judaism—aesthetically. I don't believe that is the way they take themselves.

PULCHERIA. They have the less excuse then for keeping themselves so dirty.

THEODORA. George Eliot must have known some delightful Jews.

CONSTANTIUS. Very likely; but I shouldn't wonder if the most delightful of them had smiled a trifle, here and there, over her book. But that makes nothing, as Herr Klesmer would say. The subject is a noble one. The idea of depicting a nature able to feel and worthy to feel the sort of inspiration that takes possession of Deronda, of depicting it sympathetically, minutely and intimately—such an idea has great elevation. There is something very fascinating in the mission that Deronda takes upon himself. I don't quite know what it means, I don't understand more than half of Mordecai's rhapsodies, and I don't perceive exactly what practical steps could be taken. Deronda could go about and talk with clever Jews—not an unpleasant life.

PULCHERIA. All that seems to me so unreal that when at the end the author finds herself confronted with the necessity of making him start for the East by the train, and announces that Sir Hugo and Lady Mallinger have given his wife 'a complete Eastern outfit,' I descend to the ground with a ludicrous jump.

CONSTANTIUS. Unreal, if you please; that is no objection to it; it greatly tickles my imagination. I like extremely the idea of Mordecai believing, without ground of belief, that if he only wait, a young man on whom nature and society have centred all their gifts will come to him and receive from his hands the precious vessel of his hopes. It is romantic, but it is not vulgar romance; it is finely romantic. And there is something very fine in the author's own feeling about Deronda. He is a very liberal creation. He is, I think, a failure—a brilliant failure; if he had been a success I should call him a splendid creation. The author meant to do things very handsomely for him; she meant apparently to make a faultless human being.

PULCHERIA. She made a dreadful prig.

CONSTANTIUS. He *is* rather priggish, and one wonders that so clever a woman as George Eliot shouldn't see it.

PULCHERIA. He has no blood in his body. His attitude at moments is like that of a high-priest in a *tableau vivant*.

THEODORA. Pulcheria likes the little gentlemen in the French novels who take good care of their attitudes, which are always the same attitude, the attitude of 'conquest'—of a conquest that tickles their vanity. Deronda has a contour that cuts straight through the middle of all that. He is made of a stuff that isn't dreamt of in their philosophy.

PULCHERIA. Pulcheria likes very much a novel which she read three or four years ago, but which she has not forgotten. It was by Ivan Turgénieff, and it was called *On the Eve*. Theodora has read it, I know, because she admires Turgénieff, and Constantius has read it, I suppose, because he had read everything.

CONSTANTIUS. If I had no reason but that for my reading, it would be small. But Turgénieff is my man.

PULCHERIA. You were just now praising George Eliot's general ideas. The tale of which I speak contains in the portrait of the hero very much such a general idea as you find in the portrait of Deronda. Don't you remember the young Bulgarian student, Inssaroff, who gives himself the mission of rescuing his country from its subjection to the Turks? Poor man, if he had foreseen the horrible summer of 1876! His character is the picture of a race-passion, of patriotic hopes and dreams. But what a difference in the vividness of the two figures. Inssaroff is a man; he stands up on his feet; we see him, hear him, touch him. And it has taken the author but a couple of hundred pages—not eight volumes—to do it.

THEODORA. I don't remember Inssaroff at all, but I perfectly remember the heroine, Helena. She is certainly most remarkable; but remarkable as she is, I should never dream of calling her as wonderful as Gwendolen.

CONSTANTIUS. Turgénieff is a magician, which I don't think I should call George Eliot. One is a poet, the other is a philosopher. One cares for the aspect of things and the other cares for the reason of things. George Eliot, in embarking with Deronda, took aboard, as it were, a far heavier cargo than Turgénieff with his Inssaroff. She proposed, consciously, to strike more notes.

PULCHERIA. Oh, consciously, yes!

CONSTANTIUS. George Eliot wished to show the possible picturesqueness—the romance, as it were—of a high moral tone. Deronda is a moralist—a moralist with a rich complexion.

THEODORA. It is a most beautiful nature. I don't know anywhere a more complete, a more deeply analysed portrait of a great nature. We praise novelists for wandering and creeping so into the small corners of the mind. That is what we praise Balzac for when he gets down upon all fours to crawl through Le Père Goriot or Les Parents Pauvres. But I must say I think it a finer thing to unlock with as firm a hand as George Eliot some of the greater chambers of human character. Deronda is in a manner an ideal character, if you will, but he seems to me triumphantly married to reality. There are some admirable things said about him; nothing can be finer than those pages of description of his moral temperament in the fourth book—his elevated way of looking at things, his impartiality, his universal sympathy, and at the same time his fear of their turning into mere irresponsible indifference. I remember some of it verbally: 'He was ceasing to care for knowledge —he had no ambition for practice—unless they could be gathered up into one current with his emotions.'

PULCHERIA. Oh, there is plenty about his emotions. Everything about him is 'emotive.' That bad word occurs on every fifth page.

THEODORA. I don't see that it is a bad word.

PULCHERIA. It may be good German, but it is poor English.

THEODORA. It is not German at all; it is Latin. So, my dear!

PULCHERIA. As I say, then, it is not English.

THEODORA. This is the first time I ever heard that George Eliot's style was bad!

CONSTANTIUS. It is admirable; it has the most delightful and the most intellectually comfortable suggestions. But it is occasionally a little too long-sleeved, as I may say. It is sometimes too loose a fit for the thought, a little baggy.

THEODORA. And the advice he gives Gwendolen, the things he says to her, they are the very essence of wisdom, of warm human wisdom, knowing life and feeling it. 'Keep your fear as a safeguard, it may make consequences passionately present to you.' What can be better than that?

PULCHERIA. Nothing, perhaps. But what can be drearier than a novel in which the function of the hero—young, handsome and brilliant—is to give didactic advice, in a proverbial form, to the young, beautiful and brilliant heroine?

CONSTANTIUS. That is not putting it quite fairly. The function of Deronda is to make Gwendolen fall in love with him, to say nothing of falling in love himself with Mirah.

PULCHERIA. Yes, the less said about that the better. All we know about Mirah is that she has delicate rings of hair, sits with her feet crossed, and talks like an article in a new magazine.

CONSTANTIUS. Deronda's function of adviser to Gwendolen does not strike me as so ridiculous. He is not nearly so ridiculous as if he were lovesick. It is a very interesting situation—that of a man with whom a beautiful woman in trouble falls in love and yet whose affections are so preoccupied that the most he can do for her in return is to enter kindly and sympathetically into her position, pity her and talk to her. George Eliot always gives us something that is strikingly and ironically characteristic of human life; and what savours more of the essential crookedness of our fate than the sad cross-purposes of these two young people? Poor Gwendolen's falling in love with Deronda is part of her own luckless history, not of his.

THEODORA. I do think he takes it to himself rather too little. No man had ever so little vanity.

PULCHERIA. It is very inconsistent, therefore, as well as being extremely impertinent and ill-mannered, his buying back and sending to her her necklace at Leubronn.

CONSTANTIUS. Oh, you must concede that; without it there would have been no story. A man writing of him, however, would certainly have made him more peccable. As George Eliot lets herself go, in that quarter, she becomes delightfully, almost touchingly, feminine. It is like her making Romola go to housekeeping with Tessa, after Tito Melema's death; like her making Dorothea marry Will Ladislaw. If Dorothea had married any one after her misadventure with Casaubon, she would have married a trooper.

THEODORA. Perhaps some day Gwendolen will marry Rex.

PULCHERIA. Pray, who is Rex?

THEODORA. Why, Pulcheria, how can you forget?

PULCHERIA. Nay, how can I remember? But I recall such a name in the dim antiquity of the first or second book. Yes, and then he is pushed to the front again at the last, just in time not to miss the falling of the curtain. Gwendolen will certainly not have the audacity to marry any one we know so little about.

CONSTANTIUS. I have been wanting to say that there

seems to me to be two very distinct elements in George Eliot—a spontaneous one and an artificial one. There is what she is by inspiration and what she is because it is expected of her. These two heads have been very perceptible in her recent writings; they are much less noticeable in her early ones.

THEODORA. You mean that she is too scientific? So long as she remains the great literary genius that she is, how can she be too scientific? She is simply permeated with the highest culture of the age.

PULCHERIA. She talks too much about the 'dynamic quality' of people's eyes. When she uses such a phrase as that in the first sentence in her book she is not a great literary genius, because she shows a want of tact. There can't be a worse limitation.

CONSTANTIUS. The 'dynamic quality' of Gwendolen's glance has made the tour of the world.

THEODORA. It shows a very low level of culture on the world's part to be agitated by a term perfectly familiar to all decently educated people.

PULCHERIA. I don't pretend to be decently educated; pray tell me what it means.

CONSTANTIUS (promptly). I think Pulcheria has hit it in speaking of a want of tact. In the manner of the book, throughout, there is something that one may call a want of tact. The epigraphs in verse are a want of tact; they are sometimes, I think, a trifle more pretentious than really pregnant; the importunity of the moral reflections is a want of tact; the very diffuseness is a want of tact. But it comes back to what I said just now about one's sense of the author writing under a sort of external pressure. I began to notice it in *Felix Holt*; I don't think I had before. She strikes me as a person who certainly has naturally a taste for general considerations, but who has fallen upon an age and a circle which have compelled her to give them an exaggerated attention. She does not strike me as naturally a critic, less still as naturally a sceptic; her spontaneous part is to observe life and to feel it—to feel it with admirable depth. Contemplation, sympathy and faith—

something like that, I should say, would have been her natural scale. If she had fallen upon an age of enthusiastic assent to old articles of faith, it seems to me possible that she would have had a more perfect, a more consistent and graceful development than she has actually had. If she had cast herself into such a current—her genius being equal—it might have carried her to splendid distances. But she has chosen to go into criticism, and to the critics she addresses her work; I mean the critics of the universe. Instead of feeling life itself, it is 'views' upon life that she tries to feel.

PULCHERIA. She is the victim of a first-class education. I am so glad!

CONSTANTIUS. Thanks to her admirable intellect she philosophizes very sufficiently; but meanwhile she has given a chill to her genius. She has come near spoiling an artist.

PULCHERIA. She has quite spoiled one. Or rather I shouldn't say that, because there was no artist to spoil. I maintain that she is not an artist. An artist could never have put a story together so monstrously ill. She has no sense of form.

THEODORA. Pray, what could be more artistic than the way that Deronda's paternity is concealed till almost the end, and the way we are made to suppose Sir Hugo is his father?

PULCHERIA. And Mirah his sister. How does that fit together? I was as little made to suppose he was not a Jew as I cared when I found out he was. And his mother popping up through a trap-door and popping down again, at the last, in that scrambling fashion! His mother is very bad.

CONSTANTIUS. I think Deronda's mother is one of the unvivified characters; she belongs to the cold half of the book. All the Jewish part is at bottom cold; that is my only objection. I have enjoyed it because my fancy often warms cold things; but beside Gwendolen's history it is like the empty half of the lunar disk beside the full one. It is admirably studied, it is imagined, it is understood, but it is not embodied. One feels this strongly in just those scenes between Deronda and his mother; one feels that one has been appealed to on rather an artificial ground of interest. To make Deronda's reversion to his native faith more dramatic and profound, the author has given him a mother who on very arbitrary grounds, apparently, has separated herself from this same faith and who has been kept waiting in the wing, as it were, for many acts, to come on and make her speech and say so. This moral situation of hers we are invited retrospectively to appreciate. But we hardly care to do so.

PULCHERIA. I don't *see* the princess, in spite of her flame-coloured robe. Why should an actress and prima-donna care so much about religious matters?

THEODORA. It was not only that; it was the Jewish race she hated, Jewish manners and looks. You, my dear, ought to understand that.

PULCHERIA. I do, but I am not a Jewish actress of genius; I am not what Rachel was. If I were I should have other things to think about.

CONSTANTIUS. Think now a little about poor Gwendolen.

PULCHERIA. I don't care to think about her. She was a second-rate English girl who got into a flutter about a lord.

THEODORA. I don't see that she is worse than if she were a first-rate American girl who should get into exactly the same flutter.

PULCHERIA. It wouldn't be the same flutter at all; it wouldn't be any flutter. She wouldn't be afraid of the lord, though she might be amused at him.

THEODORA. I am sure I don't perceive whom Gwendolen was afraid of. She was afraid of her misdeed—her broken promise—after she had committed it, and through that fear she was afraid of her husband. Well she might be! I can imagine nothing more vivid than the sense we get of his absolutely clammy selfishness.

PULCHERIA. She was not afraid of Deronda when, immediately after her marriage and without any but the most casual acquaintance with him, she begins to hover about him at the Mallingers' and to drop little confidences about her conjugal woes. That seems to me very indelicate; ask any woman.

CONSTANTIUS. The very purpose of the author is to give us an idea of the sort of confidence that Deronda inspired —its irresistible potency.

PULCHERIA. A lay father-confessor—horrid!

CONSTANTIUS. And to give us an idea also of the acuteness of Gwendolen's depression, of her haunting sense of impending trouble.

THEODORA. It must be remembered that Gwendolen was in love with Deronda from the first, long before she knew it. She didn't know it, poor girl, but that was it.

PULCHERIA. That makes the matter worse. It is very disagreeable to see her hovering and rustling about a man who is indifferent to her.

THEODORA. He was not indifferent to her, since he sent her back her necklace.

PULCHERIA. Of all the delicate attention to a charming girl that I ever heard of, that little pecuniary transaction is the most felicitous.

CONSTANTIUS. You must remember that he had been *en rapport* with her at the gaming-table. She had been playing in defiance of his observation, and he, continuing to observe her, had been in a measure responsible for her loss. There was a tacit consciousness of this between them. You may contest the possibility of tacit consciousness going so far, but that is not a serious objection. You may point out two or three weak spots in detail; the fact remains that Gwendolen's whole history is vividly told. And see how the girl is known, inside out, how thoroughly she is felt and understood. It is the most *intelligent* thing in all George Eliot's writing, and that is saying much. It is so deep, so true, so complete, it holds such a wealth of psychological detail, it is more than masterly.

THEODORA. I don't know where the perception of character has sailed closer to the wind.

PULCHERIA. The portrait may be admirable, but it has one little fault. You don't care a straw for the original.

Gwendolen is not an interesting girl, and when the author tries to invest her with a deep tragic interest she does so at the expense of consistency. She has made her at the outset too light, too flimsy; tragedy has no hold on such a girl.

THEODORA. You are hard to satisfy. You said this morning that Dorothea was too heavy, and now you find Gwendolen too light. George Eliot wished to give us the perfect counterpart of Dorothea. Having made one portrait she was worthy to make the other.

PULCHERIA. She has committed the fatal error of making Gwendolen vulgarly, pettily, drily selfish. She was *personally* selfish.

THEODORA. I know nothing more personal than selfishness.

PULCHERIA. I am selfish, but I don't go about with my chin out like that; at least I hope I don't. She was an odious young woman, and one can't care what becomes of her. When her marriage turned out ill she would have become still more hard and positive; to make her soft and appealing is very bad logic. The second Gwendolen doesn't belong to the first.

CONSTANTIUS. She is perhaps at the first a little childish for the weight of interest she has to carry, a little too much after the pattern of the unconscientious young ladies of Miss Yonge and Miss Sewell.

THEODORA. Since when is it forbidden to make one's heroine young? Gwendolen is a perfect picture of youthfulness—its eagerness, its presumption, its preoccupation with itself, its vanity and silliness, its sense of its own absoluteness. But she is extremely intelligent and clever, and therefore tragedy *can* have a hold upon her. Her conscience doesn't make the tragedy; that is an old story and, I think, a secondary form of suffering. It is the tragedy that makes her conscience, which then reacts upon it; and I can think of nothing more powerful than the way in which the growth of her conscience is traced, nothing more touching than the picture of its helpless maturity.

CONSTANTIUS. That is perfectly true. Gwendolen's history is admirably typical—as most things are with George Eliot: it is the very stuff that human life is made of. What is it made of but the discovery by each of us that we are at the best but a rather ridiculous fifth wheel to the coach, after we have sat cracking our whip and believing that we are at least the coachman in person? We think we are the main hoop to the barrel, and we turn out to be but a very incidental splinter in one of the staves. The universe forcing itself with a slow, inexorable pressure into a narrow, complacent, and yet after all extremely sensitive mind, and making it ache with the pain of the process—that is Gwendolen's story. And it becomes completely characteristic in that her supreme perception of the fact that the world is whirring past her is in the disappointment not of a base but of an exalted passion. The very chance to embrace what the author is so fond of calling a 'larger life' seems refused to her. She is punished for being narrow, and she is not allowed a chance to expand. Her finding Deronda pre-engaged to go to the East and stir up the race-feeling of the Jews strikes me as a wonderfully happy invention. The irony of the situation, for poor Gwendolen, is almost grotesque, and it makes one wonder whether the whole heavy structure of the Jewish question in the story was not built up by the author for the express purpose of giving its proper force to this particular stroke.

THEODORA. George Eliot's intentions are extremely complex. The mass is for each detail and each detail is for the mass.

PULCHERIA. She is very fond of deaths by drowning. Maggie Tulliver and her brother are drowned, Tito Melema is drowned, Mr. Grandcourt is drowned. It is extremely unlikely that Grandcourt should not have known how to swim.

CONSTANTIUS. He did, of course, but he had a cramp. It served him right. I can't imagine a more consummate representation of the most detestable kind of Englishman —the Englishman who thinks it low to articulate. And in Grandcourt the type and the individual are so happily met: the type with its sense of the proprieties and the individual with his absence of all sense. He is the apotheosis of dryness, a human expression of the simple idea of the perpendicular.

THEODORA. Mr. Casaubon, in *Middlemarch*, was very dry too; and yet what a genius it is that can give us two disagreeable husbands who are so utterly different!

PULCHERIA. You must count the two disagreeable wives too—Rosamond Vincy and Gwendolen. They are very much alike. I know the author didn't mean it; it proves how common a type the worldly, *pincée*, selfish young woman seemed to her. They are both disagreeable; you can't get over that.

CONSTANTIUS. There is something in that, perhaps. I think, at any rate, that the secondary people here are less delightful than in *Middlemarch*; there is nothing so good as Mary Garth and her father, or the little old lady who steals sugar, or the parson who is in love with Mary, or the country relatives of old Mr. Featherstone. Rex Gascoigne is not so good as Fred Vincy.

THEODORA. Mr. Gascoigne is admirable, and Mrs. Davilow is charming.

PULCHERIA. And you must not forget that you think Herr Klesmer 'Shakespearean.' Wouldn't 'Wagnerian' be high enough praise?

CONSTANTIUS. Yes, one must make an exception with regard to the Klesmers and the Meyricks. They are delightful, and as for Klesmer himself, and Hans Meyrick, Theodora may maintain her epithet. Shakespearean characters are characters that are born of the *overflow* of observation—characters that make the drama seem multitudinous, like life. Klesmer comes in with a sort of Shakespearean 'value,' as a painter would say, and so, in a different tone, does Hans Meyrick. They spring from a much-peopled mind.

THEODORA. I think Gwendolen's confrontation with Klesmer one of the finest things in the book.

CONSTANTIUS. It is like everything in George Eliot; it will bear thinking of.

PULCHERIA. All that is very fine, but you cannot persuade me that *Deronda* is not a very ponderous and ill-made story. It has nothing that one can call a subject. A silly young girl and a solemn, sapient young man who doesn't fall in love with her! That is the *donnée* of eight monthly volumes. I call it very flat. Is that what the exquisite art of Thackeray and Miss Austen and Hawthorne has come to? I would as soon read a German novel outright.

THEODORA. There is something higher than form—there is spirit.

CONSTANTIUS. I am afraid Pulcheria is sadly aesthetic. She had better confine herself to Mérimée.

PULCHERIA. I shall certainly to-day read over *La Double Méprise*.

THEODORA. Oh, my dear, *y pensez-vous?*

CONSTANTIUS. Yes, I think there is little art in *Deronda*, but I think there is a vast amount of life. In life without art you can find your account; but art without life is a poor affair. The book is full of the world.

THEODORA. It is full of beauty and knowledge, and that is quite art enough for me.

PULCHERIA (to the little dog). We are silenced, darling, but we are not convinced, are we? (The pug begins to bark.) No, we are not even silenced. It's a young woman with two bandboxes.

THEODORA. Oh, it must be our muslins!

CONSTANTIUS (rising to go). I see what you mean!

1876.